Changing Organizations

Organizations

Practicing Action Training and Research

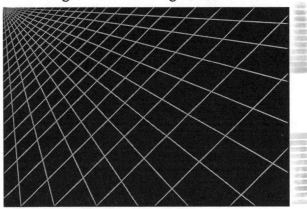

Raymon Bruce
Sherman Wyman

Foreword by Frank Sherwood

SAGE Publications
International Educational and Professional Publisher
Thousand Oaks   London   New Delhi

For information:

 SAGE Publications, Inc.
2455 Teller Road
Thousand Oaks, California 91320
E-mail: order@sagepub.com

SAGE Publications Ltd.
6 Bonhill Street
London EC2A 4PU
United Kingdom

SAGE Publications India Pvt. Ltd.
M-32 Market
Greater Kailash I
New Delhi 110 048 India

Printed in the United States of America

Library of Congress Cataloging-in-Publication Data

Bruce, Raymon R.
    Changing organizations: Practicing action training and research / by Raymon R. Bruce and Sherman Wyman; foreword by Frank Sherwood.
        p.   cm.
    Includes bibliographical references and index.
    ISBN 0-7619-1005-0 (acid-free paper). — ISBN 0-7619-1006-9 (pbk.: acid-free paper)
    1. Organizational change. 2. Action research. 3. Reengineering (Management)   I. Wyman, Sherman M.   II. Title.
HD58.8.B774   1998
658.4'06—dc21   97-339807

This book is printed on acid-free paper.

98   99   00   01   02   03   10   9   8   7   6   5   4   3   2   1

Acquiring Editor:	Catherine Rossbach
Editorial Assistant:	Renée Piernot
Production Editor:	Sanford Robinson
Production Assistant:	Lynn Miyata
Designer/Typesetter:	Rebecca Evans
Cover Designer:	Ravi Balasuriya
Indexer:	Teri Greenberg
Print Buyer:	Anna Chin

The authors wish to acknowledge the fundamental place that the journals of the late Neely Gardner have in this publication. Gardner had compiled his notes into an unfinished work, "Organization Theory and Behavior: An Approach to Managing in a Changing Environment." We owe considerable debt to these journals and to the inspiration that the memory of their author provided for this work.

To Neely and Jane Gardner

CONTENTS

FOREWORD

You will find this book somewhat different from others.

That is because its authorship is not fully covered by the two names you will find on the cover.

There is another individual whose experience, wisdom, and writing provided much of the foundation, and indeed much of the incentive, for Raymon Bruce and Sherman Wyman to invest the incredible number of hours required to bring a book of this kind to fruition.

The name of the man whose ideas and work are captured in these pages is Neely D. Gardner. Although he is not widely known, it is very important to an understanding of this book to have a real sense of this man. As you move through the book, you will find constant reference to him and the special ways in which he thought about releasing individual energies to accomplish collective purposes.

Thus, authors Bruce and Wyman felt it important that you have an appreciation of Neely D. Gardner as an innovative, exciting, and experimental individual before they expose you to the ideas he developed over nearly a half century in public management, both in the United States and in other countries.

They asked that I undertake the assignment of introducing you to Neely. The task is not an easy one because Neely moved in many circles and had associations and relationships that spread beyond a small group of friends. My own involvement with Neely occurred over a 30-year period, from 1956 until his death on March 24, 1987. We did a lot of things together, both professionally and personally, and I think of myself as a person who had a profound regard for his uniqueness. He had more ideas and a greater willingness to give them a try than anyone I ever met. Hopefully, some of the reasons for my feeling will become apparent as you read this.

ESSENTIALS ABOUT GARDNER'S LIFE

It is important to realize that Neely Gardner spent the greater share of his working life as a bureaucrat in the California state government. That in itself is worthy of note. His life is testimony to the fact that dreariness and uniformity are not all there is to our public institutions.

Though born in Texas in 1912, Gardner grew up in Sacramento, California, then a sleepy little town that woke up whenever the state legislature met. An only child, he was raised by loving parents in a comfortable situation. His father was an instructor at the Sacramento community college. In considerable degree he was a "local," having gone to school, married, and had his first job there. Sacramento was always home.

He graduated from the University of California at Berkeley in 1935 with a degree in medieval history, not the best credential for a working world in the depths of a major depression. In those days any job was a good job. After some graduate work in educational psychology and a stint on a local newspaper, Neely hooked on with the California State Department of Agriculture, and soon we find him in Blythe, California, about as unpleasant a part of the California desert as exists. He was a border inspector. It was a tough life, terribly hot, spartan quarters, and many miles from any urban center. His job was not exactly uplifting. He was really part of a California customs operation, where each incoming vehicle was zealously inspected to prevent the importation of agricultural products into the state. It was about as bureaucratic and by the rule an experience as could be conceived. In reflecting on it years later, Neely never gave it a bad rap. He remembered those days fondly.

Very likely, any feelings about Blythe were tempered by a happy family life. Two girls came first, then a boy, all welcomed by a mother and father whose own relationship was very close.

After several years in Blythe, Neely did get a transfer back to Sacramento, where his experience in training began. It does not appear, though, that Neely's career took off brilliantly. He had put in 16 years in the pits of the bureaucracy before he was put in a position to have some impact on the broader state system. In 1953, he became a training consultant in the Bureau of Training, a unit of the California State Personnel Board. There he came under the wing of a man of immense prestige, whose health problems had prevented him from becoming executive director of the state personnel board. Even with reduced energy, this man brought training to high visibility in state governmental management. And his key operative was one Neely D. Gardner.

When Bill Smith died in 1956, Neely was the logical choice to succeed him. Benefiting from the Smith legacy, Neely was now in a position to influence the management of the state significantly. In his position Gardner ignored the bureaucratic rules that imprison so many people. He made the chief trainer of the state an important resource for the top managers. In reasonably short order, they were making the phone calls to him and asking for his advice. He was not just the state's trainer; he was its major consultant. He had more contacts with the top brass than his state personnel board boss and often found himself in the position of telling the bosses what they couldn't do.

It is much to the credit of John Fisher, the board's executive director, that he learned to live with a situation where his subordinate was the one in demand and who got the approval. I remember Fisher's saying, "What do you do with a guy like Neely? He does his own thing and doesn't take my authority over him seriously. But he does a hell of a job and really helps the managers of this state. How can you knock that?"

Gardner's increased visibility as an expert in public service training made him attractive beyond the borders of the United States. In 1960, he undertook the first of many international assignments, this one under the auspices of the United Nations. He served as a consultant to the Institute of Public Administration in Egypt, and that began a series of involvements with public service improvement in a variety of nations.

Because the six years Gardner spent as the chief training officer of the state were remarkably productive, there will be a return to this period later in the manuscript. It was at the beginning of his service as training leader that I first encountered him. We rapidly developed a close association that persisted for about 30 years.

Success as training officer led to his final appointment in the state service, as deputy director of the Department of Water Resources. In this case he collaborated with a highly talented executive, William Warne, and the two provided the leadership for the largest non-federal public works project in the country up to that time.

Gardner's last 8 years of service were under a Democratic governor, Edmund G. "Pat" Brown, whose whole career had been spent in government. It was a great time for the bureaucrats. There was money to do the things that needed doing, the leadership at the top was publicly interested and supportive, and California as a whole was blossoming.

The arrival of Ronald Reagan, with his belief that government was the problem, coincided with Neely's 30th anniversary of state service. He was ready to retire at age 55, in good health, with a solid reputation, and lots of opportunities.

Though it meant moving from Sacramento, he decided to accept an invitation to join the faculty of the School of Public Administration of the University of Southern California in Los Angeles. Thus, he and I became colleagues, about 11 years after we had met.

The move to academia provided him with much greater freedom than he had known in state government. Not only was he engaged in teaching and research within the university, but he also became involved in a host of other consulting and public service projects. For the next 15 years he was an immensely busy person. It was a time when he proved himself a highly successful teacher; he mentored some brilliant people and started them on exciting careers; he engaged in the biggest consulting undertaking of his life, the wholesale reshaping of the California State Compensation Insurance Fund; he was an influential figure in the launching of a nationwide training and development service for state and local governments, modeled in some degree after his work in California; and he engaged in a major project in Iran that might have been his greatest triumph had not the Islamic revolution occurred in 1979.

He retired from the university in 1978, entirely because of an arbitrary rule then in existence that forced professors out at age 65. Yet he remained as active as ever for the next several years. In 1980, he took off for 6 months, enjoyed the beaches of Hawaii with his wife, and wrote the draft of *Organization Theory and Behavior: An Approach to Managing in a Changing Environment.* It was a lengthy manuscript that sought to capture the best of his ideas and experiences; and it is this document that serves as the foundation for the book you are reading. By 1982 Gardner's health had begun to deteriorate seriously. Somewhere along the line he had contracted ALS (Lou Gehrig's disease), and it led to his death. He was 75.

His career seems to have been divided rather neatly into three parts: (a) a very long apprenticeship of roughly 20 years in the California state government, beginning as a border inspector of agricultural goods and ending as a statewide training consultant; (b) approximately a decade as a much respected and highly effective senior executive in California state government; and (c) roughly 15 years as a university professor, consultant, and adviser to governments around the world. In sum, he was an active contributor for 45 years, and it is likely that the second half of his career was far more rewarding than the first. In his résumé, it is interesting that the first date mentioned in connection with an achievement is 1956, nearly two decades after his career in state government had begun.

Two doctoral dissertations have been written about him. The first, completed in 1967 by Anwar Qureshi, was officially concerned with the institutionalization of training in the California state government.[1] But it was basically a story of the way in which Neely Gardner had skillfully developed the capacity and the presence of training in state government. Qureshi reported Gardner's successor as saying how difficult it was to follow a man who had done so much.

The second dissertation was much more recent, and it was intendedly concerned with Gardner and his ideas. It was completed by Edward J. Jasaitis in 1992 and carried the title, *Training and Development: The Neely D. Gardner Approach.*[2]

Jasaitis reported that he was at first skeptical of Gardner as a dissertation topic because he found few references to him in the social sciences indexes. Then he went to a two-day workshop in 1990 that was specifically focused on Gardner's ideas and contributions. There he found that not everything is in the indexes; and those who had been exposed to him were absolutely convinced that Neely's thinking had critical relevance. In his concluding chapter, Jasaitis (1992) wrote:

> Gardner's approach to training and development represents a radical approach. It is distinct from the traditional approaches of his time, as well as those of today. Current approaches have not worked well . . . a different one is needed. Why not Gardner's?
> . . . During the prospectus stage of this dissertation, questions were raised about the usefulness of this research and its usefulness to the field of public administration. The doubt quickly disappeared as the research began to reveal his powerful ideas and the results of their application. (pp. 247-248)

THE STATE TRAINING EXPERIENCE: WHERE IT CAME TOGETHER

Although it has already been reported that Neely Gardner was a highly successful manager in California, that statement does little to explain what it was that made him such an unusual figure. Indeed, I still count him as by far the most outstanding practitioner of human resources development in the public service I have ever known. It is the way in which he *practiced* his craft that he was so special.

His unique talents became apparent to me early in our relationship. He was not at all like other bureaucrats. And he most certainly did not manage like them. He brought to the situation a set of personal characteristics and behaviors that set him off from others.

Most fundamentally, he started with an old-fashioned set of ethics. That included a deep concern for the democratic society, the obligations of service, and the importance of very hard work. He was indefatigable in his pursuit of the public interest. At the same time he was nonevaluative in his personal style, with the result that he had great capacity to listen actively. He often had strong feelings about what ought to happen, but he was remarkably skillful in helping people sort through their problems and establish their own recipes for action. Though he was powerful, he did not actively seek or want power. He was not regarded as a competitor but as a helper, and that made him more powerful.

Gardner had internalized the importance of learning as the essential condition for a fulfilling life, both individually and organizationally. It is probable that Neely saw learning as crucial because it provided the essential equipment to deal with the new and the different. These orientations made him highly experimental, loving the new just because it was new. It never bothered him that an experimental effort carried high risk. How else do you learn? And the predilection for learning also made him very open. There was always the fear that he had not been exposed to something that was important in understanding how best to do things.

Interestingly, Gardner's marked disdain for authority seemed only to increase his capacity to carve out a special niche for himself in a California bureaucracy that was classically Weberian in style and orientation.

You could see his effect at two levels. He was able to fashion special consulting relationships with the very top managers in the state for four basic reasons: (a) He was not a competitor and not really an participant in the power game; (b) he was a very good listener and was quite content to play that role; (c) he had ideas; and (d) he knew how to make training and development a very important contributor to managerial improvement. He reported that

> few weeks passed without inquiries from a director or deputy director concerning the introduction of some program, one in which we were able to help him . . . [by] utilizingthe knowledge we had developed concerning techniques for overcoming resistance to change.[3]

Neely never tried to build a training empire, and here again he showed his aversion to power. In his view a central training unit should operate very much in a helping role to the operating units. As a matter of fact, he saw every manager as a trainer; therefore, the real goal was to help managers throughout the system perform a key aspect of their jobs.

As a result, the bureau of training was very small, with only five consultants to work with the vast state apparatus. They did little that was routine. Much time was spent helping managers appreciate their human resources responsibilities and identify special needs within that context. Also, the small staff took on special tasks that were either experimental, particularly related to the needs of a particular top manager, or developed as models to be pursued later within the agencies.

Within this context of nonroutine assignments, it could be fairly assumed that Neely as boss would spend a lot of time counseling his five professionals on the ways in which they should pursue their highly discrepant tasks. But that was not the case at all. The management style was totally nondirective. Staff members expressed their frustration that Neely did not give them help. They were left on their own, despite the fact that Gardner's own reputation was heavily dependent on success in performing these tasks. Most amazing was that his staff, five very different people, never seemed to let him down. Further, they performed in ways that were highly congruent with Gardner's own style.

Undoubtedly, the consistency of performance by the highly individual group of training consultants derived from Gardner's influence, indirect though it might have appeared. Beyond that, however, there was a powerful mission statement that made training a central element in the work of the agencies. Training was more than putting on a few classes; it was an important vehicle for the accomplishment of organizational goals. Gardner put it in these terms:

> Our concept was that we were not emphasizing the development of individual managers—rather we were emphasizing the development of the whole organization. While this certainly meant the development of skills and attitudes by managers within this organization, we were attempting to bring about an organization impact, rather than impact on the individual. (cited in Sherwood, 1965, p. 7)

In an article that appeared in 1960, Gardner expanded further on the basic concept of California's training strategy:

> A useful notion, it seems to me, is to view the mature and effective organization as a self-actualizing organization—an organization that feels the need to contribute something to the world and to the culture in which it operates, so that the organization takes care not only of its own survival needs but also takes care of its safety, its acceptance, and its esteem (public image?). It seems to me a reasonable view that a self-actualized organization needs to be staffed with self-actualized people; and perhaps growing self-actualized people depends on operating a self-actualized organization.[4]

To distinguish between such an orientation toward the organization from classic training emphases on the individual, Gardner began using the term *organization development*. Jasaitis believes that he may have coined the term, which rapidly gained wide acceptance in the late 1950s and continues to be the favored label for organization change undertakings. There is evidence, Jasaitis (1992) reports, that Gardner was using the term as early as 1953 (p. 153).

The importance of training in the organization change process basically separates Gardner's work from others. It was a point of reference that he observed consistently throughout his lifetime of practice and teaching. That is why those very distant times in California have relevance to a reading of this text. You will find in the following pages that his organization change strategy depends heavily on the development of a learning community where there is a constant search for new understandings and an equally high commitment to the sharing of those findings. To put it in terms that are reminiscent of Frederick W. Taylor, it is not enough to find the one best way. There is the imperative to insure that everyone understands how to use the one best way. Gardner would go further: The learning organization is continuingly engaged in discovering new one best ways and making sure that such discoveries are shared. Thus it is no happenstance that Gardner labeled his approach "Action Training and Research."

CALIFORNIA DEPARTMENT OF WATER RESOURCES

Gardner's 4 years of service as deputy director of the Department of Water Resources were largely a reaffirming of the concepts he had developed in his training role. He was, of course, no longer a consultant and an observer. He was engaged in one of the most complex projects ever undertaken by a state government.

The Department of Water Resources was new, having emerged from a much smaller unit. Its new size and status were a direct result of the decision to export water from northern to southern California, financed by a $1.75 billion bond issue. About every management issue conceivable was to be found in this huge enterprise: tight time schedules, no tolerance for failure, the need to recruit a highly diverse and substantially technical staff, and the necessity to accommodate all such imperatives within a framework of high collaboration and coordination.

William F. Warne, the director of the new department, and Gardner formed a highly effective leadership team. In an interview with Jasaitis in 1990, Warne declared that he appointed Gardner deputy director because of his recognized ability to attack, organize and orchestrate complex problems as the state training officer. The two had known each other well because Warne had served as chairman of the state training committee, which recommended policy for the bureau of training. Warne also reported to Jasaitis that from the very beginning Gardner assumed responsibility for departmental management while Warne dealt with the politics of the enterprise. "Warne credits Gardner," Jasaitis (1992) wrote, "for much of the success that was achieved" (p. 35).

There was one element of the management environment that Gardner later said he had not appreciated in his days as training director. It was the degree to which power motivations, most of them negative, dictate attitudes and behavior in organizations. If anything, he would have thought that power would have been less a factor in Water Resources, with its highly technical staff and its very specific mission. That was not the case, however.

The attitudes of the old Conquistadors were alive and well. Gardner came to see power behaviors as the single most destructive factor in achieving the kind of cooperation required to bring together the many disciplines of the department within a very tight time frame. As a result of the seriousness of the problem, he became personally engaged. He wrote a programmed learning text, set in a society of cavemen and designed to show how even primitive people moved easily to personal power agendas. As might be expected, such self-aggrandizing personal behaviors had their disastrous effects in caveman society. The book was fun. It made its point in Gardner's typically indirect way.[5]

Asked later how effective the programmed learning had been in correcting Water Resources' problems, Gardner was characteristically reticent. It had done some good, he judged, but not nearly enough. The unbridled quest for personal power continued in Water Resources; and he concluded that it was far more endemic in management than he had ever realized.

Because Neely had always emphasized open communications and participation, it is possible that the Water Resources experience led him further along that path. You will find in this book that much Gardner's quest was to develop ways in which all members of the organization can take part in setting its agenda and achieving its objectives. To seek power, he seemed to conclude, is human. And the best way to handle things is to establish an arena in which everyone has a reasonably equal opportunity to pursue the power motivation.

The Water Resources experience ended his 30 years of service to the State of California on an exceedingly high note, and it provided a very solid base for his second career of consulting and teaching. He now had the absolute assurance that the ideas he had provided operating managers were solid. He had been in the thick of things himself, and he knew his approaches worked.

As has already been reported, Gardner's second career involved approximately 15 years of service as a professor in the School of Public Administration at the University of Southern California. He began that assignment in 1967, just after he had retired from the state. It was a period of high productivity, with many involvements inside and outside the university. For the readers of this book, three pieces of this remarkably active period seem particularly pertinent:

1. The consulting engagement with the California State Compensation Insurance Fund
2. The involvement with the National Training and Development Service
3. Gardner as academic: his students

REFORMING THE CALIFORNIA STATE COMPENSATION INSURANCE FUND

Of all the activities in which Neely Gardner was engaged during his years as an academic, none is as consequential as his consulting assignment with California's State Compensation Insurance Fund, which began in 1967 and formally lasted about 5 years. In reality, however, his informal association with the Fund continued over many years.

Why was this undertaking so important? In effect, he was given free rein to take the lead in developing an organization that would really have the capability to learn and change and thus to cope with a rapidly transforming environment. It was a chance to put his ideas to the ultimate test, with no prescribed limits on experimentation. Of course, the project was constrained by the general human aversion to risk taking, but at least there was the assumption that anything was possible.

As it turned out, the State Comp Fund met many of Neely's expectations. Through an excruciating chain of steps, it moved from a hidebound bureaucracy to an exciting, changeful organization with a very different mandate. It achieved levels of success never attained before, and that special quality persisted for nearly 30 years. It is a premier example of a successful effort at organization development, one which has received a considerable amount of attention in professional circles. In my view it stands alone as an OD event that was truly organizationwide, was theoretically consistent, and did become a demonstrably different kind of organization.

You will find that the State Comp Fund is liberally reported in this book, though not so much in terms of the specifics of the organization as in terms of the lessons learned. Gardner himself recognized that he was engaged in a project that held a tremendous learning potential. He kept extremely meticulous notes, later transferred them into a journal, in which he described precisely what was happening in the organization, how he developed his own strategies and undertook to discharge his special consulting role, and the ways in which the various events transpired. He summarized this material in the book manuscript he completed in 1980. Even the summary runs 125 pages and is a major part of the book.[6] It was evident that Gardner saw the State Comp Fund as his great laboratory experiment—one which had gone well and from which a great deal of learning was gained.

The State Fund was a very unlikely candidate for such experimentation. It was founded just before World War I as a self-supporting activity in the California government. The period was one of progressivism, in which there was a lot of optimism about government and correspondingly great suspicion about business. In this climate, the state took on the task of providing the local governments of the state with workers compensation insurance, essentially at cost.

As California grew and prospered, so did its local governments. With its niche monopoly, the State Comp Fund enjoyed a long and relaxed period of easy living. Because it was a good and secure place to work, it attracted its share of talented people. It had, incidentally, grown to the point that it was the 44th largest insurance company in the United States. Because it had plenty of money and was limited in the salaries and perks it could provide as a state agency, it tended to put more emphasis on the development of its people. It was a thoroughly professional organization, with which Neely Gardner had many associations in his days as state training director. Conversely, Gardner was known and respected in the Fund. Despite all its professionalism and investments in training, though, the Fund remained a tedious, overcontrolled, by-the-numbers bureaucracy.

From its monopolistic perspective, the Fund became confused about its relationships. It seemed to assume that the local governments operated to serve its needs. A bright, energetic director of finance in one of the state's largest municipalities, Long Beach, took the seemingly outrageous position that the Fund had service obligations to its customers. When the Fund asserted its monopolistic privilege and refused to budge on the matter, the Long Beach official took the only path available to him. He withdrew from the Fund. Long Beach became the first city to self-insure its workers; that is, it had become its own insurer. The idea caught on rapidly. When the gigantic County of Los Angeles self-insured, it became clear that the game was up for the old State Comp Fund.

With its survival at stake, Al Young assumed the presidency of the Fund. In his desperate situation, Young turned to Neely for help—just as had many other managers in state government.

At the 1969 national conference of the American Society for Public Administration, when the OD project was well under way, Young and Gardner described the events that were unfolding. It is particularly interesting to read what Young said at that time:

> The Fund, and myself personally, owe a tremendous debt to this man sitting down the table, Neely Gardner. As Training Officer for the State of California, Neely mounted a training program for management which has never been equalled before or since. He assembled a tremendous faculty of guys who were able to bring to it the top management support

and a large spectrum of training opportunities at a time when this was not the most popular subject to talk about in governmental circles. Organization, communication, group dynamics, conference leadership. And all of these constructed in a way which encouraged maximum participation. You never went to more than two of these without finding yourself on the staff of the third one.

I was so personally impressed, maybe because this had not previously occurred in our organization. I was so impressed by the value of some of the things I saw and heard, some of the mentalities that we were exposed to, that very soon almost every member of our organization from the front-line supervisor up had been exposed to modern management technique. All Fund managers had been to an in-depth sensitivity training experience. Without this injection, without this exposure to some of the wide spectrum of new skills, new training, new concepts, I doubt very much we could possibly have moved into the experiment."[7]

In his speech at the conference in 1969, Gardner made his goals very clear. His intent was not to change an organization but to create a changing organization. His general belief that authority systems, as found in traditional hierarchies, destroyed real collaboration was emphasized. The big issue, he said, was whether the Fund could "institutionalize change or, in fact, institutionalize de-institutionalization." At another point, he asked, "How do you organize to stay loose, to avoid habitualism, to respond quickly to the environment, and at the same time keep the organization output-oriented? In other words, how do you develop a changing organization?"[8]

Gardner's view was that organizations are in constant flux. The problem is that people either cannot or will not face that reality; they want to freeze something that cannot be frozen. One of his biggest irritations was organization charts, which always depicted a set of relationships that were out of date. At Miami Beach, he reported: "Today's Fund is depicted on what may be one of the most unusual organization charts you have ever seen. It is printed with disappearing ink." Earlier, he had raised the question with President Young, "What would happen if we forgot the organization as it exists today?"

His experience at the Department of Water Resources made him particularly alert to the power dynamics of the Comp Fund. He described President Young "as a queen bee surrounded by warrior bees."

It bears repeating that Neely's grand experiment was in an organization where survival was the issue. The Fund had lost much of its old business. It had to reform itself into a service organization that would meet the needs of the customers who remained; and it had to be entrepreneurial in finding new sources of revenue that were needed to keep the Fund solvent. In effect, the basic goal was to create an organization that was sufficiently savvy to know where its opportunities lie, was sufficiently entrepreneurial to take advantage of such opportunities, and was sufficiently supple and motivated to compete successfully with private sector organizations.

It was a situation where many of the Gardner ideas had substantial face validity. There was a bottom line. Revenues had to be produced; there could be no reliance on taxes to make up the difference. Further, there was nothing sure about what the business of the Fund would be. It had to find niches where it could outstrip the private sector, both in services and efficiencies. It had to have a very fast reaction time. This was a case where the human potential of the organization had to be used to its fullest, as Gardner believed ought to be true in every organization. Here, however, the failure to exploit the Fund's full human potential could mean its demise. It was a challenge Gardner relished.

There is a happy ending to the story. The organization did change, more than even Neely might have hoped. The Fund did find new ways to market itself; it was launched on a new growth curve; and it competed with great success against private sector organizations. The experience showed, however, that such gains do not come easily and there is no such thing as a complete victory.

The key to success lay in the Fund's transformation into a changing organization. Perhaps for the first time, this idealistic concept took on real meaning. The essential message of this book is its specification of the steps involved in creating a changing organization, as they were discovered by Gardner in the State Fund experience. Since you will be exploring these strategies in depth, it is necessary here to provide only a summary of how the transformation was achieved.

A critical first step was to deal with the values of the Fund, which were rooted in hierarchical authority and which entailed wide status differentials. Rank in the organization denoted power. These distinctions, rendering many employees powerless, did not just reduce the motivation to perform; they profoundly inhibited communication; they created difficulties at many of the points where organization members transacted with the larger society; and they certainly reduced the sense of ownership. Largely because of the influence of President Young, a number of steps were taken to reduce these differentials and thus to introduce greater equity into power relationships.

The solutions were largely structural, but that only could occur because of a reasonably broad consensus in the organization that greater equity in power relationships was necessary and desirable. The structure was amended in a number of fairly classic ways: (a) the development of formal institutions that provided for much greater participation of the membership; (b) a revamping of central staff operations to make them less powerful as controllers and more important as supporters; and (c) a consequent expansion of the authorities of the district offices where the main contact with the Fund's publics occurred. Neely sought even greater power equity through the introduction of a variety of market mechanisms but these were successfully fended off by central staff.

Greater power equalization, however, was only the necessary foundation for the building of a changing organization. Once there was greater engagement in the enterprise by its members, with appropriate rewards for contributions, it was possible to begin the process of handling change in quite a different way. Ways of thinking and acting had to be internalized that assumed the organization was in constant flux, continuingly responding to new imperatives and challenges.

It was through an emphasis on learning that Gardner sought to instill a new mind-set in State Fund employees. In various configurations, Fund members were licensed to learn about their environment, to examine the issues they faced, and to bring their discoveries back to a larger group. In effect discovery became a way of life. It was reported years later that, when a problem was encountered, it was still the State Fund response to say, "Let's see what we can learn about it." To a surprising degree, the act of discovery was a real turn-on.

It was critical, of course, that the Fund learn how to use its new information. That involved at least three major steps: (a) processing the data openly and comprehensively; (b) acting on it effectively; and (c) evaluating the experience so that more learning could be obtained and first steps could be taken to deal with the next set of problems.

To build these needed skills in the State Fund, Gardner initiated a training center. It was built on his experience as State training director, where his training of trainers program was attended by many operating managers. They found the values, attitudes, and tools to which they were exposed highly beneficial. That is because the manager's basic job is dealing with people, and the skills and competences needed for that job were exactly what Gardner thought trainers should have. His training placed high emphasis on self-awareness, goal setting, needs analysis, data gathering, communications, listening, and evaluation. The investment in this kind of training in the State Fund had a big payoff. Competences were developed in working together and using the information that was being acquired.

One other feature of this learning, changing community deserves mention. This was not an environment in which there were teachers and students. Not long after an individual had gone through the training of trainers program, he/she was likely to be back in the classroom—this time as a trainer. In this fashion, State Fund members developed skill not only in learning for themselves but in helping others learn.

Although one is tempted to write a great deal more about the State Fund transformation, it was the creation of a learning community that made Gardner's ideal of a changing organization a reality. The State Fund stands as testimony that it is possible to build a changing organization, and its experience recently suggests the job is never done. Organizations have all kinds of reasons to reduce their degree of openness, and, with that, there comes an end to the learning community.

NEELY AND THE NATIONAL TRAINING AND DEVELOPMENT SERVICE

By the time Neely Gardner became involved in the National Training and Development Service (NTDS) in 1970, much of the thinking you will find in this book had been articulated. He was now speaking and writing of Action Training and Research as a philosophy and an approach for building the changing organization. In considerable degree, NTDS was a convenient vehicle for bringing his ideas to national attention.

Gardner had high credibility in national training circles largely because of his California achievements in training, not because of the work in the State Comp Fund. That was still developing. Gardner was a busy man!

Back in the late Johnson and early Nixon years, there was considerable opinion that the nation's system of federalism needed extensive refurbishing. Among other initiatives, one was directed toward improving the quality of people working in state and local governments. The Intergovernmental Personnel Act, largely a federal grant-in-aid program, was passed at that time and was expected to place considerable emphasis on training and development.

Fred Fisher, a former manager who had joined the International City Management Association as its training director, saw great opportunities in these movements. The need was certainly there, and now it appeared money would be available. It was he who conceived and arranged a major conference in Maryland in early 1970 to make a proactive effort to shape the way the federal government supported human resources development in state and local government. From that conference emerged a major study and a recommendation that there be established something called the Continuing Education Service. While Neely was active in these early days, he was not center stage. Yet his influence was clear. A December 15, 1971 *ICMA Newsletter* declared that the main thrust of the CES was "to establish action training and research as an integral part of the management process."[9]

Just a word about Fisher. He is one of those high-energy, very bright, and thoroughly nice people whom you encounter only once in awhile. Neely really changed his life, and he internalized Neely's values, philosophy, and approaches to such a degree that Action Training and Research has been the fixture of an extraordinarily successful career. He has worked his magic in a great variety of countries around the globe. And he has never forgotten his debt to Neely.

Fisher had this to say about the early days of the National Training and Development Service (which was called the Continuing Education Service for only a short while):

Gardner's influence on NTDS was evident from the start. The ICMA newsletter quote, defining the proposed organization's thrust as establishing 'action training and research as an integral part of the management process,' was pure Gardner philosophy. I suspect that few of those midwifing the NTDS effort (except perhaps Frank Sherwood) understood what that statement really meant. I didn't understand it, in Neely's terms, although I may have written the news release for ICMA at the time. Meaning was only to become clear as Neely worked his magic on the NTDS program in his subtle, quiet, unobtrusive ways.

I have painted a brief history of NTDS . . . to emphasize Neely's influence on the NTDS philosophy and program as a driving force from the very beginning. It is this influence I want to dwell on because it helps define Neely Gardner and his larger contribution to the theory and practice of organization behavior. (Fisher, 1992, p. 198)

Although Neely Gardner had a great deal to do with the initial conception of NTDS, the translation of the highly successful California model to a national scale somehow got lost along the way. NTDS tended to become just another training resource, delivering its own set of programs. However, the 4-week *Managing Change* program was pure Neely Gardner. Presented first in Aspen, Colorado, in 1972, it was designed around Action Training and Research methodology. Participants were a combination of training professionals (including R. Bruce, co-author of this book), department managers, and local government executives.

Neely had a phenomenological perspective that each of us constructs our own reality; and we value these constructs very dearly. To secure any real changes in the ways in which we behave in organizations (and it must be understood that at heart Neely was a revolutionary), it would be necessary to get these individual reality constructs out in the open where they can be clarified, discussed, and subjected to development. Thus, much of the Gardner emphasis in the seminar involved securing data on perceptions and feelings about membership in the organization. In many ways the Aspen program was the first real formalization of his Action Training and Research method.

Fisher extolled the *Managing Change* program. He wrote,

Of all the NTDS programs, and there were many (335 in the first three years of operation involving a minimum of 10,000 individuals), the four week *Managing Change* seminar was the flagship of the fleet and, from many perspectives, had the most impact and influence.

> *Managing Change* was not without controversy. . . . [But it] was more than just controversial. It was a platform for Gardner to subvert the conservative nature of local and state government training. (p. 203)

> *Managing Change* was a complex, multi-layered, fast moving, omni-directional learning experience that had Neely written all over it. Action research, self-discovery, and ever-widening definitions of participation as a learning *and* societal goal, conflict, diversity, controversy, sharing, growth, and always, learning by doing. It was a very special time in the lives of the many who attended. Without a doubt, it still remains, for many, the signature of NTDS. It became indelibly inscribed on their own lives and the lives of their organizations. (p. 205)

NTDS had a short shelf life. Its Ford grant ran out and was not renewed; the money from the federal government began to dry up. By the mid-1970s, NTDS was gone and generally forgotten. As Fisher observed, however, the memory of the *Managing Change* seminar remained very much alive. At workshops held in the 1990s on Gardner and his work, graduates of the seminar appeared in the largest numbers and announced themselves Neely's greatest admirers.

Neely Gardner never was the leader of the NTDS and cannot be blamed for its demise, but Fisher (1992) declares he was "surely the intellectual soul of the organization and its most valued mentor" (p. 205).

NEELY'S STUDENTS

Even limited contact with the worlds in which Neely moved produces abundant evidence that everyone was his student. Generally, you did not know that you were in such a relationship with him. He was not a Socrates delivering the message. And it was not even that he was consistently contriving situations to place you in the position of learner. The process was much more subtle, and it often was un-planned and highly participative. Only afterward did you realize that real learning had occurred.

Within this reality it is dangerous to single out anyone as especially Neely's student. But it is a fact that he taught for more than 15 years at the University of Southern California in a formal academic setting.

This particular venue provided him the opportunity to touch a substantial number of people who later practiced and taught public administration with his particular style, philosophy, and ways of building more effective organizations.

One such person is Camille Cates Barnett, who enjoys a distinguished career in local government management over two decades. She is currently the chief management officer for Washington, D.C. This post was created by the city's Control Board to dig the city government out of its financial and physical chaos. With her local government expertise to provide technical assistance to a variety of foreign countries as a consultant at the Research Triangle in North Carolina.

In 5 years as city manager of Austin, Texas, she achieved an international reputation for her innovative and skillful performance. Many acknowledged her as the best city manager in the country, male or female. Before assuming the Austin position, she had occupied top management jobs in two other major Texas cities, Dallas and Houston. She is a Fellow of the National Academy of Public Administration and has received many awards in her now rather lengthy career.

In 1992, Barnett wrote an article for a symposium on Neely Gardner. It is one of the most exciting statements of a student's debt to a professor I have ever read.

She begins by recalling an incident when she first encountered Neely as a consultant, before she had begun her own doctoral work. He had been contracted to perform a training activity in a city where Barnett was then working. She found him early in the morning rearranging the chairs in the meeting room. She reported the interaction that followed:

> "Neely, you shouldn't be doing that! Here, let me help. Shall I get someone in here to do that?"
>
> "No, Camille, it's my job. You see . . . It's one of the most important things I do: arrange the chairs."

She wrote that she thought he must be joking. "He was not. Even when Neely joked, he was not joking" (Barnett, 1992, p. 180).

In her essay, she dealt specifically with the ways in which she used Gardner's Action Training and Research process when she became

Austin city manager. It was another case where AT&R really made a difference. One reason is that she saw AT&R as a theory of leadership; and, since she was moving into a major leadership position, it was only natural that she should use it.

She wrote, "When he taught it to me, I never considered it a theory of *training* [italics hers]; it always seemed to be a theory of "leadership . . . I have spent the 20 years since Neely taught me this finding ways to make it work in cities. It is a leadership theory that can bring both success and significance" (Barnett, 1992, p. 181).

This is how Barnett characterized Neely Gardner and her debt to him:

> Neely cared what happened. He cared particularly about government, organizations, and leaders who did not do their jobs. His response was to show how. He changed organizations and taught people.
>
> Neely was a model of a learning leader. He melded theory and practice. He managed me like I would like to manage others—by not *managing*; he *led*. It never crossed my mind that he did not care. He believed in people.
>
> He taught me to think differently: to empower others; to see patterns, not just events; to trust my intuition; to find the order in chaos; to do what I really cared about.
>
> Leadership for Neely was in the arranging of the chairs: create the environment; focus the energy; facilitate the interaction; take care of the people.
>
> Thank you Neely. (p. 187)

CONCLUSION

When Neely Gardner went to Hawaii and wrote the draft of a book on his philosophy and techniques for creating a changing organization, he was already suffering from Lou Gehrig's disease. One of the curious aspects of the malady is that it profoundly affects motor capacities but has essentially no impact on the brain and the capacity to think. The life expectancy of those with the Gehrig disorder is unfortunately short. Undoubtedly, Neely sought to leave a record in 1980 while he still had the capacity to do so.

Although Gardner lived 7 more years, there was a continual diminishment of his physical capacities. He had neither the energy nor the finger dexterity to edit a manuscript. His important, unfinished work essentially disappeared from sight. Then, in 1990, Sherman Wyman took the initiative in organizing the first of several workshops on Gardner's life and work. One of those who participated in that first workshop (and all subsequent ones) was Raymon Bruce. He had been one of Neely's early collaborators at the State Compensation Insurance Fund, where he was a career officer.

Aside from bringing together the two people who would be the authors of this book, one of the consequences of the 1990 workshop was to reinstate Neely's manuscript as a highly important resource in the management literature. A few copies were found, and Xerox machines were kept busy. It became very clear that Gardner's philosophy and learnings should become a public resource. A book had to be published.

Ten years had passed since he wrote his manuscript. In today's world that is a millennium. There is genuine skepticism about ideas set forth even a year ago. If a book were to be published for wide public use, it had to be updated. Also, Neely's manuscript was truly in draft form. Significant as the State Comp Fund experience was, it seemed that Neely had explored it in excessive detail. Such an event had to be placed within the broader context of applying AT&R.

This book is an effort by authors Bruce and Wyman to provide you with the essential Gardner and also to place it in a current context. They have been successful in that effort. In the remaining pages you will be able to explore the richness of Gardner and at the same time see how his ideas apply today.

—Frank Sherwood
Professor Emeritus
School of Public Administration and Policy
Florida State University

NOTES

1. Anwar U. Qureshi, *California State Training Division: A Study in Institution Building.* Doctoral dissertation, University of Southern California, Los Angeles, 1967.

2. Edward J. Jasaitis, *Training and Development: The Neely D. Gardner Approach.* Doctoral dissertation, Florida State University, Tallahassee, 1992.

3. Frank P. Sherwood, *The Genesis and Growth of Training in the State of California: The Role and Philosophy of Neely D. Gardner.* Los Angeles: University of Southern California, 1965, mimeo, p. 14.

4. Neely D. Gardner, "Mr. Training Director: His Job." *Journal of the American Society of Training Directors, 9,* (August, 1960).

5. The program was titled *Summitry* and was originally printed in mimeographed form for internal use in the Department of Water Resources. It achieved a much wider circulation, however, and was recognized as very useful. It was subsequently published by the National Training and Development service. Neely D. Gardner, *Summitry.* Washington, DC: National Training and Development Service, 1974.

6. Neely D. Gardner, *Organization Theory and Behavior: An Approach to Managing in a Changing Environment.* Los Angeles, 1980, typescript, pp. 277-403.

7. Comments by Al Young, President, California State Compensation Insurance Fund, at the 1969 National Conference of the American Society for Public Administration, Miami Beach, Florida, May 21.

8. Comments by Neely D. Gardner at the 1969 National Conference of the American Society for Public Administration, Miami Beach, Florida, May 21.

9. Fred Fisher, "And the Memory Lingers On," *Public Administration Quarterly, 16,* 197 (Summer 1992).

10. Camille Cates Barnett, "Leadership: Arranging the Chairs—Reflection on the Lessons of Neely Gardner," *Public Administration Quarterly, 16,* 180-187 (Summer 1992).

PREFACE

The genesis of this volume is the work of Neely Gardner and the influence that he and his work have had on those of us fortunate enough to work with him on his project to develop changing organizations. More particularly, this volume arises out of his unfinished manuscript, *Organization Theory and Behavior: An Approach to Managing in a Changing Environment* (1980). Gardner fashioned this manuscript out of the journals he kept while developing his Action Training & Research methodology as a consultant to a public agency in California. Indeed, through the generousness of Neely Gardner's daughters, Joanne Gardner Kamiya and Neita Gardner, we have been able to include much of Gardner's seminal work in each of the chapters of the second part of this volume under the subtitle (or variant of) "From the Journals of Neely Gardner." Therefore, it is appropriate and altogether fitting to include segments of Gardner's manuscript preface in the same format.

From the Journals of Neely Gardner:
Achieving A Changing Organization

My purpose in writing this book has not been to add my voice to those of profound world citizens who have become concerned with emerging problems. Rather it is to take seriously the role of a resident of this planet in trying to contrive ways to meet the terrifying prospects of the years ahead.

Any person interested in such an undertaking must do so humbly. For I take to heart the words of Einstein, "I really do not know very much," as applying manyfold to those of us of lesser competence.

I try to focus on some of the more interesting organizational and interpersonal theories, theories which want much more testing, and attempt to show how these theories might be translated into action in ways that would be productive to society. The plan is to deal with organizing to achieve a changing organization capable of meeting the wants and needs of its environment while enhancing the physical and psychological well-being of its employees. Further, the intent is to provide a cognitive map as to ways communities, corporate and public organizations, and voluntary associations might become changing structures. All of this requires giving attention to change itself.

The concept of *changing,* increasingly discussed in the literature, differs from concepts which concern methods of affecting specific change. In the process of changing, one recognizes the necessity for and the inevitability of changing. The effort then must be to see that the changing that occurs benefits the citizens in both our country and the world. In arriving at this point, I am indebted to almost everyone I ever knew. This includes an expression of gratitude to my parents, to whom I owe many debts beyond creation, including learning the meaning of love; to my wife, Jane, who has been a major influence and educator in my life and who has helped me in my effort to become a human, human being; to my children; to my teachers in school; and to my associates in the organizations which I have worked. . . . I should like to mention Frank P. Sherwood, from whom I have gained so much personally and conceptually.

Gardner's acknowledgments apply equally to the current authors. Our own wives and familes have had a similar influence on us. Sharon Bruce contributed both as a co-practitioner and in offering substantial insightful advice. Christine Wyman has lent active support to this project as well. Also, in particular, Michelle Wyman's timely and valuable critique was very substantive in getting us on the right path. Jesse and Joshua Dudley were constant sources in shaping our philosophical outlook. Frank Sherwood, of course, is the mentor behind this whole enterprise. It is always the burden of the authors to create a work worthy of their mentors. To be sure, we have only touched a part of what Gardner and Sherwood have envisioned. Let it suffice to say that we hope that our effort can be considered as a modest beginning to sharing our experience with their ideas and methods.

In the spirit of AT&R we need to acknowledge that the most substantial contributors to this book are the people in the organizations we used as models of the ones we describe. These contributors are represented by key people that practiced action training and research in developing their respective changing organizations. They include R. A. Young, Jerry Marsh, the late Jack Wiebers, K. C. Bollier, Norm Hansen, Jim Tudor, Preston McCoy, Gary Foss, Moses Ramarui, the late president Haruo Remeliik, Dr. A. Yvonne Russell, Ph.D., M.D., Shirley Zimmerman, Robert Jensen, the late fire chief Warren Isman, fire marshal Stephen Smith, Ted Austell, Geraldine Rodriguez, and James Clark.

Clearly, we find ourselves indebted to the insightful critiques of such knowledgeable people as Henry B. Kass (Budd Kass), Portland State University; Camilla Stivers, Cleveland State University; Meredith A. Newman, Washington State University at Vancouver; Ralph P. Hummel, The University of Akron; Blue Wooldridge, Virginia Commonwealth University; and Robert Abramson, Organization Development Consultant, Sacramento, California. Where we clearly benefited from their shared knowledge, we may not have fulfilled all of their expectations. Therefore, wherever the book falls short in this regard, it is, of course, the responsibility of the authors.

Other participants that were participants in the actual creation of this volume include two tireless graduate assistants, Chang Huang, at Florida State University, and Phyllis Behrens at the University of Texas at Arlington. Without the visionary support and guidance of Catherine Rossbach and Sage Publications, this volume would not have appeared.

PART I

HISTORY AND THEORY
OF ACTION TRAINING
AND RESEARCH

Today, many organizations are seeking ways to be more flexible. Total quality management, reinventing government, and business process redesign are some of the approaches being used to enable the people doing the work to participate in organization development. The primary question becomes, "What is development?" However, there is a second question, "How can we do this development for ourselves?" Part I explores briefly some of the history and theory developed from these two questions. Part II presents and examines a methodology that can be used as a guide for people who wish to develop their organizations into organizations that can change for themselves.

1

CHAPTER 1

BACKGROUND ON DEVELOPMENT

A recent study by the Congressional Budget Office—The Role of Foreign Aid in Development—asked the question, "What is development?" The study defined it as follows. "Development means change. Most analysts would agree on that point. But defining development more precisely than that is problematic" (U.S. Congress, "Role of Foreign Aid," 1997, p. 3). In the case of human development efforts, Kurt Lewin defined development as change—but a change that is opposite to regression. "The indirect way of studying the dynamics of development by studying regression may prove fruitful for the whole theory of development" (Lewin, 1951, p. 87). Fruitful indeed. Lewin developed the useful development tools, which include action research, force field analysis, and reeducation. In this book, we will define *development* as change associated with individuals or organizations growing in order to meet their true potential.

HOW DO WE BRING ABOUT THIS DEVELOPMENT FOR OURSELVES?

In 1967 Neely D. Gardner began a research experiment using Lewin's discoveries to form the core of his Action Training and Research (AT&R) methodology for developing what Gardner referred to as *changing organizations* (Gardner, 1969, pp. 32–38).

Gardner believed that as society entered into what he called an era of discontinuity, organizations would be in constant need of change from within.

Gardner was one of the pioneers in organization development (OD) within public organizations. In Michael McGill's history of OD he cited Gardner's work at the Training Division of the California State Personnel Board as the first articulation and implementation of a program of organization development in the public sector.

McGill's history goes back to just after World War II to search for the beginnings of OD and in so doing, McGill found reason to include the activities, writings, and conceptualizations of Leland Bradford and Neely Gardner. Both Bradford and Gardner were engaged in training and development activities in large organizations and conceived of the necessity to develop both the individual and the organization (French, Bell, & Zawacki, 1983, p. 13).

McGill cited Gardner describing the outline from the salient features of organization development as conceived by the Bureau of Training Division of the California State Personnel Board in 1954: "Since the word 'training' apparently means different things to different people, the Training Division has sketched, in brief, some concept of what constitutes proper training in State service. Training viewed from [their] standpoint might well be called organization development" (McGill, 1974, p. 104). Although Gardner published his use of the term in a 1957 article, "Training as a Framework for Action" (Gardner, 1957), he gave credit for originating the term *training division* back in 1954 to the Bureau of Training Division itself (Jasaitis, 1992).

Gardner's Action Training and Research (AT&R) approach focuses not so much on how to change organizations but how to develop organizations that could constantly change themselves without requiring the oftentimes traumatic intervention by outside consultants as change agents. In short, Gardner wanted to create an organization in which each employee was a trainer and each employee was an agent of change. Gardner wanted to develop *changing organizations*.

Changing organizations are organizations that have developed the capacity of ongoing organizational learning that allows them to evolve through responsive changes to the increased pace of change in their environments. Responsive change means that the organization does not merely react to changes that happen to it, but is a proactive agent in its own environment. The organization sees itself as a part of it environment not an objective observer of it.

Change will come if we do nothing at all, it will come due to influences our presence incites, and it can come from actions we initiate ourselves. The primary value in this attitude is to focus the organization on owning its part in the major changes emerging in the environment of which the organization itself is an integral part. We are participants in our environment, not independent observers. This means that we do not "observe" our environment, we explore it (Ittelson, 1973). Exploring our organization in its environment is the ultimate source of new knowledge and organizational learning.

These environmental changes may include changes in the organization's clients' or customers' needs, innovations in work processes and tools, and changes in the human resources involved in doing the work. Environmental changes can also include changes in the market economy or political structures, changes in the laws or regulations that govern the organization, and changes in the organization's mission.

Clearly, organizations cannot mount massive organization development efforts in response to every change that may occur in each of these areas, nor can they institute every management fad that comes down the pike. It is also unrealistic to forecast all of the significant changes that will most probably have significant impact on the organization. Gardner saw that a changing organization must deal with such organizational questions of change, including how to

1. Constantly sense the environment to pick up the indications, trends, and patterns of change

2. Explore the indications, trends, and patterns of change that the organization should respond to

3. Identify and solve the problems and opportunities that emerge from these change issues

4. Accept the new knowledge that changes proffer to the organization

5. Change the organization through developing the people involved

6. Design and implement appropriate responses to the problems and opportunities that are most important to the organization's evolving growth through organizational learning

In the changing organization, Gardner envisioned an organization that seeks to constantly transform itself to deal with the organizational questions of change. To further this vision, he proposed that the members of the organization, from the executives to the line worker, should take an entrepreneurial attitude toward their work, how their work fits into the organization, how their work meets the client/customer's needs, and how their work fits with the changing environment within which it must operate and serve the greater community.

The organization and all of its employees must view their situation as an extended organization that includes its client/customers, its industry including its competition, and the community at large. The executives and management must recognize that the knowledge of the work is vested in those employees that perform it and must keep a proper perspective on their management ignorance of that knowledge. The changing organization must understand that work performance information—about resourcing, process, and results—is vital to employees who are expected to be entrepreneurial about their work; this information should be readily available to them in a form that will help them to improve their results and to redirect their efforts to influence the changes in their situation.

In Gardner's original view in 1954, a changing organization would be one that balanced resource allocation for change between the work process resources and the training of the human resources that would enact the changes to new work processes. This is necessary in order to initiate the self-management of the employees and units doing the work. Therefore, the changing organization would devolve power and responsibilities from management to these self-managed employees and work units. With this devolution of organizational power to the people doing the work, management takes on the major responsibility of training; every manager is a trainer and a provider of training. The people doing the work have the work knowledge and management provides for the development that the people doing the work need in order to capitalize on their knowledge. This relationship is the core of organizational learning in the changing organization. To operate the changing organization there would have to be resource allocation, work process monitoring, and results evaluation information systems that are an equally useful feedback for management and for the people doing the work.

THE INTERNATIONAL ASPECT OF AT&R

Gardner envisioned AT&R as being especially useful in organizations within developing nations. This international dimension emerged out of the work he and the California State Training Division performed in the 1950s. Robert Abramson and other Training Division colleagues and students who were associated with Gardner subsequently worked extensively overseas in developing countries performing work based on the AT&R methodology. These diverse nations included countries in the Caribbean, Micronesia, and Africa, and in Pakistan, and more recently several post-Soviet nations in Eastern Europe. Gardner also integrated the Training Division's approach into the University of California's International Training of Trainers (ITOT) program. He developed most of the modules in that program into an international comparative administration perspective. ITOT is based on the principle that development of changing organizations in developing countries cannot take place unless it is a self-sustaining process of selecting objectives for change that are perceived as beneficial and provide changes that are realistic accomplishments within the local social context. They will not be effective if they are based on a series of imported foreign beliefs, values, and practices (Jasaitis, 1992). Gardner practiced his approach to changing organizations in a number of overseas programs including programs in Egypt, Pakistan, the Caribbean, Iran, and Brazil. Abramson and other Training Division colleagues who were associated with Gardner subsequently worked extensively in developing countries using the AT&R model, using participatory approaches to promote ownership by managers/employees of the problem solving and action planning of this change process (Abramson, 1978; Abramson & Halset, 1979).

Gardner also developed a manual for the United Nations, "Guidelines for the Trainer of Professional and Technical Personnel in the Administration and Management of Development Functions" in

1970. However, his principles of process consultation, systematic approach to changing organizations, decentralization, and the devolution of power through participation on the part of the employees engaged in the service delivery was too revolutionary for the United Nations at that time and the manual was suppressed. Nevertheless, in more recent years both the United Nations and the World Bank have embraced many of the principles Gardner put forth in his "Guidelines for the Trainer of Professional and Technical Personnel in the Administration and Management of Development Functions" and AT&R methods (United Nations Development Program, 1995).

CHAPTER 2

ACTION RESEARCH IN THE STUDY OF ORGANIZATION AND MANAGEMENT

The story of Action Training and Research (AT&R) begins with the work of Lewin and his development of action research methods to help people learn to change their behavior in their social organizations. However, viewing organizations as social creatures that can be developed began in the late 1800s. Two dominant movements or schools emerged in the study of organization and management: classical bureaucratic and scientific (adapted from E. Schein, 1970). Along the way there have been some mini-movements such as sociometrics and role and systems theory. But with the exception of systems, most have faded after a decade or two of popularity.

MANAGEMENT DRIVEN AND PARTICIPATORY DRIVEN CHANGE

Classical authors such as Henri Fayol, James Mooney, and Max Weber advocated a formal, hierarchical, machinelike approach to organization, with scant attention given to the needs of employees—and most early twentieth-century managers followed suit. Frederick Taylor focused his theories and methods on a scientific analysis of the work process and people's performance of the work. Later, the legendary General Electric studies of Elton Mayo and associates brought recognition of the importance of peer acceptance and support in informal groups and to the significance of the norms of these groups for work performance (Mayo, 1945).

During and after World War II, a third management movement emerged in the field of behavioral science. Three remarkable behavioral scientists—Kurt Lewin, Carl Rogers, and Abraham Maslow—provided core theoretical contributions to the study of the needs and behavior of individuals in organizations. They have been followed by a host of able, applied–behavioral scientists who have measurably enriched the theoretical base and provided practical concepts and techniques for use by those actually engaged in changing organizations. (For a contemporary but by no means exhaustive list, see the assortment of behavioral scientists and their contributions in Golembrewski, 1993.)

The concepts and values of these schools or movements are still very much in evidence in organizations today. We still typically organize work in a hierarchical, structured fashion. The scientific analysis of our work and decision-making processes still provides continued innovations. Informal groups are important sources for workers' performance norms and for their social needs. And many managers attempt to meet individual needs (as well as organizational goals) by employing different mixes of participative and collaborative techniques and styles. Given this history, specific attempts to change organizations can be seen as featuring values, structures, and behaviors that fall somewhere on a continuum from management-driven change at one extreme to nonmanagement employees participating in changing the organization at the other (see Figure 2.1).

Management-driven change is typically executed by managers employing a variety of techniques and personal styles ranging from authoritarian to participative, depending on their preferences and the nature of the situation. But of primary importance with management-driven change, much, if not all, of the power remains with management. Examples of contemporary techniques that are heavily management driven include total quality management (TQM), work process redesign, reinventing government (REGO), strategic alignment, management by objectives, and program evaluation (Lindsay & Patrick, 1997).

Participatory change, on the other hand, is premised on a genuine sharing of power and responsibility for change between employees and management. Change approaches that advocate this sharing are

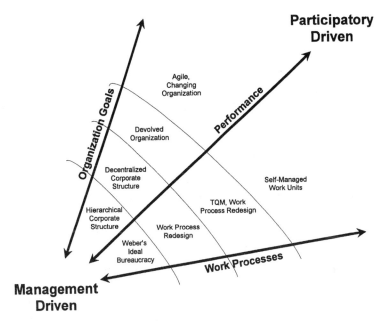

Figure 2.1. Management Driven and Participatory Driven Change

members of the closely related family of action research, organization development, and action training and research. Participation encourages employees to participate fully in innovation, fact finding, analysis, problem identification and solving, response–strategy development, and evaluation of results. These efforts typically feature ongoing employee collaboration with immediate managers as well as top-level executives.

A critical point of distinction between these two approaches centers around whose values dominate the change agenda and process. If the key elements of an organizational downsizing plan or the final goals for a strategic plan reflect principally the values and aspirations of management, clearly the change process is management dominated. But when both management and employee concerns and proposals are equally articulated in the process as well as in the final objectives, a genuine collaborative effort is likely underway (Gardner, 1969).

To be sure, many management-driven change techniques, such as TQM, work process redesign, and reinventing government include a variety of participative techniques or interventions (see Wolf, 1992). But, as Gardner often admonished, the values and concerns of both parties must be well embedded in both the process and the agenda of a genuine shared change effort.

Participatory change, however, is not without a number of genetic defects. In organizational change experiences, who really controls the agenda may be difficult to ascertain. Moreover, the focus of control may shift from "shared" to management driven during the process. Accusations from employees of "manipulation" by those who are at the same time professing "participation" are not uncommon. And the agenda itself may be heavily influenced by a small group of employees or one or two managers "having things their way." Finally, the history of management-driven and participatory change includes glaring examples of attempts by both employees and management to dominate or manipulate practitioner–consultants to achieve their personal aims (Eddy & Saunders, 1972).

There are many shelves full of research proposing a rich assortment of approaches and personal styles for changing organizations. Some espouse techniques that are clearly management driven and others advocate that management pursue varying degrees of employee participation. A lesser number, including this volume, advocate strategies that are genuinely employee–management-based with ongoing collaboration and power sharing as key values.

Of course, immediate situational imperatives may force even the most collaborative manager to adopt a more authoritarian style for some short-term change events. Clearly, the reverse holds true for authoritarian managers. However, the probability of lasting success with pervasive change efforts is dramatically enhanced with significant management–employee collaboration and the pursuit of a logical, phased strategy for change.

KURT LEWIN AND ACTION RESEARCH

Two individuals are credited as the principal founders of action research. John Collier, a practicing public administrator, served as Commissioner of Indian Affairs from 1933 to 1945 and advocated action research as a process for attempting to resolve race relations.

The other was Kurt Lewin, a mathematician turned social psychologist, a German immigrant who, as noted earlier, had a profound impact on the behavioral science community (French & Bell, 1995).

Lewin believed that the key elements of action research were what he called reconnaissance, fact finding, changes in planning, and action based on a correctional feedback system that linked action to facts (Lewin, 1947). In the Lewin tradition, applying action research to an organizational setting calls for the joining of organizational members and internal or external practitioners in a continuous collaborative process of reconnaissance, fact finding, planning, action, and evaluation.

Action research and organization development are both derivatives of applied behavioral science. Further, both are action-oriented, data-based, problem-solving social inventions. Both call for close collaboration between organizational insiders and outsider practitioners. "This is why," Michael Peter and Vivian Robertson wrote, "we believe a sound Organization Development program rests on an Action Research model" (cited in French & Bell, 1995, p. 71).

Action research as a methodology for helping people to change their behavior in their organizations is similar to coaching a football team, dance troupe, or a new employee learning the job. The *unit of research* is the performance of the people involved. In each case, the coach seeks to provide the players, dancers, or new employee methods of observation, feedback, and analysis of their performance in order for them to change—in other words, improve their performance of their actions being examined. Action research works for the people that are willing to change their status quo for themselves. In the AT&R method, *the action* is the effort by people in the organization to change themselves in terms of their work goals, behavior, structure, and performance through a learning process supported by *research* of their own actions.

In summary, whether deployed in an organizational setting or elsewhere, there are typically three major characteristics common to an action research effort:

1. It is change oriented: It is problem focused and aims at improving some existing condition or practice, usually in terms of resolving issues, solving problems, or realizing some opportunity for innovation.

2. It is organic: It is a reiterative research process that consists of a series of systematic, iterative steps of fact-finding, reflection, and planning, strategic action, and evaluation.

3. It is collaborative: It is research conducted as a joint, cooperative effort among the participants (Peter & Robertson, 1984, as cited in Luke, 1992).

As a behavioral scientist Lewin was intent on erecting a firm bridge between the abstract and the concrete, between social theory and social action (Allport, 1946). Lewin's later work emphasized the use of action research to ensure the practical application of the theoretical aspect of social research—in other words, people in action.

The research needed for social practice can best be characterized as research for social management or social engineering. It is a type of action research on the conditions and effects of various forms of social action and research leading to social action. Research that produces nothing but books will not suffice (Lewin, 1948, pp. 202–203).

Along with action research, Lewin advanced his concept of reeducation as a change in culture as a critical element of changing behavior in social groups (organizations). Here he put forth the basic dynamics of organizational change. Besides his classic change strategy of unfreezing the organization, changing it, and then refreezing it, Lewin included his reeducation component.

> The reeducative process affects the individual in three ways. It changes [1] cognitive structure [new knowledge], the way he sees the physical and social worlds, including all his facts, concepts, beliefs, and expectations. It modifies his [2] valences and values, and these embrace both his attractions and aversions to groups, and group standards, [one's] feelings in regard to status differences, and his reactions to sources of approval and disapproval. And it affects [3] motoric action, involving the degree of the individual's control over [one's] physical and social movements. (Lewin, 1948, pp. 59–60)

Changes in organizational behavior will not occur without a change in all three of these elements. And, in addition they must be voluntary.

Much stress is put on the creation, as part of the reeducation process, of an atmosphere of freedom and spontaneity. Voluntary attendance, informality of meetings, freedom of expression in voicing grievances, emotional security, and avoidance of pressure all include this element. Carl Rogers's emphasis on the self-decision by the client stresses the same point for the psychotherapy of the individual (Lewin, 1948, p. 65).

Lewin's students and followers continued his work at the Center for Group Dynamics. J. Barton Cunningham pointed out there were many other training designs and programs that combined action research and training that Lewin's students developed after Lewin's death in 1946. Most notable was the National Training Laboratory (NTL) in Bethel, Maine, led by Leland Bradford in 1949. NTL emphasized the T-Group (Training Group) and sensitivity group's aspect of reeducation.

> [Another] such program was carried out at the Training Division of the California State Personnel Board in 1954. The training emphasis sought to develop a climate for facilitating the use of training in the organization. . . . The training division used the word "organizational development" to describe its activities which emphasized individual training to alter attitudes and behaviors. (Cunningham, 1993, pp. 21–22)

Gardner was the manager of the Training Division that Cunningham mentioned. "Both Leland Bradford and Neely Gardner were engaged in training and development activities in large organizations and conceived of the necessity to develop both the individual and the organization" (French et al., 1983, p. 13).

Gardner held that management should assist, prod, cajole, and model appropriate change behavior. But he often reiterated the axiom that without ongoing and genuine employee involvement in all phases of a change experience, from problem identification to response implementation and evaluation, broadly supported, durable change was unlikely (Gardner, 1969).

ORGANIZATIONS DO NOT REALLY CHANGE, ONLY THE PEOPLE IN THEM DO

The paramount principle of Gardner's AT&R is that organizations do not really change, only the people in them do. If the people do not change through some process of reeducating themselves, then the organization cannot really change. If the people in the organization do not learn, the organization does not learn either. By the same measure, if the people do not or will not change, then they are open to be exchanged through reinventing, right-sizing, lean-&-meaning, agilizing, and other popular management-driven strategies for moving people in and out of the organizations in question. The same applies to the organization itself. For example, if it is around 1920 and the organization is a buggy whip firm employing leather crafters, then it should probably be striving toward reorganization. The employees and the organization may want to start learning to make new leather products such as leather upholstery for the motor cars that will begin to crowd the streets.

WHY ACTION RESEARCH?
IF IT IS NOT "NEW," IT IS NOT LEARNING

Action research is just that: researching people in action (i.e., working). But rather than simply bringing in professional behavioral scientists and industrial engineers to study the people working, action research also seeks to provide the people involved in the action being researched with the tools they need to participate in researching the action themselves. These methods include survey feedback instrumentation, force field analysis, consultative interview techniques, and meaningful practice exercises.

Learning in the AT&R method is based on two models of change in human behavior: self-reeducation as described in Lewin's approach to action research (see Benne, 1976), and Rogers's (1969) consultative approach to helping people change themselves (i.e., grow). Lewin's self-reeducation approach to changing human organizations is based on those people in the organization who will be affected by the change learning to change themselves. The three areas that Lewin argued must be brought into the change process research include (1) new cognitive structures, (2) new valences and values, and (3) new motoric action (Benne, 1976) are translated in the AT&R method to (1) new knowledge of the organization's issues, problems, and opportunities; (2) new values to meet the changing needs of the organization's clients; and (3) new ways to perform the actions required. Self-reeducation is not learning just any change. It is learning to accept new values according to the new knowledge gained. Self-reeducation validates those new values through experiments and practicing of new ways to work. In short, the people involved in the change become the learning organization. Clearly, if it is not "new" it is not learning.

Gardner also relied on Rogers's ideas of the importance of participation and involvement to create ownership of the change by those involved (Gardner, 1974). This ownership was required to provide the foundation of Gardner's governance by consent model that moves the management of the organization away from the authoritarian rule of the classic bureaucracy toward a more democratic one.

Rogers's approach to change involves a facilitative approach that allows the participant to learn to find his or her own way to deal with problems. The resolution is within the individual, in other words, but for some reason, the individual cannot seem to get at these solutions. The AT&R practitioner can only try to help each individual find his or her own solutions.

Finally, Gardner also relied on Sherwood's concepts of outcome resource allocation and an entrepreneurial approach to internal organization management. Sherwood's approach includes a shared analysis and agreement on the organization's aspirations for change, the outcome expected of the change in the organization, as well as an equitable sharing in those outcomes (Sherwood, 1968).

WHY TRAINING IN ACTION TRAINING AND RESEARCH?

Why add training to action research? Action research, even with its participatory nature, still connotes a single intervention or a single organization change, which might include many interventions. Training emphasizes the consultant's obligation to transfer his or her organization change skills, knowledge, and abilities to the people in the organization before that organization can become a changing organization—in other words, one that can change itself incrementally whenever the situation indicates and not just wait for some dramatic event to force the change. As Bennett and O'Brien (1994) observed, in order to deal with today's knowledge explosion and the galloping pace of change, organizations must transform themselves into learning organizations—organizations in which people continually expand their capacity to create results that they truly desire by continually learning and changing (Senge, 1990)—and training is one of the key building blocks of a learning organization:

> Training and education efforts play a key role in transforming an organization's practices. Training is an integral, complementary component of change and growth. . . . In a learning organization, training programs focus on helping people learn from their own and others' experience and becoming more creative problem-solvers. . . . Action learning incorporates the real key to using training and education as a building block: It not only teaches skills, it teaches innovative thinking and how to learn, as well. (Bennett & O'Brien, 1994, p. 46)

Adding training to the action research approach recognizes that the people involved construct their social reality (Berger & Luckmann, 1967). Therefore, people must change if the organization's social reality is to change. The client organization's employees themselves need to acquire the skills and methods to undertake appropriate AT&R processes for themselves. For any action research program that does not provide the means for the participants (employees as well as management) to change and grow, the resulting organizational change will be symptomatically oriented at best and mostly cosmetic at worst.

Therefore, AT&R practitioners have a need to direct considerable attention to the development of the skill and methods among the people of the organization so that they can constantly change as needs and the environmental situation shift. Indeed, if the organization is to become a changing organization, it must be able to transform itself in anticipation of the changing needs of the people that its products and services support. The organization must assume a more proactive entrepreneurial posture that anticipates changes, rather than a mere reactive or responsive one that passively waits for changes to happen.

As a measure to increase the training component of AT&R, Gardner added the dimension of training of trainers. The unique purpose of this component was to focus practitioners on transferring their training skills to the client organization to change itself. The ultimate purpose of AT&R is not only for organizations to improve themselves but to improve their effectiveness by helping the people who receive their services or products to improve themselves.

Gardner asked,

> What if the only valid measures of the success of your organization were to be the improvements in your client's own situation and in the improvements in their work behavior? How would you go about improving your own organization by these measures? (quoted in Bruce, 1994, p. 125)

The answer Gardner intended for this rhetorical question was that the AT&R practitioner had to train the client organization to be AT&R practitioners to their own client organizations. The true measure of success for the client organization would be measured in the successful changes in their client's organization, and so on.

Gardner's training-of-trainers approach to AT&R actually added a new dimension to the proverb, "Give a man a fish and you feed him for a day. Teach a man to fish and you feed him all his life." If you "Train a person to train others to fish, you will feed the whole village, and the generations to come!" (Bruce, 1994, p. 142).

CHAPTER 3

THE ACTION TRAINING
AND RESEARCH CYCLE FOR
CHANGING ORGANIZATIONS

The action training and research cycle of 12 transition stages is split into two phases (see Figure 3.1). The first six stages make up a strategic decision-making research phase and the last six stages make up the change implementation action phase.

THE AT&R MODEL

In the research phase the (1) orientation stage sets the geopolitical grounding for the AT&R practitioner and the people in the organization to consider as a mutual action research project. This stage may include a discussion of the organization's current mission and organization in terms of goals, processes, and performance.

The (2) contract stage involves situation assessment. It initiates the original trust, based on mapping the establishment of mutual values and scope of the enterprise by mutual agreement of all parties concerned. We will look at action research a state agency used to find ways to help its people be more open to change and innovation in the workplace. During this stage, the client organization and the practitioner need to agree on the role and expectations of AT&R methodology in the organization's particular situation.

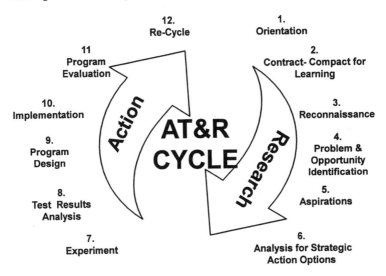

Figure 3.1. Two-Phase AT&R Cycle

The (3) reconnaissance stage involves exploring the issues of the client organization. The participants examine the regions outside the frame of the organization's current social territory. It is often in these regions that they must find new knowledge, values, and options for strategic change in the way the organization does business. This stage is similar to the issue agenda stage of the strategic management process (Nutt & Backoff, 1992). We will look at AT&R's research on three different kinds of thinking: exploration thinking, intuitive thinking, and rational thinking for the organization's strategic decision-making process for developing information technology conducted at an East Coast County government.

The (4) identification problems and opportunities stage provides the menu of areas open to the strategic decision makers. AT&R method provides interesting insights into the nature of problem solving in organizations. This stage looks at the organization's issues explored in stage 3 to determine the potential problems and opportunities those issues can pose for the organization.

The (5) aspirations stage brings together the strategic decision making for a change from the status quo to an envisioned future. The AT&R method places this stage of setting the organization's goals for changing itself deep into the AT&R cycle of stages because it relies on the research of the first four stages to put the organization's aspirations for what it wants to become in a more sobering reality than the classic "vision–mission statement" exercise usually associated with operational planning. Usually, there are more issues with their attendant problems and opportunities identified in stage 4 than the organization has the strategic resources to address. Strategic resources are those resources an organization has left over after allocating resources to accomplish the organization's mission. Selecting the problems and opportunities to address with the organization's resources available for changing itself constitutes the core of the organization's strategic decision-making process for changing itself. In most cases, these strategic resources for change are quite limited. They represent the limits of the organization's ability to invent its own future.

In the (6) analysis stage for strategic action options, strategic decisions are detailed by the commitment of organization resources to specific action options. In this stage the organization comes to grips with the limits of human decision making. There are many decision-making tools to aid organization decision makers in this process. Lewin's force field analysis is an excellent and often used tool in this process. In any case, the action aspect of AT&R requires that the research and analysis must transform to actual resource allocation and action. Usually this transformation occurs in the form of the organization's strategic resources being allocated to specific projects, task forces, or start-up organization units with new objectives for change, beginning in the next stage.

The (7) experimentation stage examines and tests the key assumptions involving the decision for changing the organization. This stage represents the first commitment of action resources to the change project. It is clear that the somewhat arbitrary divisions of the AT&R cycle into phases means that there is not always a clear-cut distinction between research training and action in each of the stages. In many instances the start of some actions can be traced back to the very first stages. Quite often it begins in the problem and opportunity identification stage. Once a problem is identified, organizations tend to grab it—like a dog with a bone—and chew it until it is solved.

However, just as often, experimentation is required because research in the earlier stages of AT&R includes some untested key assumptions about the organization's capabilities. It is also required because people, their livelihoods as well as the organization, are at risk. Therefore, careful experiments, usually in the form of pilot projects, need to be designed and conducted. Later we will look at an AT&R design used to set up a program to research and test innovative fire and rescue equipment and methods.

The (8) test results analysis stage serves to revise and polish the plan for change and provides vital experience and training for those involved. At this stage, certain decision assumptions and political quarrels can be put to rest in as far as committing organization resources to action is concerned. These disagreements can now be put into organizational perspective with the organization's own *experiential data* along with the organization's conventional wisdom, professional analysis researched in journals, practitioner analysis, and surveys of other organizations.

The (9) program design stage translates the various parts of the strategic plan into discrete action steps, often encompassing a series of concurrent and interlinked projects. Program design can range from a formal strategic plan to a *request for proposal* design with clear measurable objectives, specific action steps, evaluation criteria, progress measures, and monitoring. In some cases it may include a "back of the envelope" plan, a "quick hit" or "cherry picking" project that has been hanging around waiting for permission to be implemented.

The (10) implementation stage, of course, is the accomplishment of the change actions selected. In organizations it is often hard to say when implementation begins and ends. But in most cases, physical implementation begins with the allocation (assignment) of resources to effect a given change. Implementation ends when the change is achieved to some degree and is either maintained or abandoned by the organization. Sometimes implementation is abandoned because the allocated resources are used up before the change is fully or even partially in place.

The (11) program evaluation stage is often an important stage that is most often neglected, if it is even done at all. It is the process of the organization realizing and celebrating its achievements and owning up to its mistakes. However, to conduct a proper evaluation, criteria of evaluation must be identified somewhere along the line—it is hoped at the goal-setting stage of aspiration or at least at the project-planning stage. Without some criteria of evaluation this stage can become a self-congratulating exercise of the organization's achievements. This stage is most important because it is an accounting for the resources allocated. It must become the measure by which strategic resources are allocated in the future. In many cases, this is the major source of the organization's learning. Without evaluation, the organization can learn, but it cannot know what it learned for the next time.

The (12) re-cycle stage keeps the organization in the process of learning from its achievements and its mistakes. The next orientation stage will thereby have a more realistic and comprehensive situation analysis experience.

A MENU, NOT A RECIPE

This action stage approach to teaching, learning, and developing changing organizations is presented in this book in 12 stages as Part Two: A Practitioner's Guide to Changing Organizations. Each of the 12 stages of AT&R opens with a *menu* of the stage involved. This menu then tells about that stage in terms of how it was used in various instances by AT&R practitioners.

The 12 AT&R stages can be used by teachers, trainers, students, practitioners, managers, and employees alike to guide them through the development of their organizations into more democratic and entrepreneurial endeavors. AT&R is intended to be a guide through the transition steps involved in changing organizations. It is not a magic formula for successful change but a template to help people bring some level of common sense to the project as they go through the process of changing their organizations. Whether people decide to go it on their own or bring in a consultant, or use any of the multitude of management, problem-solving, and human behavior methods available, AT&R is intended merely to be a map to guide people through the obvious steps involved in any organizational change effort. There are many methods and tools at hand to use for each step in the changing process, each having varied results (Micklethwait & Wooldridge, 1996). Many such projects for change that fail do so because the people involved get bogged down on a particular step or cannot find their way to transition to the next step. AT&R focuses on the transition between the steps of change. It is valuable both because it can be useful as an adjunct support to many methods and because it operates at the nodes between the steps of change. AT&R is not for every situation. It is a map or guide, and to continue this metaphor it should never be mistaken for the country it represents. As a map, it is by definition vacuous and without substance. However, to the degree it represents the substance it tracks—namely people working together as an organization—it is hoped that it can be a useful method for those people to make the most of what resources they already have to meet the changing needs of the people they hope to serve.

The practitioner's guide can help with the how and where in looking for new knowledge, values, and innovative practices. By practitioner, we mean people who use AT&R or other methods to help organizations change. A practitioner can be a professional consultant, an internal consultant, a knowledgeable employee, an expert from the academic community, or an expert from some other peer organization lent to the client organization. The practitioner functions more as a trusted sounding board and trainer than anything else. The practitioner's contribution for the most part reflects back to the client what they understood the client was saying as faithfully as the practitioner has understood it. This way, the person can see what they are saying from another point of view. The practitioner can raise the group's awareness of their organizational blind spots, but the group itself must learn to see.

AT&R cannot be a cookbook of recipes or discrete action steps for practitioners to use to change organizations. Those looking for AT&R to be a set of instructions on conducting the AT&R stages will be disappointed. We furnish the stages as Gardner described them along with hints and examples of how AT&R was applied since.

The purpose of AT&R as a method focuses more on helping the people in the organization to develop menus for healthy living rather than providing them step-by-step recipes for cooking the good dishes to be served. Or, to return to a previous metaphor, AT&R is a map for the transitions between the action steps of changing organizations.

Most organization changes ultimately have to go through the transition stages outlined in AT&R informally, if not formally. AT&R

practitioners, as many consultants have experienced, are often brought into the situation after the actual organization change process has started and encountered difficulties. It is not uncommon for the practitioner to be brought in as an agent for change after quite a mess has been created. It's like the customer who tried to fix his computer, fails, and then takes the pieces to a computer repair shop in a cardboard box full of electronic boards and disassembled parts. Therefore, when the practitioner is invited in as a change agent to "facilitate" change, AT&R is valuable as a map to find out in which stage of the organization's change process they are entering. In turn, AT&R can be used by the practitioner to guide the organization around to AT&R's initial stage of orientation.

In practice it becomes clear that AT&R is an organic process. Not only do the AT&R stages overlap each other, the research in each stage often generates feedback results that are valuable to previous stages. For example, when "if we only knew then what we know now!" is the feeling in the exploration of the issues in the reconnaissance stage, it is clearly an invitation to go back and revisit the situation analysis of the orientation stage or the value analysis of the contract-setting stage. In AT&R there is always this opportunity to rewrite history in a dynamic iterative process, at least to improve the organization's emerging understanding of its own history.

This is not to say that AT&R is the only resource that should be used for changing organizations. Clearly, there is a rich history in action research that provides numerous methods for people and their organizations to learn to adapt to their changing environment.

THE ACTION TRAINING AND RESEARCH
PRACTITIONER AS AN AGENT FOR CHANGE

The AT&R method is a cyclical process that invites the practitioner (internal or external) and the people in the organization to participate in the collaborative design, implementation, and institutionalization of change in the organization. The AT&R practitioner's major resources are experience, knowledge, methods, models, and skills. Many of the capacities used by practitioners are interpersonal skills applied in both one-on-one, group, and intergroup situations. In addition, the practitioner needs to be able to provide clients with historical, theoretical, and practical models that help them examine their own values, theories, work processes, and findings. The AT&R practitioner needs to have a clear understanding of how traditional and experimental organizations really work and how the dynamic, political aspects of organizations affect the total environment. To be most effective, AT&R practitioners must be knowledgeable in the areas of organizational theory, work processes, administrative behavior, and social psychology, and possess strong facilitator skills. Above all, AT&R practitioners need to become avid students of others' cultures.

As the practitioner shares his or her experience, knowledge, and skills with the client organization, there is an advancement both of the research necessary to design needed changes the client organization should consider and of the training of the client organization's employees in methods of research and implementation of change. The common efforts of the consultant and client are brought together through the various action research stages of changing the organization. Of course, participant-oriented action research is generally not intended to reflect all of the requirements of rigorously applied pure empirical research. Action research was first proposed by Lewin (1947) as a mode of social research intended to overcome some of the shortcomings of positivism (Baburoglu, 1992).

In action research, the action assumes greater importance than the purity of research; experimentation with proposed problem solutions takes precedence over searching for the optimal solutions. Action research is nonetheless scientific, but in Rogers's terms it does assume the ideas that are investigated are more important than performance of rigorous procedures. It further assumes that significant observations of important problems far outweigh sophisticated research designs (Rogers, 1969).

ACTION RESEARCH, AT&R, AND
ORGANIZATION DEVELOPMENT

Reflecting the problem-solving focus of action research, most organization development (OD) efforts are built around the core action research elements of data collection, problem identification planning, action, evaluation, and feedback (Boss, 1983). In addition, many OD techniques and values owe a historic debt to the T-Group and self-analysis experience of a group of social psychologists who established the National Training Laboratories in the 1950s. It is interesting to note that one of its early members, Edgar H. Schein—now a distinguished OD scholar–practitioner—recalls that the initial purpose of the Bethel, Maine, experiments was to "teach leaders how to be better leaders, that is, how to manage human systems more effectively" (Schein, 1990, p. 19). Only after experience with T-Groups did Schein and many of his associates conclude that nondirective therapeutic approaches advocated by Rogers and others "were far more effective as interventions than suggestions, directions, and other forms of 'active' leadership" (Schein, 1990, p. 19). A common theme of early definitions of OD emphasized the organization as a whole, a systemic approach to organizational innovation, problem solving, and change. But beyond this common ground, practitioners evidence little agreement on how to change behavior and whether one's focus should be at the interpersonal, group, or intergroup level (Warren, 1966). Other differences occur around the issue of whether the focus should be on encouraging a generic, incremental response or, as Warren Bennis's suggested, to develop a "complex educational strategy to change beliefs, attitudes, values and structures" to enhance an organization's ability to adapt to the imperatives of change (Kirkhart, 1972, p. 76).

Two central OD scholars, Wendell French and Cecil Bell, have provided a definition that they admit may not be "right" but that attempts to convey where OD is and where it is going:

> Organization development is a long-term effort, led and supported by top management, to improve an organization's visioning, empowerment, learning, and problem-solving processes, through an ongoing, collaborative management of organization culture—with special emphasis on the culture of intact work teams and other team configurations—utilizing the consultant-facilitator role and the theory and technology of applied behavioral science, including action research. (French & Bell, 1995, p. 144)

The practice of OD by creative internal and external practitioners over the past 30 years has produced an ever-expanding inventory of what some call *techniques* and others *interventions*. These can be classified into groups or family clusters, although specific OD applications may feature interventions from one or several clusters. They include

1. *Diagnostic activities* to identify the status of a problem, the 'way things are.' Methods range from proactive devices such as 'build a collage that represents for you your place in this organization' to the more traditional data collection methods of interviews, questionnaires, surveys, and meetings.

2. *Team-building activities* are designed to enhance the effective operation of work teams. They may relate to task issues, such as the way things are done, the needed skills to accomplish tasks, the resource allocations necessary for task accomplishments; or they may relate to the nature and quality of the relationships between the team members or between members and the leader.

3. *Intergroup activities* improve the effectiveness of interdependent groups. They focus on joint activities and the output of the groups considered as a single system rather than as two subsystems.

4. *Survey feedback activities* are similar to the diagnostic activities mentioned in that they are a large component of those activities. These activities center on actively working the data produced by a survey and designing action plans based on the survey data.

5. *Education and training activities* are activities designed to improve skills, abilities, and knowledge of individuals. They may be directed toward technical skills required for effective task performance or may be directed toward improving interpersonal competence.

6. *Techno-structural or structural activities* are designed to improve the effectiveness of the technical or structural inputs and constraints affecting individuals or groups. The activities may take the form of (a) experimenting with new organization structures and evaluating their effectiveness in terms of specific goals or (b) devising new ways to bring technical resources to bear on problems.

7. *Process consultation* is an approach in which the client is given insight into the human work processes in organizations and taught skills in diagnosing and managing them. Primary emphasis is on processes such as communications, leader and member roles in groups, problem solving, decision making, group norms, group growth, leadership, authority, intergroup cooperation, and intergroup competition.

8. *Grid organization development* is a six-phase, three- to five-year change model involving the total organization. This approach starts

ith individual managers' skills and leadership abilities, moves to ̲am improvement activities, and then to intergroup relation activities. Later phases include corporate planning for improvement, developing implementation tactics, and an evaluation phase.

9. *Third-party peacemaking* is conducted by a skilled consultant (the third party). It is based on confrontation tactics and an understanding of the processes involved in interpersonal conflict and conflict resolution.

10. *Coaching and counseling* features nonvaluative feedback given by others to an individual and the joint exploration of alternative behaviors.

11. *Life- and career-planning activities* focus on life and career objectives and how to achieve them.

12. *Planning and goal-setting* include theory and experience in planning and goal setting, utilizing problem-solving models, planning paradigms and ideal organization versus real organization "discrepancy" models.

13. *Strategic management* focuses on their organization's basic mission and goals and environmental demands, threats, and opportunities and engages in long-range action planning.

14. *Organization transformation techniques* are changes including management philosophy, reward systems, the design of work, the structure of the organization, organization mission, values, and culture. Total quality programs are transformational; so are programs to create high-performance organizations or high-performance work systems.[1]

As we will illustrate later, many of the interventions employed in these families are equally useful in AT&R. However, a note of caution:the relative importance of techniques in modern OD ought to be considered. Edgar Schein argued eloquently that many practitioners have forgotten the original OD vision's focus on process, attitudes, and values and have become fixated on the elaboration and imposition of techniques. He suggested that OD must be premised on a set of assumptions about, "How things really work and how they ought to work." Schein cautioned,

> The essence of OD was the underlying theory about the learning and change process, the philosophy and attitude that one had to figure out how to help the client system to help itself. The use of any given technique did not guarantee that it was being used with the right attitude or

assumptions, hence the identification of OD with particular techniques implies from the outset a misunderstanding of what the "essence" of OD was, and, in my opinion should continue to be. This essence was for many of us a new vision of how one could work with and improve human systems, but my fear is that such a vision and the attitude that it generated are being lost in the mass of technologies that today connote OD. (cited in Schein, 1990, p. 14)

These concerns readily apply to the entire family of action research, OD, and AT&R. Although techniques or interventions are the nuts and bolts of these approaches, they must not displace the primacy of a genuinely collaborative and generic employee–management-based approach. Schein warns that whether the practitioner is a line manager or an inside or outside consultant, if he or she possesses only intervention skills without a knowledgeable commitment to the helping nature of OD process and values, the experience "is not only likely to be a waste of time but downright dangerous" (Schein, 1990, p. 25).

STORYTELLING AS CASE HISTORY

During the 1950s through the early 1970s, Gardner had a researcher's discipline of keeping personal journals of his ongoing experiences at a state agency he referred to as the State Fund. It was during this State Fund project that he developed his method for changing organizations that he would later call AT&R. Recounting some of his experiences can provide valuable insights into the origins of AT&R. The experiences of the other AT&R practitioners that have been using AT&R methods ever since can provide insights into the practical application of AT&R as well. In addition, the results of their research and development of AT&R have provided refinements on the methods. Their experiences and research can provide practical examples of some of the key points and pitfalls practitioners encounter in the various stages of using the AT&R methods to help organizations transform themselves into changing organizations today. Therefore, the experiences of Gardner and the authors as practitioners are not presented as formal case histories. They are presented in a narrative style of storytelling in order to give the events-as-process a flavor of the human social dynamic that appears as background in case histories, but is the primary substance of the process of people changing their behaviors and thereby their organizations.

As a convention for this section of the book we have chosen to refer to many of the organizations involved in generic terms in order to observe the privacy and confidentiality of those involved. For example, some descriptions involve a large West Coast County and others involve a large East Coast County, and so on. Also, certain critical facts may have been changed for this purpose as well. In addition, the experiences that are described are those of the authors', sometimes as outside consultants, sometimes as inside consultants, sometimes as line employees. As a convention we do not differentiate between the authors, and will refer to our part as actors in the events as "practitioners."

CHANGING AT&R

AT&R as a method for creating changing organizations is itself a changing thing. It has been continually developed by AT&R practitioners learning from the client organizations as well. Therefore, in this handbook section on AT&R, various stages of the AT&R process are described not only as they were first formulated by Gardner, but also as they have been researched and developed by AT&R practitioners and clients in the field. Gardner explained it this way:

> Lewin's contributions to normative reeducation strategies of changing stemmed from his vision of the required relationship between action researchers, educators, and practitioners. In AT&R the scientist and trainer (interveners) are part of the field to be examined, the problem, and the experimental solution. (Gardner, 1974, p. 107)

The research aspect of AT&R provides practitioners a means for discovery of new knowledge to continually improve the AT&R methods. The reeducation aspect of AT&R creates an environment for practitioners to link action research methodology to other resources for changing organizations such as organization development (French et al., 1983), strategic management (Nutt & Backoff, 1992), total quality management (Wolf, 1992), re-engineering the corporation

(Hammer, 1997), reinventing government (Osborne & Gaebler, 1992), the learning organization (Senge, 1990), and perhaps now the agile organization (Roberts & Paul, 1995).

NOTE

1. These clusters and definitions are condensed versions from French and Bell (1995), pp. 163–166. Cluster 7 is based on Schein (1988). The definition for cluster 8 is premised on the work of Blake and Mouton (1970). Cluster 9 is based on Walton (1969).

PART II

AT&R AS A METHOD FOR DEVELOPING CHANGING ORGANIZATIONS: A GUIDE FOR PRACTITIONERS AND PARTICIPANTS

This guide is designed to provide basic information about each stage, narrative accounts of the stage in use, and notes from Neely Gardner's journals describing the process of developing the AT&R stage in a research project. Throughout, an attempt has been made to include as much of Gardner's ideas and thoughts as possible. Therefore, we have designed the AT&R cycle as a map of the changing organization territory (see Figure II.1).

A menu for each AT&R stage is provided at the beginning of each stage. The menu includes four modules. The first module is action. This module is a description of the change action that takes place in that stage. The training module is an abbreviated list of training that should be considered during that stage. The AT&R approach emphasizes the role of training as the foundation for change. Whatever "magic" attaches to the process seems to be generated by the involvement of those who will be affected when changes are made. The research module is a narration of the research and experimental activities that should take place. The outcome module describes the expected outcome of the stage.

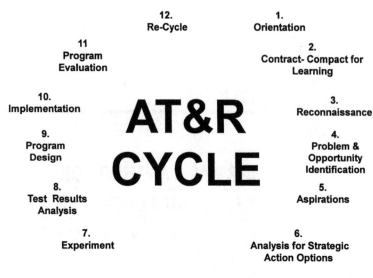

Figure II.1. AT&R Cycle

Together these four modules are intended as a guide for practitioners in using the AT&R approach to changing organizations. The stages are organized in recurring cycles in order to emphasize the iterative nature of the process. It is not meant to be linear or sequential. Many stages may be active concurrently, and subsequent stages are meant to influence prior stages. Therefore, there is nothing significant in having twelve stages over some other number. It is clear that the overall change process can have as many subsets of stages as seems practical. In any case, the steps must lead to new personal insights, group values, and beliefs and bring about a changing of values and norms. Each stage along the way is accompanied by an educational process, either experiential or cognitive or both. Each cycle of learning is supportive of a progressive level of change, and each level of experience and learning creates the basis for even further change. As the participants develop, the organization becomes a learning organization and therefore, a changing organization.

CHAPTER 4

AT&R STAGE 1: ORIENTATION

MENU FOR AT&R STAGE 1: ORIENTATION

Action   *Orientation should provide a time for raising and answering questions that help in developing the level of trust between intervenor and client. It is also a time of learning about the nature of the field to be examined and the manner in which the activity will be conducted. Trust must start with modeling on the part of the intervenor. He or she is obligated to be open about his or her values so that the intervenor cannot in any way be charged with undertaking manipulative activities. All clients should be aware that AT&R has a participative thrust, and that by its very nature it tends to enhance the position of the individual and to diffuse the sources of power. Effectiveness should be viewed from the perspectives of the individual, the organization, and society (Gardner, 1974).*

Training   *Participatory management; the consultative approach to change; establishing trust; the AT&R Process: What it can do and what it cannot do.*

Research   *Discuss with the client(s) the perspectives toward making organizational change from the point of view of:*

1. *The people who most likely will be involved in or by change: Who are they? And what has been their overall past experience and involvement in change within the organization? Key Individuals: The person of contact/Client, Executives and Managers, Employees/Participants.*

2. *The organization's capabilities to deal with change: structure, processes, service/products, and resources.*

3. *The organization's external climate for change: clients/customers, suppliers, the organization's industry, field, or social context in general. Write up a view of the situation and review it with the client to create a joint situation statement.*

4. *The organization's mission, goals, and objectives: Do they incorporate the need for change or are they aimed at keeping the status quo?*

Outcome   *Situation analysis statement.*

WHERE DOES "CHANGING" START?

At the University of Montana there was an English professor who always opened his lecture on Hamlet with the question, "Where does the play begin?" The students would offer everything from when the Ghost walks on the battlements to when the murder of Hamlet's father had occurred, which was sometime before Act I. After rejecting all of the students' suggestions, and with a grand Shakespearean flourish, he served up the answer: *in medias res.* Like Hamlet, most organization change begins right in the middle of things. The function of the orientation stage is to get a sense of the organization's current situation.

In this first stage the practitioner is contacted by someone in the client organization. Who that person (or persons) is usually depends on the practitioner's relationship to the client organization. If the practitioner is a professional outside consultant, she or he will most probably be contacted by some official of the client organization. If the practitioner is a professional internal consultant within the client organization, they may be approached directly by executives, managers, or employee groups for assistance. If the practitioner is not a professional consultant but a manager, he or she may simply apply the method as part of the management approach. If the practitioner is not a consultant but a member of a line work unit, the AT&R methods can be introduced to the team's development. Or anyone with these AT&R skills can use them as individuals in the performance of their work. Finally, many practitioners have found these methods useful in their own individual life and family development. Although this book will be presenting AT&R in an organizational setting, practitioners can be anyone who can use the AT&R methodology as a guide to changing human organization—and this includes organizations that are personal; family related; work-unit related; departmental; corporate; agency related; and county, state, federal, or international related.

This stage makes "first contact" and gets the lay of the land. It can simply be an informal conversation of a few minutes to an organization-wide survey and feedback effort. Each engagement will be different. But the purpose will be the same: to assess the situation.

EXAMPLE IN PRACTICE:
REORGANIZATION IN A LARGE WESTERN COUNTY

Some years ago, an AT&R practitioner was "lent" by a state agency to help the director of personnel of a large, fast-growing county in California's Silicon Valley to help the county reorganize its bureaucratic Department of Personnel (Foss, 1987). The director had attended Gardner's National Training and Development Service seminar for Action Training and Research in Aspen, Colorado (Fisher, 1992). The director wanted to use action training and research methods to develop the department into an organization that could meet the constantly changing needs of county agencies and the citizens that use their respective services. In this case, the practitioner had already developed an all-important relationship of trust with the director.

The director ushered the practitioner into the executive offices of the county and introduced him to the County's chief executive officer (CEO). "Howard, this is the practitioner in action training and research I've been telling you about. I've convinced his agency to lend him to us for our OD project."

"Oh," the tall, angular CEO replied, scrutinizing the practitioner, "I hear, you're the 'OD' guy that's going to go in there, wave his magic wand around, and straighten out all those personnel people!" The County CEO's initial reaction was not atypical.

An action training and research practitioner coming in to help an organization change is first treated as a "foreign body" with which that organization must cope. The practitioner can expect to be viewed as a potential pathogen vector until the organization's "auto-immune system" determines differently. As part of the initial orientation stage of action training and research, this entry event became an opportunity for the practitioner to explain briefly to the CEO the principles of the action training and research process. For the CEO this briefing included a description of the skill transfer of the action training and research methods from the practitioner to the people in the department. It also included underscoring the importance of the participative nature of action training and research and having the people affected by the change brought in on the decisions for the changes needed.

The CEO sat down to hear what his visitors had to say. The director of personnel explained that the people in the personnel department would be learning how to change their organization themselves as an ongoing process after the practitioner had completed the initial action training and research process.

"You see," the practitioner explained to the CEO, "What I need to do is to go in there and try to pass out magic wands to everybody." The CEO became more relaxed and shared his personal vision for modernizing the County's personnel department and other county agencies as well.

This "passing out of wands" is more commonly described as *empowerment*. Empowerment is the crux of action training and research. The core of this notion is to give those people who will be involved in the organization's change the skills and tools required to identify the organization's need for changing, and let them do it for themselves. They then will have the necessary tools to continually change their organization as the needs of their client agencies and the county's citizens change in the future.

In the orientation stage, the AT&R practitioner as the change agent always faces the dilemma of the impact of their physical insertion into the organization's status quo. William Bergquist (1996) described this impact as

> the effect the measurer has on the phenomenon being measured (the so-called Heisenberg [uncertainty] principle). Thus, an organization that brings in an outside consultant to study its culture will be subject to the particular perspective (including distortion) of the consultant's own culture. To turn around and study the consultant's culture in order to gain a better perspective on the consultant's report would require the hiring of yet another consultant to study the first consultant—or would require that client organization study the consultant's culture. The first approach would lead to infinite external regression (a consultant for the consultant for the consultant, ad infinitum); the second would lead to an internal regression (like looking at mirror images of mirror images of mirror images, ad infinitum). (1996, p. 582)

AT&R takes the second approach described by Bergquist, fully acknowledging the regressive pitfall involved. The change agent functions as an organization mirror in order to reflect back the organization's view of itself, while at the same time modeling the values of the AT&R process to develop internal "consultants." This behavior modeling is an example of the "T" of AT&R. The change agent can show others how to perform this mirroring function as part of the skill transfer of the AT&R methodology in order to enable the organization to change itself whenever needed in the future—in other words, to become a changing organization.

The infinite regression described by Bergquist can be avoided to the degree that the change agent is able to keep from contaminating the organization's action research efforts with (1) his or her own personal bias and ideas about what the organization's situation is, (2) what ought to be done about it, and (3) refraining from contributing any of the client's data gathered in the process. Without the training aspect of action research the change agent practitioner can be open to the constant challenges by various members of the client organization demanding that the change agent defend her or his right to intervene in the organization. Often people in the organization who question the intrusion of the AT&R practitioner may try to get the practitioner to contribute his or her "data" to the process in order to test the practitioner's method or to label the entire effort as the practitioner's personal agenda.

EXAMPLE IN PRACTICE: GOVERNMENT TRANSITION IN THE REPUBLIC OF PALAU

An action training and research practitioner was "lent" by the State Fund to the U.S. Department of the Interior's High Commissioner of the U.S. Trust Territories in Micronesia. In this case the action training and research intervention was for the practitioner and his wife, also an action training and research practitioner, to help the Trust territories' district administrator of Palau and the Palauans in making the transition from being a nation dominated first by the Spanish, then purchased by the Germans, then by the Japanese as a League of Nations Mandate, and then by the United States as UN Trust Territory, and now changing itself into the free nation of the Republic of Palau (Belau).

On the way to the islands (go West from Hawaii to Guam, turn left and then on past Yap) the practitioners stopped off to interview the presidents and governors of the other island groups of Micronesia that had already made this transition. Actually, the first stop was at Johnson Island, a lonely outpost south of Hawaii that the U.S. military was using in their nuclear program. Everything was built underground. The one small standing building that served as an airport had a sign that read, "NO, THIS IS NOT THE END OF THE EARTH! BUT YOU CAN SEE IT FROM HERE!"

The remaining stopovers included the Marshall Islands, Ponape, Guam, Siapan, and Yap. The officials from these island governments graciously shared their advice and experience in their already completed transition efforts. This travelogue progress of the practitioners was managed and monitored by teletype messages through the Trust Territory network that stretches thousands of miles across Micronesia.

Palau is located in the Pacific about 4° north of the Equator. Palau itself is a group of some 200 small islands set like emeralds in a diadem

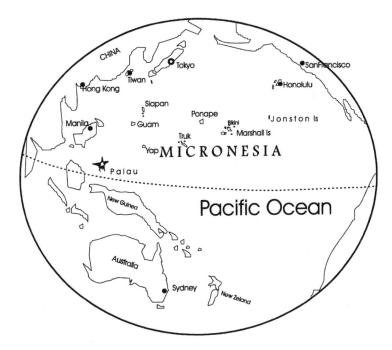

Figure 4.1. Palau in Micronesia

of a large oval coral atoll that is about 30 by 80 miles across (see Figure 4.1).

Some of the islands are the size of a house, with a few palm trees, a white coral sliver of a sandy beach on a crystal sapphire lagoon. Others are several miles across with mountains and surrounding mangroves. Koror, the capital, has a population of some 7000 people and is located on an island 7 miles long. The remaining 8000 Palauans live in small villages situated on some of the other 200 islands.

When the practitioners arrived in Koror, Palau's capital, they met first with the district administrator to become oriented on the current situation, at least as the district administrator understood it. In 6 months the Palauans would elect their first president. The practitioners' job was to help the Palauans organize their new government.

The day after the new president of Palau was inaugurated, the district administrator left the islands. The AT&R practitioners now faced a new or second intervention entry process with the new national government of Palau. Although the contract to help in the transition was originally with the U.S. Department of the Interior, the "client" was now the Republic of Palau.

Within the first week of the president's administration four people from the president's transition team showed up at the AT&R practitioners' office. This was a classic example of the beginning of Bergquist's infinite regression pitfall of consultants analyzing consultants.

The four Palauans came into the small office of one of the practitioners. The individuals were busy in the creation of their new nation. In retrospect, they were not unlike the teams that the practitioner would encounter years later as process historians of the 1992–1993 Clinton–Gore Presidential Transition Team (Bruce, 1996).

The leader of their transition team did most of the talking.

"We understand that you were hired by the High Commissioner to come out here to tell how to run our new government. So now, will you tell us that, please?" The four islanders then sat in silence, waiting for the practitioner to tell them how to run their new nation.

In Palauan culture, it is important to know that it is considered impolite for a person to ask another person a direct question. In Palau it is everyone's responsibility to tell others what they need to know without the other person having to ask direct questions. If a direct question is asked, it means the person asked is suspected of hiding something or that they have been remiss in their responsibilities. Therefore, the transition team leader's direct question was not to be interpreted by the practitioner as a particularly friendly one.

The practitioner described how he and his wife met with the community for the past 6 months. They had been talking with the people in Koror and the other villages in order to help them identify what they felt were the most important issues that the new government should address when elected. He pointed out to the transition team that there were nine basic national policy issues that emerged. "You may remember," he suggested, "the president included these several national issues in his inaugural address."

The four members of the transition team replied with a series of Groucho Marx–like eyebrow-raising gestures. In the Palauan culture, this facial gesture is equivalent to Western culture's nodding, "yes." The practitioner had a copy of the president's inaugural address on his desk. He opened it and read aloud the national policy issues to the visitors:

The national issues our new government will address first are,

1. How we get the skills and knowledge we will need to do everything for ourselves,

2. How we go about developing our nation's resources to achieve self-reliance without really becoming more dependent to foreign aid,

3. What standard-of-living level or level of infrastructure services should be available in the community,

4. How we develop our national leadership, our management, and our development talent among resident Palauans,

5. How we ensure that the national government supports and shares the resources, public service responsibilities, and funds with the states in a fair and equitable manner,

6. How we ensure that our cultural identity will not get lost in the shuffle between self-reliance and economic development,

7. How we ensure that the development of national resources is for the benefit of the whole community, yet still reward the entrepreneurial few who take the risks to develop resources on their own,

8. How we promote and control our finance in the face of economic development and foreign investment,

9. How we build on the strengths of our tradition's culture, economy, government, and justice instead of replacing them. (Remeliik, 1981)

"What I will need to know," the practitioner continued, "is the president's position on these ten national policy issues, and then I can help you with ways you might want to consider to organize your administration." The four men rose and left the room without a word.

The next week brought a rerun of the same scene. "OK," the transition team leader opened, "You were hired to show us how to run our government. You're a professional in this. So tell us."

The practitioner had expected their return. All along, he and his wife had been developing three models of administration representing a spectrum of possible organizations. The practitioner pulled out the chart to show the transition team. At one end of the spectrum was the classic hierarchical bureaucracy; at the other end a loose, collegial organization such as a university. In the middle was a project-oriented organization.

"There are many organizations you can consider," the practitioner said, explaining the chart. The one at this end of the scale," he continued, pointing to the bureaucratic model, "is how you were organized by the district administrator. Now, if your president wants to bring in light industry, make hydroelectric dams, and modernize the infrastructure you might want to look at this project organization in the middle of the scale. On the other hand, if his position is to protect the island culture at all costs, then perhaps you should look toward the other end of this chart. In any case, there is a fourth model that is not pictured on this chart, and that is the one you will design yourselves for Palau. It may include alternatives beyond the spectrum I have drawn here."

"You mean like our council of chiefs?" he asked. "How can we choose?"

"I can help you there. But first, you need to consider the president's position on the national issues in order to determine where on this scale of organizations you will want to start." Once again, the four men left in silence.

The third week the transition team returned again, this time with a new articulation to their demand. "You are a professional in this organization business. You have talked to everybody. You know much about Palau now. You have met in our council of chiefs many times. You have to have some idea about how you regard these national policy issues of the president's own speech. Don't mind if we want to bring industrial equipments in. You should at least be able to tell us how you would run our country. You should have an opinion on the best way on your chart for you. Will you tell us that?"

The practitioner felt himself finally pinned. They had succeeded in putting the question to him in a form he could not honestly avoid. He knew that if he answered the question as asked and told them how he would run the country, he and his wife might as well get on the next plane and leave the islands. He thought to himself, "How would Neely Gardner handle this?" *Creative confrontation* flashed in his mind as he replied, "Yes, you are right. There is one model on the chart that I prefer to the others. And I'll tell you what it is, but first you must make me one promise." The practitioner waited for the transition team leader to respond.

"Promise? Yes, of course, what is that?" The team leader's eyes never lost their calmness.

"You have to make me king. You make me king and I'll tell you how I'll run this country." The entire transition team was taken aback. "And I'll tell you something else."

"Oh," the leader gasped, "What's that?"

"I'll probably run this country better than you will. And I'll tell you something else," he said leaning close to the transition team leader, whose eyes had lost some of their calmness.

"What?"

"You're not going to like the way I run it." Again the transition team left without a further word.

The next week, the practitioner was appointed as special advisor to the president. Months later, during a boat trip to the transition team leader's village, he confided to the practitioner that they were trying to get rid of him, because he would not tell them how to run their country. "You were? OK!" he said.

"And you know," he explained, "We did come up with a fourth model ourselves. We organized the president's cabinet like our council of chiefs. You were right, we did it ourselves."

The practitioner as a change agent can respond to such challenges by providing the knowledge, values, and practices of AT&R, showing the practitioner's role is to help the challengers to learn to perform the action research process for themselves. The practitioners were resources there to help the Palauans learn to use their own resources. This was accomplished by the practitioners as experts in the field reflecting back the client organization's progress and training them in organization research methods.

THE PRACTITIONER AS AN ORGANIZATION MIRROR IN PRACTICE

In addition, during the orientation stage the practitioner can help the people address organization taboos they may have about discussing certain organizationally sensitive issues. The practitioner, as an organizational mirror, can reflect such issues into the action research arena that otherwise may not be addressed.

For example, last year an assistant department director in a large East Coast county had concerns about a small branch of his public agency. He invited an AT&R practitioner to help them work better as a team. It is not unusual to be approached by a potential client who has a perceived solution contained in the invitation. By having an orientation stage precede the contract setting stage, the practitioner has the opportunity of gaining his or her own perspective on the situation before agreeing to participate.

In this case, during the orientation stage with the branch it became evident that the nature of the group discussion was very guarded. At first the practitioner thought that this was a symptom of the effect of his entry into the group. Then, when the group discussion approached a serious subject, one of the members erupted with unacceptable behavior by most groups' interaction norms. The group sat as the person vented and then the group discussion went on as though it had not happened at all. Then the group dialog shifted to more task-oriented considerations.

Apparently, no one in the group would ever bring up this person's unacceptable behavior in group discussions. The group discussion always avoided that person's "hot buttons." When the practitioner asked for the group's reaction to this behavior, there was stunned shock. However, in the ensuing group discussion, they decided that all the members of the group had been enablers of the situation. By not dealing with the "unacceptable" behavior, it became de facto, acceptable denial behavior for their group discussions.

Once the group was able to restructure their group norm to make it also "acceptable" to deal with the member's behavior in group meetings, they found that they had much more fundamental issues that were making them dysfunctional as a group. One member of the group suggested they had been using the one member's strange behavior as a mask to avoid confronting their real and more substantive differences, which made working as a team difficult. Primarily, these differences involved the fact that as a group of six professional people and two part-time secretaries, the branch was involved in three somewhat competing functions. Beyond maintaining a certain level of civility in order to share the space and secretarial support, the group was able to admit that "teamwork" was not really required of the branch as a group. They were in a collegial association of professionals and technicians that shared the same space. As a result, two of the functions were reassigned to another department in the county, and the other was reassigned to another branch of the original department. The practitioner's main function in the group was merely to help the group raise its awareness of its own behavior by helping the members research their interactions with each other in the group, to mirror their actions back to them in the group, and to encourage them to take the responsibility to handle it themselves.

INITIAL ENCOUNTERS:
EVERY INTERVENTION IS A CHANGE

The initial entry of the change agent into the client organization is most important. As in the case of quantum physics, the mere act of an outside person coming in to look at an organization changes the status quo. Organizations initially tend to treat the practitioner as an outsider, usually with all the hospitality to which "outsiders" are entitled within the organization's cultural norms. This initial politeness ensues because the people in the organization are unsure at that initial point whether the change agent is a vector of disease, a vaccination virus, or whether the practitioner will help the organization plant the seeds of innovation that will determine the nature of the fruits of their efforts.

This entry situation recurs with each organization's subgroup as the practitioner enters deeper into the organization to the people in the work units. As in the case of the dysfunctional department branch, the first entry was with the assistant department director, and then again with the branch itself. In the case of the county personnel department, there were multilevel entries, the department director, the CEO, the various branches in the department such as pay and classification, employee relations, recruiting and testing, and so forth. It is clear that in Palau a major shift occurred after the inauguration of the new president.

When the AT&R practitioner becomes involved with any of these organization work units, they are in themselves to be considered as organizations. Each work unit creates its own culture, group norms, and leadership. The same is true for departments, divisions, and so on. Each organizational entity will have its own orientation stage, and so on, if it is to participate in the organization changes involved. Clearly, if AT&R methods are not provided to these organization work units involved in the change, they will not learn how to change their work unit organization for themselves in the future.

FROM NEELY GARDNER'S STATE FUND
JOURNALS: DEVELOPING THE ORIENTATION STAGE

In 1967 Gardner moved from government to the University of Southern California (USC) for a career in academia in order to work on the type of action research he called change *agentry*. He saw an opportunity to research and test his research at the State Fund. His work at the State Fund became the development arena for creating what he would later call action training and research (AT&R). The initial dialogue between himself as the change agent and the president of the State Fund became part of the orientation stage of AT&R.

The practitioner's initial entry as a change agent is very problematic for all concerned. This is true in Gardner's case as well. Originally, he had dealt with the State Fund before his AT&R intervention in the role of the state training officer. He had developed working relationships with a number of the State Fund executives during these training sessions. Even so, it was one thing to be the deliverer of expected executive training services delivered from another state agency and quite another to have Gardner come in as a practitioner from USC to facilitate the organization's metamorphosis from a staid hierarchical state agency into a "changing organization." Although the president had invited Gardner in, not all of the executives were happy about this intervention. However, the AT&R intervention is not only part of Lewin's "unfreezing" process. Gardner saw it as an excellent time to train the client organization, particularly the executive groups, in the principles and practices of AT&R. Gardner noted,

> As an outside practitioner, I was aware that I must attend carefully to the way in which I entered the organization. I felt there was a high level of trust between me and the [State Fund] executive group. They knew me and had some feel for my values, experience, and capabilities. Even so, I thought it best to be very sure we understood each other. They should know that my bias was for participative forms, open communication, distribution of power, and toward autonomous work groups and away from hierarchical structures. We discussed these issues openly. As nearly as I could tell, only one of the eight members of the executive group was covertly agitated. The comfort level of the others was sufficiently high that I felt encouraged to move ahead.

During that stage the president explained to Gardner that when he became president of the State Fund in 1966, he recognized that the workers' compensation environment had been in a state of rapid change because the entire market situation of the 1950s and 1960s had grown dramatically in California. He told Gardner that, through the years, the State Fund had prospered and maintained its competitiveness without losing sight of its legislated mandate: to constantly set the standards for the workers' compensation industry.

As the years went by, the job of the State Fund became more and more difficult. In the beginning, private insurance carriers were not interested in compensation insurance, but as time passed, escalating medical costs made workers' compensation insurance become a significant part of the policyholder's cost of doing business. Private insurance companies discovered this as a new business opportunity for themselves. Not only did the competition with the State Fund increase, but private carriers were able to encourage greater and greater legislative restrictions on the Fund.

The State Fund was organized much like private mutual insurance companies with various district offices located around the state in northern and southern divisions that were subdivided into regions. The district office managers reported to the regional manager, who reported to a central division chief, who reported to the executive vice president, who reported to the president. The State Fund also had the traditional organizational pyramid of hierarchical "stovepipe" staff departments in the home office located in San Francisco. They too were subdivided into two divisions, one for insurance-specific functions such as underwriting, policy accounts, billing, and safety. The other division included more general administrative functions such as personnel, finance, training, computer systems, and internal audits.

As a state agency, the State Fund employees were civil servants covered by the State Personnel Board rules and regulations. The State Fund also came under most of the other rules and regulations of a state agency in terms of budgeting, purchasing, and property management.

However, the State Fund is an enterprise fund. This means that it receives no revenues from the state. The State Fund has to earn its operating revenues from the premiums paid by policyholders. In fact, like any private insurance carrier, it pays taxes to the state in the form of a premium tax. In addition, California employers do not have to purchase their workers' compensation insurance from the State Fund. They can buy it from any insurance carrier that agrees to sell it to them.

The State Fund did have one area of monopoly. All the local public agencies in the state had to insure with the State Fund. However, that began to erode in the 1960s. Laws were changed to make it easier for public agencies to insure themselves and outsource their claims and safety service functions to the private sector. For example, the City of Long Beach was experiencing vast increases in disability cases among police officers.

The finance director of that municipality regularly lambasted the Fund, with a great deal of emotion, because he regarded the Fund as wasteful and unresponsive.

> At the time the city was being hit with a great many disability claims . . . the city's claims experience worsened and the premiums to the State Fund grew. [When the finance director] pointed this out to the Fund people and asked for technical help in finding solutions for mitigating the problem . . . he was stonewalled by the Fund. He was told it was not a Fund problem. And it was within this context that he subsequently took the city into self-insurance as a less costly way of handling the problem. Other jurisdictions followed suit, including the giant County of Los Angeles. (Sherwood, 1990, p. 1)

One by one, these large public agency accounts were disappearing from the State Fund's portfolio. Meanwhile, the State Fund had retained much of its original organization from when it was created in 1914. Even after bringing in practitioners from Stanford Research Institute, the disconnection between the State Fund and its policyholders continued. The president explained that

> We were experiencing trouble in keeping up with recruiting and training. A number of longtime executives were reaching retirement. A number of minor personnel administration brush fires broke out in various parts of the organization. Many of us became convinced that the highly centralized, pyramidal organizational structure was placing an impossible load on the [president] and creating serious blocks to necessary communication. A number of vertical organizational structures based on

technical or professional specialization were tending to compete with one another and a number of rough interfaces resulted. And finally, strong regional rivalry existed between the northern California and southern California Divisions, occasionally verging on open warfare. (Young, 1969, p. 1)

At this time Gardner found the State Fund was a conglomerate of management philosophies from an authoritarian hierarchy to the new participative management style just coming into vogue, and all the points within that universe. Almost all managers at significant levels in the Fund participated in various educational programs. They included the management development program that was initiated by Gardner's Training Division of the State of California. It stressed the virtues of the participative model that was at the core of what would later become his AT&R method for building changing organizations. Other management development programs the State Fund managers had attended included those held by the University of California at Berkeley Business School. Virtually all attended laboratory or sensitivity training not once but a number of times. Team development laboratories were common. The executives experienced various T-Group sessions with Carl Rogers and Robert Tannenbaum. They attended the UCLA Leadership and OD Labs. Continual management development efforts included training in the Kepner–Tregoe decision-making and problem-solving process, attendance at American Management Association Conference seminars, and many other programs in mid-career education and training.

Gardner felt that perhaps as a consequence of the management training the president had received, he felt it was best for the State Fund to move toward an open participatory approach. And the president did so even though he was operating in an organization that evinced fierce competitiveness, both internally and externally as a competitive insurance agency. The president felt the need for counseling in order to understand the concept of OD. He believed that most major functionaries of the State Fund also needed such help. Gardner, Rogers, and Tannenbaum helped provide this counseling as part of the orientation stage of AT&R in Gardner's State Fund experience.

Gardner's sensitive orientation work at the State Fund provided the foundation for the AT&R practitioner's initial contact with the client organization. First, he begins his training of the organization/client by modeling the AT&R principles at the outset. Second, the entry experience of other practitioners demonstrates how this entry stage recurs as the practitioner delves deeper into the organization. In addition, it is clear that each intervention is different and defies the practitioner to come into the organization with a cookbook approach to change the organization.

Throughout this stage, and as we will see in the following several stages of the research phase of AT&R, an organic approach is called for. This organic approach allows the practitioner to guide the people in the organization through the unique situation they find themselves in, and to learn the methods they need to change it for themselves.[1]

GARDNER'S INTERVIEWING
TECHNIQUES FOR SITUATION ANALYSIS

The initial stage of orientation requires the practitioner to learn the client organization's situation. Usually this information is obtained through a personal interview process with people at various levels of the organization. However, in all the phases of the action training and research project, the interview is a significant part of the process. It will be one of the practitioner's most used and most important skills and is applicable to both counseling and data collection activities. In action training and research, it is important for members of the client group to participate as principals in the process; therefore, one of the practitioner's obligations is to help clients develop the greatest possible interviewing skill.

TYPE OF CLIENT INTERVIEWER

There are situations in which those to be trained will not be highly educated or oriented toward behavioral science. In fact, the participant researcher may be a member of an indigenous group in a core city or of the population of a developing country and may have very little formal education. Frequently, the indigenous action researcher becomes an excellent interviewer. It is possible that such a person will possess sensitivity beyond that achieved by some highly trained persons. Further, the indigenous researcher may find it easier to develop the trust of the persons interviewed than an outsider might. This is important, because the reliability of data sometimes depends as much on the level of trust that exists between interviewer and interviewee as it does on research capability. Given the motivation that frequently comes from participation, the indigenous researcher often becomes surprisingly capable in applying interview processes appropriately.

In most organizations in western countries, the type of client participant one encounters today is fairly well educated but is not necessarily familiar with a behavioral science approach. Experience in training such people suggests that the difficulties in developing competence in interviewing are less than one might expect. Time and time again, the client action researcher does a better job of eliciting information from the respondent group than a well-trained outsider practitioner.

MOTIVATION OF RESPONDENT

If the interview is to be productive, it is important that the respondent be motivated to cooperate. Motivation occurs when the perceived situation is compatible with the respondent's needs and goals. There are both extrinsic and intrinsic motivating factors that can stimulate a cooperative response in the action research interview. Extrinsic motivational factors include the following.

1. The interviewer is seen as someone who is there to help.
2. The subject matter of the interview is related to the change the respondent desires.
3. The interviewer is not relating to the respondent as an authority figure.

Intrinsic motivational factors include the following.

1. A good relationship develops with the interviewer.
2. Responding to the interviewer is in conformance with a social norm.
3. The interview offers the respondent a rare opportunity to talk and to be heard with understanding.

To develop a situation in which the motivational factors are maximally present, it is important to build a climate in which understanding and trust prevail. In building this climate, it helps if the respondent knows the answers to the following questions:

1. What is the purpose of the interview, so that the respondent can ascertain that the interview really relates to his or her situation and so that needs and goals may be personalized?
2. What is going to happen to the data provided by the respondent?
   a. Is it to be kept confidential?
   b. Who will see and review the data in the analysis process and in what form will it be published?
   c. Is anyone in managerial and leadership positions in the respondent's organization serious about using the action research findings that come out of the interviews?
3. In a general way, what does the researcher expect of the respondent in the course of the interview?
   a. What are the questions to which the person will be asked to respond?
   b. Is the interviewee competent to respond to such questions with reasonable success?
   c. How should the interviewee proceed in order to answer the questions?
   d. How much time will the interview require?
   e. What will be done with the notes taken during the interview and the summary of those notes that will be recorded in the action researcher's journal?

In community and organizational settings, respondents are likely to be inhibited in the interview. They need to have a feeling that what they say will not be attributed to the respondent. In the training given to client–researchers, the ethics of the confidential relationship between interviewer and interviewee needs to be emphasized. In working with hundreds of client–participants, Gardner found that there is great need for confidentiality. In most training sessions the discussion of the need to protect the respondent has been generated by the training group itself. An innate understanding of ethics of interviewing can be assumed to exist across the board, in both sophisticated and virtually illiterate workers.

INTERVIEWING

One of the most important things an interviewer can learn is an appreciation of the nondirective interviewing process and the skills required. In training client researchers to conduct patterned interviews, the practice has been to build as much proficiency in the use of nondirective skills as possible. This is done to ensure that many of the needed understandings and skills for conducting loosely structured, patterned interviews will have been partially achieved.

Some patterned interviews are more standardized than others. Both the focused interview and the nondirective interview are nonstandardized, with the interviewer being free to develop the situation in whatever way is deemed most appropriate (Phillips, 1966). There are few standardized questions. The nature of the questions should be dictated by the problems in the organization being researched.

There are three types of questions that generally elicit a great deal of data without impinging too greatly on the free flow of ideas or influencing by preconception the answer of the respondent. For example, when the State Fund sought to determine the views of the district managers and employees on the organization's progress, the following three questions were posed.

1. What are the things about the Fund organization and its operations that you would like to see continued and enhanced?
2. What are problem areas that you believe should be looked at with the view of improving the organization and its operation?
3. If you had the power to change the Fund with "a stroke of the pen" tomorrow morning, what changes would you make?

TYPES OF QUESTIONS

In patterned interviews, the broad topical questions cause the respondents to attempt to provide information within the parameters set by the question. Still, within these terms, they have considerable scope to explore problems on their own terms. Detailed questions allow the respondent less freedom of response; they are likely to result in data that are not as useful as might be desired. The reason is simple. The questions are constructed to meet the researcher's needs rather than the client's needs.

Organizational action researchers trained in the survey of the National Training and Development Service for State and Local Government were asked to operate within a framework of no more than three or four major questions. In their practice interviews, they were permitted to supplement these questions, provided the supplementary queries interfered only minimally with the input of the respondents. There are several types of questions with which trainees were asked to become familiar:

1. Yes/No. One was the very typical question that can be answered "yes" or "no," a type of question that is commonly used in the courtroom. Although yes/no questions can establish an answer to a very specific situational event or idea, they do not generate much data. In fact, yes/no questions sometimes prevent respondents from pursuing their own lines of thought. The yes/no question is derived from the preconceptions held by the interviewer, and the answers do not necessarily flow from the values, feelings, or experiences of the person being interviewed. In the action training and research preparation sessions, the use of yes/no questions is discouraged.

2. Leading. The *leading question* is also manipulative, because it limits the interviewee's choice and answers. Although not all such questions are as blatantly unfair as the classic, "When did you stop beating your spouse?" they do tend to skew the type of information that emerges from the interview. Another example of a leading question might be, "Explain why most employees in the respondent's union seem to be dissatisfied with their boss." The leading question may have the virtue of producing uniformity among respondents along the specific dimensions in which the investigator is interested. However, the reliability of the data thus obtained is questionable. The investigator who happens to have keen insights regarding the sources of problems or opportunities might obtain confirming information that might prove the investigator to be on target. Nonetheless, the manipulative nature of the question is inconsistent with the ethics of the AT&R approach.

3. Fixed-Alternative. There are also fixed-alternative questions that tend to elicit standardized information. An example of a fixed-alternative question would be, "With which one of your siblings do you relate the best? Your older brother? Your older sister? Or your younger sister?" Fixed alternative questions frequently appear in questionnaires. Although there are reasons that such questions must be used in some types of questionnaires, we have discouraged the use of fixed-alternative questions in action training and research.

4. Open-End. The two types of questions that trainees are encouraged to use are the open-end and the reflective questions. The open-end question is one that cannot be answered "yes" or "no." For example, "How do you feel about your job?" Although in this question there is a presumption that a person feels some way about the job, it does not indicate whether the interviewer believes the respondent feels either favorable or unfavorable. The person being interviewed must respond with a declarative statement of some kind.

5. Reflective. The reflective question, which grows out of the interview itself, is an attempt on the part of the interviewer to support the respondent and let the respondent know that what has been said is understood. As an example, the respondent might say, "I'm really uptight about the fact that I can't begin to get all my work done." The reflective question would be, "Are you frustrated because you haven't time to do everything that is expected of you?" Frequently, on being understood, the respondent is able to move more deeply into the subject area. If the interviewer's reflective questions do not in fact capture the thoughts and feelings of the respondent, respondents generally make a clarifying statement to straighten out the perceptions of the interviewer.

NATURE OF QUESTIONS

Interviewers need to be aware of the different types of questions, such as these listed:

1. Nonquestions. In addition to what has already been said, one must note that many questions are nonquestions (1959). For example,

"Don't you think" questions frequently mean, "I think"; probably the interjection should be set forth as a statement, for it really is not a question. It is hard to trace the genesis of the nonquestion habit, which is rampant in our culture. People who use the nonquestion take advantage of the person to whom the question is posed. It is relatively safe to say, "Don't you think we'd better be getting to the airport?" when one's colleague is carrying on a conversation with acquaintances and one is concerned lest the plane is missed. In a sense the burden is placed on the colleague for one's own anxieties and one's own ideas.

2. Probes. Probing questions nearly always proceed from a preconceived cognitive map held by the person who is making the inquiry. For example, the broad-pattern question might concern problems in the personnel system and the interviewee might begin to respond, "For one thing, the personnel process is very slow. I have been up for reclassification for 7 months now. It was just 7 months ago when the personnel analyst made my desk audit."

For the sake of argument, let us say that the respondent had some very significant things to say about the personnel classification system and the rather costly and cumbersome procedures used in its administration. But the interviewer, who was convinced that most personnel analysts were too young, inexperienced, and unsympathetic, chose to take the following attack on the questioning:

Interviewer: Were you interviewed by one of the junior personnel staff?

Respondent: I suppose you could say so. I think the analyst has worked in the section for about a year and a half.

Interviewer: Did you get the impression that he approached the desk audit objectively?

Respondent: That was several months ago, but as I recall the analyst seemed to be working from a checklist and didn't seem to understand some of the information that I was trying to give him concerning the difficulty of my job. I think this has something to do with the personnel department's point-evaluation system.

Interviewer: Then in addition to not being objective, you had a feeling that he really wasn't interested in your job?

Respondent: It is sometimes hard to talk to analysts. They seem to be living in a different world.

If one accepts the assumptions given about the respondent and interviewer, one can readily see that the probing question, rather than eliciting information on the personnel system, was being controlled by the interviewer in a way that precluded an exploration of the problem as seen by the respondent.

3. Hostile questions. Many questions are hostile. The most obvious are, "What did you mean by that?" "Whatever gave you that idea?" "Please tell me what you're up to." As we learn to hear what is being communicated, it can be observed that many subtly phrased questions are attacking in nature. As one listens, one finds that the questioner is frequently the aggressor, and the recipient often exhibits discomfort when attempting to cope and defend against the question. Even when an attack is not intended, questions cause some people discomfort to the extent that they modify their own communications.

For example, I might be saying, "I was hoping your report would be ready by noon because I could very well use it to advantage in this afternoon's meeting." At the moment I was making the statement, a noisy truck was passing, a jet was going overhead, and you actually did not hear what I was saying. Therefore, you said, "I didn't hear you. Would you mind repeating what you just said?" This, in turn, would cause me to rephrase my statement as follows, "I don't want to bother you because I know you are very busy, but if your report is ready, I would like to have a copy to use in a meeting this afternoon."

The object of focusing on the nature of questions with a training group is twofold. First, trainees need to be aware of the impact of their own questions on respondents and others. Second, they need to sharpen their own hearing to understand the portent of questions posed to them. These interviewing techniques need not be limited to situation analysis. They can be useful in most of the stages in which the practitioner needs to elicit information from people in the client organization.

SUMMARY

The orientation stage involves the first encounter with the client organization and a situation analysis that can range from an informal discussion to a series of interviews to a full-blown participant survey effort. The purpose is to establish a working relationship with the contact people in the client organization, to get some understanding of the organization's current situation, and to begin to assess whether AT&R might be appropriate in helping the organization to become one that can change itself—namely, to help it become a changing organization. At the same time, this stage is designed to allow the client organization, or at least those persons with which the practitioner is in contact, to gain a good understanding of the AT&R methodology and to assess whether they want to learn how to change their organization for themselves and whether the AT&R methodology can be adapted to their organization. This research provides the basis for working out the agreement to proceed in the second stage, contract setting.

NOTE

1. Each AT&R chapter includes a section from Neely Gardner's journals. The substance and quotes are compiled from his notes and journals, which he put together in an unfinished manuscript, *Organization Theory and Behavior: An Approach to Managing in a Changing Environment*.

CHAPTER 5

AT&R STAGE 2: CONTRACT SETTING

MENU FOR AT&R STAGE 2: CONTRACT SETTING

Action *The contract need not be a written one, although a memorandum of understanding can be useful when drawn in a spirit of trust. Contracts probably should be considered psychological agreements, derived through open- and tough-minded interaction. During the contract-setting period the participation is made meaningful to the extent that the intervenor is able to model and elicit effective and authentic communication (Gardner, 1974).*

Training *Listening, leveling, values analysis.*

Research *Desired management and time frame: what the client expects or sees as the role of the intervenor.*

The client's and intervenor's level of commitment: nature of their personal participation.

Resources furnished.

Willingness not to manipulate the process and participants.

How will we keep score on our achievements?

Values comparison.

Write up a memorandum of understanding with the client outlining the scope of the change being considered.

Outcome   *A memorandum of understanding.*

AN AGREEMENT TO PROCEED

Whether the practitioner is an external or internal consultant, a manager, or member of a work unit, employing the often invasive methods that might be used when using the AT&R method as a guide requires agreement on the part of the other people involved. This is not only because AT&R methodology requires open participation but also because changing human organizations means humans changing themselves to the extent of the project at hand. Therefore, it is paramount that not only do the officers of the organization agree to the project, indeed initiate it, but as the project involves organizational entities and work units within the organization, this contract setting must be resumed there as well.

"Contract" may be too strong a word for many AT&R projects. Clearly, external consultants will often have a business contract to set the legal and business expectations of the project. However, this is not the contract we are referring to in this stage. The contract is the agreement between people to work together in changing themselves. It is the agreement to create an interpersonal relationship for changing the people's organization.

AN EXAMPLE IN PRACTICE: STRATEGIC PLANNING FOR INFORMATION TECHNOLOGY

"I don't know why you are willing to go over there and work with those guys," the fire chief said. "That's a bunch of wily rascals, you know." He had developed the Fire and Rescue Department from a sleepy rural volunteer company into one of the top urban Fire and Rescue Departments in the country. For example, he brought the AT&R practitioner in to organize their program to research and test innovative fire and rescue equipment and methods. Now, at the request of the County Executive Office, he was reluctantly agreeing to lend the practitioner to the county executive to help his strategic management team in their strategic planning for the County's information technology development.

"Well, maybe," the practitioner replied. "But as the saying goes: At least they're our wily rascals. Anyway, Chief, they're talking about developing a strategic management team to provide a better organization of the county's computer resources to meet the fast pace of change in that area."

"They wouldn't know strategic management if it sat on the conference table in front of them." the fire chief corrected. The fire chief had often been a target of their "bureaucratic concern" in his efforts to build the county's world-class Fire and Rescue Department.

"Sure," the practitioner replied, "but that's why they may need help in changing the county's organization of its information technology resources. That's a beginning strategic decision in itself."

"You just watch out," the fire chief warned. "They all seem to be at each other's throats just now. You'll be 'small change' if you get in their way."

The fire chief described the strategic management team as consisting of the deputy county executive for management and budget, the budget director, the director of general services, the personnel officer, the director of information technology development, and the director of computer operations and networks. The fire chief warned the practitioner that few if any of these people had a penchant for participative management, at least in the sense that it is used in AT&R. He felt that the only cohesiveness in this strategic management team was between the deputy county executive and the budget director. They had set up this group of organization adversaries in an effort to reconcile their differences and develop a strategic computer resource development plan for the 1990s.

The practitioner met with the county's budget director who was the de facto leader of the strategic management team. She had been the one to ask the fire chief for the loan of the practitioner to help them. The director said she had a mandate from the chief and deputy executive officers to make a systemic change outlined in her proposed new model for strategic management of information resources. She told him about her recent report to the county executive officer. It also had been distributed to all agency and department directors. "The success of our strategic management depends on the shaping of all organizational aspects toward a common vision of the future," she explained. "We need both a fundamental change in our approach to the process of information resource development and structural reorganization as well."

"We recommended that a new approach to developing information systems incorporate strategic thinking at every level. . . . A reorganization is recommended to provide an adequate structure to support a new operational model, as well as the integration of culture and controls." The practitioner replied that the mandate provided a good arena for AT&R methods and agreed to join the strategic management team.

FORMAL AND PSYCHOLOGICAL CONTRACTS

Gardner explained that the AT&R contract for changing organizations does not have to be a written one, although a memorandum of understanding can be useful if drawn with a spirit of trust. Clearly, if the practitioner is not a member of the organization, a written contract is usually required for business and legal reasons. However, this is not the contract that Gardner has in mind. Contracts for changing the organization can instead be considered psychological agreements derived through open and candid interaction. During the contract-setting period the organization's participation is made meaningful to the extent that the practitioner is able to model and engage the people in the organization in effective and authentic communication (Gardner, 1974).

The word *contract* is loaded with a lot of legal baggage and seems a questionable term for this second AT&R stage. However, considering its original roots—*tractus:* to draw something along; *con:* together with someone else—it is quite appropriate. In addition, training has the same root, *tractus* (Partridge, 1958). Because Kurt Lewin's reeducation process is the underlying theory for AT&R's methodology to develop changing organizations, AT&R uses the term *contract setting* in this light.

At the core, contracts involve a sharing of an opinion, a willingness to travel the same path, to pull the same load together—in other words, a consensus among the parties to the contract. Typically it is an agreement to exchange or change values, sometimes goods, sometimes services, sometimes behaviors. The contract-setting stage involves primarily comparing and reconciling of values into a mutual understanding of the organization's situation through situational analysis in terms of strategic management (Nutt & Backoff, 1992). In this values analysis process the practitioner facilitates a discussion of the basic values of AT&R involved in the managing of change in an organization. At the same time, the clients articulate the basic values of their organization. This can be done in informal discussions or in a workshop setting in which the organization values are listed alongside the key values of the AT&R practitioner. The comparison has two purposes. First it shows that there can be honest differences of values and different legitimate points of view. Second, if the values are severely divergent, then it will be apparent to all that some reconciliation will have to be accomplished if the AT&R method is to be useful in the situation of this organization. This comparison approach is also useful because it allows for the involvement of large groups of people. The lists can be compared and the apparent disconnects can be discussed and reconciled.

Another important function of values analysis is to be a source of evaluation criteria for decision making about choosing alternative solutions and action options in the following stages of AT&R. The values analysis can also be a good source of criteria for evaluating program results, as well as evaluating the entire AT&R effort in the last re-cycle stage.

EXAMPLE IN PRACTICE: VALUES ANALYSIS
WITH THE STRATEGIC MANAGEMENT TEAM

The orientation stage with the county's strategic management team occurred in the semiweekly meeting in which the deputy county executive ruled the group like a Venetian Doge reclining on a divan. He was reputed to have treated the previous director of information technology development in a nonparticipatory manner. That director often had to make presentations about information technology problems to the deputy county executive. The deputy county executive was primarily a finance expert. He professed little understanding of the technical workings of the computer systems of the Information Technology Development Department. He had two large cards in the top drawer of his desk. Whenever the deputy county executive got lost in what he called "computer gibberish," he would pull one of the two large cards and hold it up for the director to read from across the deputy's executive desk. One card read in large black letters: "WHO CARES?" If the director persisted in his presentation much longer, the deputy held up the other one that read: "BORING!!" Needless to say, the beleaguered director finally quit.

The deputy county executive and the director of Office of Management and Budget (OMB) dominated the strategic management team's meetings. Because the department directors had no coherent vision for the future development of information technology, a field that was changing rapidly in front of them, the deputy county executive and the budget director constantly castigated the other department heads for making a mess of the county's aging computer system. The other major concern the deputy county executive and budget director flailed the other members with was the county's impending move to a new three-building complex in a year. They were concerned about what computer equipment and systems would be needed.

However, there was general agreement among the group that the county's situation with its information technology was in terrible shape and that the near future looked even worse for them. The dialogue from the semiweekly meetings revolved around disagreements about whose fault it was that the system was in such poor shape and what ought to be done to fix it. Fueling this diatribe was a change in the revenues coming to the county's budget. The county had been riding on an accelerating revenue growth boom from mushrooming property values for the past 15 years. Like many other government entities, they experienced was a subsequent decline in property values. For the first time, the county revenues were going down instead of up.

The practitioner suggested that the group do a values analysis of the county's management values as seen by the members of the strategic management team. At the same time the practitioner listed his values in using AT&R methods. Then each list was evaluated with

TABLE 5.1 Values Comparison Analysis

AT&R Values		*County Strategic Action Team Values*	
H	Participation	H	Triple A Bond rating
M	Risk Taking/Trust	H	Order
M	Open Communication of Feelings	L	Professionalism
H	Action Research as Experimentation	M	Effective Systems
L	Entrepreneurial	H	Cost Conscious
L	Program Budgeting	H	Budget Control
H	Public Service Delivery	M	Compliance
H	Development as Reeducation	L	Training as Employee Benefit
M	Survey Feedback & Accountability	M	Efficiency

regard to the four or five most important values (H), and the lowest 1 or 2 values (L). The rest automatically were rated in the mid-value range (M). The primary object of this exercise was to see which, if any, of the AT&R values would be most useful in guiding the group to develop a coherent strategic plan for information technology. The results are shown in Table 5.1.

The differences between these lists serve as an opportunity for the practitioner to relate the AT&R process to the organization's situation as the strategic management team sees it as individuals and as a group. It is also an opportunity for the practitioner to train the group in the basics of the AT&R methodology. Any such list will be somewhat abstract. This is usually because the values espoused by the organization in mission statements, policies, and rules do not always match the values enacted in the organizations' day-to-day decisions and actions. However, with both points of view in mind, a more open dialogue can begin in the sharing of values. For example, the practitioner discussed that trust without risk taking can be a dead end. One element needs to build on the other. Otherwise, it poses the group with the dilemma: "How can we earn trust if we are not allowed to take risks in the first place?" Without risk, trust can become simple blind obedience.

The practitioner used the many apparent disconnects between the two lists as a tool to explain how the values of the AT&R method work in dealing with changing the organization. In addition, the group's awareness was sharpened in discussions about the many disconnects, such as whether people are an employer's assets or whether they are partners in the organization. Because the practitioner shares personal values, the value analysis can provide a forum for the group to express their own individual values as well. The degree that openness develops also helps the practitioner assess the group's propensity for change and to gage the potential usefulness that AT&R methods may have for the group.

The practitioner and organization psychological contract is a primary example of a risk–trust relationship. In the case of the strategic management team, there was a lot of executive taunting and repressed managerial anger seething in the group. As the fire chief cautioned, the practitioner would be "small change" should open warfare break out. It was apparent that some members looked on the practitioner as just another power play by the deputy county executive and budget director to control the group. At that time, the major group norm was general distrust. The values comparison provided the practitioner a way to guide the group in questioning their own values in open discussion. For example, "When does 'Mutual Trust' become blind obedience?" Or, "When does 'cooperation' really mean 'If you do not do what I say you are not cooperating?'"

At the AT&R level, the process involves comparing and reconciliation (if necessary) of cultural values regarding how the organization functions. Implied in this comparative analysis of values is the idea that the organization (and probably the practitioner, as well) will engage in changing its values as part of the anticipated change process. The organization will more closely align its values with action research values, and the practitioner will become more aware of AT&R's inherent limitations for the situation.

During this contract-setting stage the practitioner functions mostly as a representative for AT&R values, at the same time trying to estimate how closely they track with the organization's values. The practitioner must work on two value tracks: the organization's espoused theories and values and its enacted theories and values (Argyris & Schon, 1978). Often, organizations have policies, slogans, and mottoes to espouse the accepted organizational values of the moment, whereas in practice they enact values that represent a quite different organizational culture. An organization may profess to be an open, participative firm that claims its employees are its best assets and that puts the customer–client first. At the same time the organization's management may be quite cavalier about manipulating the employees and customer–clients for profit or career advantages.

AT&R is not a panacea for every organization that seeks to change. Clearly, there can be considerable space between AT&R values and those of the organization. However, there needs to be sufficient coincidence of values to make a convincing and compelling case for the organization and the practitioner to agree that there is a willingness for the organization to change its values. This is the primary function of the contracting stage and the prime responsibility of the practitioner to make the ultimate decision in this regard. Not infrequently, consultants are called in to create a "stir-up" in an organization so that the client management can "ride in to the rescue" to make the controversial changes they had in mind in the first place. The consultant, in effect, performs the function of a "hatchet" person for the client. Once gone, the consultant becomes the scapegoat.

FRAMING THE TERRA COGNITA: THE ENTERPRISE MODEL

Another function for the practitioner is to help the organization become aware of its form and to agree on what the organization actually is. Usually the values analysis exercise leads to discussions regarding the organization's reason for being. What is its mission, its mandate? What is the organization and what is it not? The differences among the group's members emerge as they analyze their various values. At that point, it becomes important for the group to be able to describe what they think that the organization is, what it does, and who it serves. Early research at the State Fund found that having the group create a diagram of its organization as an enterprise model was a useful approach to help groups describe their organization. This enterprise model is simply a visual depiction that can show, on one page, the organization, its parts, its stakeholders, and its general environment. Figure 5.1 depicts the enterprise model that the strategic management team developed for itself. The procedure is to follow two tracks with the group. Track one: follow the money and track two: follow the mandate.

The strategic management team focused on the fundamental purpose of administering the public's interest and commonweal of public

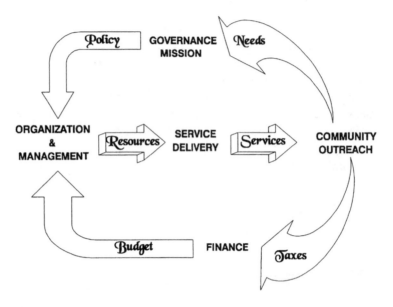

Figure 5.1. East Coast County Enterprise Model

goods. Each of these became components of a learning module designed to expand the group's understanding of the county's public
administration. Each module initiated a dialogue about the administration and those it governed, namely the citizens of the county. In
the long run, it is the consent of the governed that determines the
proper nature of the governance required. Governance was seen to
encompass the notion of service delivery founded on the economy of
scale: that the many can take better care of their public affairs by
pooling their resources. Therefore, there needs to be a sense of community within the practical public administration. To the degree that
there is not this sense of community in the administration of the
public's interests and well being, administration becomes self-serving.
Community refers to the county's strategic management team's larger
community: people living together in the county. People have needs,
people deliver services, and people use the services. This is the fundamental process that models the county's administration on the
public's interests.

The practical aspects of democratic governance in current public
administrations are usually organized along the so-called corporate

product/service delivery model. In the case of the county, the finance aspects (money track) of administration follow the revenue sources in terms of taxes and fee-paying citizens and the budgeting of those revenues to organize and manage human, physical, and fiscal resources required to develop and deliver the government services that the citizens need.

The practical public administration must be responsive to the changing needs of citizens by researching and training for the appropriate changes in services to be delivered. This change information is transmitted along the mandate track in the enterprise model. This track begins with the citizens and their changing needs reflected by the electorate in changing the members of the board of supervisors or the board of supervisors changing the laws, rules, and regulations by which county services are administered. They, in turn, change county service delivery policy in their instructions and budget approvals to the county executive officer's administration. It is then up to the administration to define and make the appropriate changes through its managers and other employees in the agencies that will have to deliver the changes in the service delivery to the citizens of the county.

The enterprise model also serves as a framework for the strategic management team's planning. Whatever actions they propose need to be evaluated in terms of how the change benefits this "county universe." The pet projects of any particular member can be judged in light of how they support the overall project of developing the county's computer resources to this end. For example, when a pie chart was made of the allocation of computer resources in the previous budget years, most of it went to finance, budget, and personnel. Very few of the computer resources went to serve the agencies that were delivering the county's services. Researching the impact of a more equitable allocation of computer resources closer to where the services were delivered to the citizens was seen to be in order.

Another value of the enterprise model is that the team players could agree on their "place in the sun." Although the members of the strategic management team were aware of the dynamics of the model, especially as they affected their departments or executive functions, they were mildly surprised to see them so graphically depicted. They could now see to agree on their general relationships to the other departments. The enterprise model and the values analysis exercises provided the practitioner the information needed to decide whether to participate in the strategic management team's project to develop a strategy to move the county's information technology resources toward the next century, or at least to their new government buildings.

Another example of an enterprise model was developed by a West Coast County Medical Center. When the AT&R practitioner met with the director and her internal organization development consultant to initiate a reorganization of the medical center, they started with the question, "What is it we can do?"

"I see at least three viable alternative answers to that question," the director said. She had been a commander in the Navy and was a practicing physician. She also had a PhD in public health and was teaching pediatrics at Stanford University. "We could be in the hospital business, of course," she said, "serving the local doctors and their patients. We could also be in the medical clinic business . . . and we could be a sort of specialized hotel business. I understand that some hotel chains actually run some hospital installations." At the time, the medical center was a 600-bed county hospital that also served as a teaching hospital and medical research center for Stanford University.

The director's reorganization group defined a *medical clinic* as an enterprise owned and operated by physicians to treat and cure their patients. In this model the patient is the client and the doctor as clinic owner is the service provider. The *hotel alternative* was defined as providing a special medical environment for physicians and their medical staff to bring their patients to receive medical services. In this model the doctor, the medical staff, and the patients are the clients and the hotel–hospital is the service provider.

The director defined a *hospital* as an organization that provided a special medical service delivery environment in which doctors can bring their patients to receive medical services. The doctors have dual roles. They represent their patients as clients and diagnose their medical situations. In some cases, such as with surgeons, they administer treatments as well. However, many of the medical services in the form of administered treatment, testing, and drugs are furnished by the hospital medical staff. Therefore, in the hospital situation the doctor and the patient are the clients. The hospital and its medical staff deliver the hospital's services.

Hospital Business - Centers of Control in Patient Care Delivery Cycle

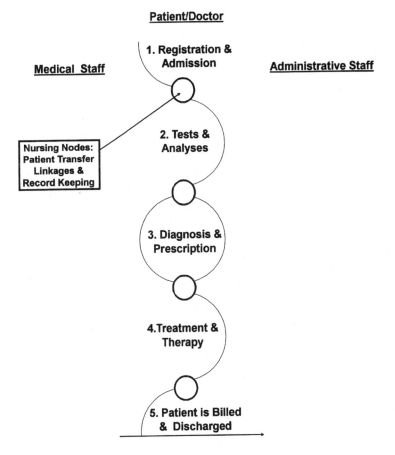

Figure 5.2. West Coast County Medical Center Model

The director's planning group decided that it was most instructive to create an enterprise model of the medical center from the point of view of the patient–doctor client as shown in Figure 5.2. Three important insights came from their model. First, there was a dual hierarchy of management in the medical center: the medical staff and the administrative staff. Control, from the point of view of the patient–

doctor switched from one to the other, depending on where the patient was in the medical service delivery process.

During admission the patient dealt with the administrative staff. During examination and testing, the patient dealt with the medical staff, and so on. The continuity for the patient was the nursing staff. At each node of the model's process the patient dealt with the nurses.

Second, as mentioned previously, the planning group defined *patient* as not just any person but one needing medical services as defined by his or her special relationship to a physician. Namely, a patient could not get admitted or released from the medical center without the physician's authorization. The physician–person dyad was the real client of the medical center.

Third, the physicians exerted a very strong management influence in the operation of the hospital, but under the definition of patient they were, in reality, client–customers of the hospital. Their strong management influence over the operation of the hospital could be considered a conflict of interest in regard to the administration of the medical center as a hospital.

Fourth, although the nursing staff represented the continuity of the hospital health care delivery service, they were not active participants in the executive decision-making process of the medical center as a hospital. They tended to defer to the doctors. With the doctors mostly in charge, the medical center was, in effect, organized more like a medical clinic than as a hospital.

Some of the changes that the director made in the reorganization of the hospital included selecting the hospital alternative as the medical center's business, bringing nursing staff into the executive management team, and getting the physicians to set themselves up as an independent corporation under contract with the hospital.

LEADERSHIP, ACTION TRAINING, AND RESEARCH

There is a risk when one assumes an either/or stance in regard to rigorous or participatory action research. This need not be. In action research certain boundaries prevail because of the nature of the participant group: the time frame within which the research takes place, the cost factors, the state of readiness of the organization, and the nature of the organization's leadership.

In this regard, leadership of the AT&R project must always remain with the people in the organization. One of the major pitfalls for AT&R practitioners is to assume a leadership role, just to get the project started. If the practitioner is unsuccessful in transferring leadership to the organization, the commitment to the change program will probably leave when the practitioner leaves. It is painful for the practitioner at first, but if the practitioner can wait out the people in the organization, they will assume the leadership and the change effect for themselves. If not, then leading an AT&R project must become the practitioner's first order of business for the skill transfer process. AT&R can be useful in organizations with any variety of management styles and cultures. Clearly, less participative leadership styles and authoritative values are not conducive to supporting change, least of all from the bottom up. However, that is the challenge of the AT&R method. For it, the only requirement is a need and commitment to change, recognizing that the practitioner's methods do embody particular values about people and organizations.

There is one important caveat in this leadership question that was pointed out by Robert Denhardt in regard to the leadership function with training people in behavioral science methods for changing organizations, such as AT&R:

> Behavioral science efforts at planned change, often discussed as organization development (OD). . . . may indeed move the organization's members toward greater openness and trust, there is always the possibility that they may simply enhance managerial control. . . . one is again left with the feeling that the human relations school is simply providing, even if unintentionally, a greater range of techniques for managerial control, techniques that can be sold to workers on an ethical basis. (Denhardt, 1993, pp. 116–120)

The ultimate ethical evaluation of providing people new and more effective means to change human organizations is part of any research scientist's dilemma when he or she has discovered secrets that can later be used destructively. The practitioner should be able to use the AT&R methods effectively even in organizations that are initially not very open to the AT&R values. Nevertheless, it is still the ethical and professional responsibility of the practitioner to exercise his or her judgment about whether the organization's leadership has invited her or him in simply to better manipulate the people in the organization. Not only should the practitioner confront the organization on this issue, but he or she should initiate a process to disengage from the AT&R project if necessary.

AN EXAMPLE IN PRACTICE:
ON THE NOTION OF LEADERSHIP IN PALAU

The notion of leadership for the AT&R practitioner was well expressed during an AT&R project to help the people of Palau set up their new nation in Micronesia. In the process of conducting the AT&R for national policy issues, the practitioners were taken by a blue and white Boston Whaler outboard motor boat across the smooth crystal waters of the coral lagoons to meet with the chiefs of the many outlying villages. Visiting villages was an interesting process. It is not proper for Palauan people from one village to walk directly into another village. The custom is to tie up the boat and wait in an *asumba,* a small platform near the dock provided by the village to receive all visitors. The *asumba* was made from large unsplit bamboo poles, and usually shaded by coconut palm trees. After a while, people would drift down from the village to sit and chat with the visitors and hear the latest gossip. Some would bring candied cassava, taro, peppered papaya, and other treats wrapped up, Japanese bento-box style. Fresh cut coconuts were brought for drink. After an hour or so, the visitors would be invited into the village to conduct whatever business was at hand or to visit with relatives. Some of the AT&R interviews were conducted with the various village chiefs at the *asumba,* or if the meeting was to be with all ten chiefs of the village, the visitors would be given a place to sleep in someone's house and then meet later in the men's meeting house in the village.

In this case, the paramount chief came down to the *asumba* himself to talk about the ensuing transition from a UN Trust Territory to becoming the Republic of Palau. His regal silver hair and dark skin framed his distinguished appearance. He carried the ubiquitous pandanas boo basket, which contained the materials and accessories for chewing betel nut.

When the subject of Palauan leadership of the new nation came up, he explained that there were different kinds of Palauan leadership among the village's council of chiefs, all of them useful in different ways. He looked out across the clear blue lagoon waters to the out-lying atoll reefs. The open sea was at a high tide and the ocean crashed in long white rolling breakers over the reefs. These living barriers were all that protected Palau's low coral islands from being swallowed up by the ocean.

"When we fish for yellowfin tuna-fish in the open sea," he explained, "We often take our young sons in our *belas* [a dugout canoe with a single outrigger] out past those reefs. It is dangerous, but we go for our yellowfin, of course. Sometimes, when the *belas* returns from fishing and the sea is at a changing tide, we must guide the *belas* carefully back through those reefs we see out there. Otherwise our family and fish can be lost."

The chief took a fresh pepper leaf out of his basket. He then placed an already split betel nut and a broken half of a cigarette on the deep green leaf. He then sprinkled quicklime over the contents, and then he rolled them all up into something that looked like a stuffed grape leaf. He chewed the package for awhile and then continued.

"To return, of course, one time a man will get behind his *belas* and push it through the reefs if the tide is rising. Another time he will get in front of his *belas* and pull it through the reefs, maybe if the tide is still falling, of course. But, at a difficult tide he must walk alongside his *belas* to know exactly the reef as he guides his *belas* through.

"I can explain, of course. Our council of chiefs, like our village, has two sides," he said, looking back toward the village of wooden houses with corrugated tin roofs. "The Other Side you see beyond the main path there and the 'Side across from the Other Side' where we are now. We use these names, I can explain, because we do not say 'Them' and 'Us.' It has no meaning here; we are all of the same village, of course. But it is useful to divide ourselves in this way. You see, on important questions for the village the chiefs from the 'Other Side' push the village, and chiefs from the Side across from the Other Side' pull, depending on the question. Sometimes it is, how do you say it, 'the other way around?' It is the responsibility of the paramount chief to walk alongside the village chiefs to hear the agreement building on both sides. When I am satisfied that I have heard a coming together, I pronounce it as my decision. But now, perhaps we may have to learn new leaderships for our new nation."

For AT&R practitioners, the leadership way of the paramount chief was most instructive. Although there is usually no shortage of leaders in an organization that are pushing and pulling it toward change, the practitioner's leading is done best by modeling the AT&R principles of open communication, good listening, and sharing the experience of change with the people changing it.

FROM NEELY GARDNER'S JOURNAL:
DEVELOPING THE CONTRACT-SETTING STAGE

Gardner presented the contract-setting stage as covering resource commitment, assurance that those involved in the project will "own" their own data, agreement that communication to those affected will observe carefully the organization's confidences, and an expression of willingness on the part of the client to use findings to the greatest extent possible. One of the knottiest problems between an organization and the practitioner is setting the contract. Gardner explained.

> I found on this occasion, as I have on others, that developing a financial and service contract is easier and in no way the same as developing a psychological or commitment contract. In my opinion it is a mistake to make the psychological contract until an estimate of the situation has taken place. Generally, organizations require a written contract prior to services being performed. The service contract or agreement should be phrased in such a way as to accommodate the probable time and work adjustments which may become manifest after a reconnaissance has been conducted.

The work contract and the psychological contract are usually quite different. The practitioner not only postpones the psychological contract to a time somewhat later when more data are available to guide the transaction, but must often renegotiate it as circumstances change. In addition, new psychological contracts must be struck with those suborganizations within the parent organization that the practitioner must work with in getting to the people doing the organization's product development and service delivery.

Gardner's opening contract was with the State Fund's president. The president was an impressive but unpretentious person. Gardner wrote, "He is a discontented optimist. He is deeply interested in social causes, and willing to take risks to achieve improvement. Some subordinates claimed to find him overpowering at times, but this may have been as much their problem as his. I think he could be described as an idealist."

For Gardner in his work at the State Fund, his first level of psychological contract-making was with the president. After discussing the potential fit of action research at the State Fund, the president asked him,

> If you can, I would like you to work with us in a practitioner role and see what we can do about this crazy organization. We have problems and, I think, we are doing the wrong thing in the wrong way at the wrong time. I do not think that our current organizational structure is efficient and effective. I would like to take my term in office to see if we can't do some things in the Fund to improve communications, interpersonal relationships, and to find an organizational structure that either enhances or beats what we are doing. (cited in Jasaitis, 1992, pp. 151–152)

This is a classic example of a psychological contract. It is an open-ended agreement to change the organization's status quo and to take a proactive view to build an organization that can continually address the changing needs of the people it serves and at the same time meet the changing needs of the people providing the service. It is a contract to build a changing organization—namely, an organization that can continually transform itself to anticipate and meet the changes that the future thrusts toward them. For the changing organization, the status quo is a benchmark for changing.

TERMINATING THE CONTRACT: ORGANIZATIONAL DIVORCE

Like any contract arrangement, there can come a falling out of the parties, or one side may breach the contractual agreement in some significant way. If the organization so decides, it can buy out the formal contract, if there is one. More commonly, the client organization simply does not renew the practitioner's contract. For the practitioner, it is more difficult. Therefore, it is realistic to have at least an informal agreement that allows either party to cancel the relationship at any time. Sometimes AT&R practitioners, for some reason or circumstance, become organization issues themselves. When this occurs, the organization and the practitioner can usually part by mutual agreement.

Sometimes the organization moves away from the original project, or new management is appointed and decides to take the organization in a direction that is not tenable for the practitioner. The practitioner must then think about whether to initiate a separation. For example, during the strategic management team's project, the county chief executive officer and the budget director retired. The assistant county executive officer was appointed by the new CEO to take over management of the strategic management team from the retiring budget officer. The practitioner prepared an accounting of the activities, plans, results, and AT&R methods used by the strategic management team to date.

The strategic management team's information technology strategy had been mostly implemented; therefore, the strategic management team began to redirect its strategic attention to "reinventing government" in the county's human services area. Other, outside consultants were brought in to "reinvent" the several human services agencies into one interdisciplinary organization. However, they took over the smallest of the last information technology strategic research pilot projects, researching rapid application development. They expanded it, on an order of magnitude, as a solution to their project to downsize human services. The assistant county executive officer asked the practitioner to help on the new project. He declined. The assistant county executive officer asked why. "Two reasons," he responded. "First, these new consultants, are using very different methods, methods that I don't think will work very well with the AT&R methods I showed you that the strategic management team has been using."

"How so?" the assistant CEO asked.

The practitioner described one meeting in which one consultant project leader came to a group meeting and placed a large whip on the table. He made it clear that this was his enforcer to get compliance and speedy results out of civil servants. "Their idea of participative decision making is: here is the decision and here is how you are going to participate in implementing it," he responded.

"But, more important," he went on, "is that one project the team had in mind was to test an assumption about building computer applications rapidly in weeks or months instead of the five years the county is used to."

This was in 1992, and although many software vendors claimed that they could build computer applications in a few weeks, no one had actually succeeded at that time. The practitioner explained how the strategic management team's strategy was to authorize a modest $55,000 pilot project to test this claim by using the new software to build a small working application in human services.

"But now," the practitioner continued, "this untested approach has been expanded to include all human service agencies. It is costing more than a million dollars just to build a prototype. It will not even deliver a working application as we had intended. The result can be expected to arrive in the form of a Request for Proposal for $12 to $15 million dollars. Only after that will we find out if it is possible. Rapid application development will not happen. Building the whole human services system will still take 6 years, not 6 months. Therefore, it will be obsolete at start-up—if it ever starts up. Worse yet, the department of information technology development will have to come back for more and more funding for the vendor to get a practical system running to meet the new requirements that have emerged in the ensuing six years. What will the public say when they find that out?"

"The kind of changing organization you have been talking about is very noble," the assistant county executive officer admitted, "but it is not possible in this political climate and with the new CEO," he responded. "It's always taken a long time for those systems. That's the way it is here."

"But look," the practitioner replied, "I signed on to help develop a strategy for information technology, not to reinvent the county's government. It's not that I can't be useful in that endeavor. AT&R methods can often work well with reinventing government, TQM, and other approaches for improving organizations. As you know, you loaned me to help out with one of the National Performance Review projects on franchising internal government services.

"However, it's the values of the way these approaches are being used to motivate the people doing the work I have a problem with.

I'm even willing to consider that participative management methods could possibly be the management practice dinosaurs of our times. But frankly, I don't think the Cretaceous period of organization change methods has for us arrived yet. However, as a professional in this business of organization change, I am obliged to know better. I find the actions being initiated to change human services as incompatible with AT&R. Therefore, I cannot participate in that project."

"But, let me suggest a compromise," the practitioner continued. "We have just about finished all our strategic projects for information technology. We have succeeded in almost all of our strategic objectives in our plan. We have moved the county to a wide area network and client server environment with relational database on the mainframe computer. However, we are about to snatch failure from the jaws of success."

"How so," the assistant county executive officer asked?

"We have one last piece of software we need our current vendor to put on the mainframe computer in order for the people in the agencies to easily access their databases on the mainframe computer through their personal computers and local area networks. This access software will turn our mainframe systems into a kind of data warehouse and at the same time extend their life for a decade or so."

"So, what's the problem?"

"The managers in the department of information technology development and the department of computer operations and networks, are dead set against this software."

"Why?"

"I think it's because they have always been fighting with the vendor. They really would like to get rid of them, not get more of their software. But, send me down there, and let me help conduct a thorough cost–benefit analysis for this software and test it out. I know that the database administrators in that department are convinced that the software will deliver accessibility without much additional cost. There're for it. If we take it through the AT&R process, we can then let the county executives decide on the basis of our database administrators' results testing it with county systems." The assistant county executive officer assigned the practitioner to the computer department. The database administrators were able to prove the case with actual test results and with the cost–benefit analyses of several successful pilot projects in diverse county agencies.

Contracting to develop a changing organization using AT&R methods is basically a meeting of the minds. It is an agreement to travel together using the AT&R to map the way to become a changing organization. The contract-setting stage is a natural continuation of the situation analysis of the orientation stage. Contract setting works to create a psychological agreement between the practitioner and the client organization, which is based on a mutual trust and a willingness to provide the people involved in the changing with the methods, tools, and training they need to change their organization for themselves. The values analysis also provides a source of criteria for later decision making.

The contract-setting stage also charts their organization's territory as a lead-in to exploring the organization's issues in the next, reconnaissance stage. At the same time, because of many people who may not have been party to the contract, the psychological contract is always under construction and can be terminated by either party when necessary.

FROM THE JOURNALS OF
NEELY GARDNER: LISTENING AND LEVELING

In using the nondirective approach, the practitioner will also come to the interview equipped with a full set of perceptions and biases. An important part of training the participant group involves exploration of values and norms. This exploration not only leads to the development of skills but also helps participants conduct their interviews with integrity and empathy. Much of the values training focuses on helping participants look at their own values. One of the reasons for examining values is to make incipient practitioners aware of the possible influence their own biases might have on the nature of the data they collect, even though the biases may not interfere overtly with the respondent's contribution. However, they certainly will be a block to the interviewer's active listening. Thus, awareness of the interaction of values and ability to listen is a necessary part of the training.

LISTENING STEPS

Here are some of the recommended listening steps:

1. Look at one's own attitude. Each person, living in a private world, carries on an almost continuous internal dialogue. Frequently this dialogue becomes so interesting that the private world excludes stimuli from the external world. An interviewer's preoccupation with self (personal values, needs, goals, motives, and perceptions) distorts or prevents the practitioner from hearing what the respondent is trying to communicate. Communication is facilitated when the practitioner
   a. Sees the world through the eyes of the interviewee
   b. Accepts what the respondent says as being valid from the interviewee's point of view, avoiding if possible an internal conversation which evaluates or challenges what is being said
   c. Keeps in mind that none among us ever knows the other person's intentions.
2. Be attentive. In so doing, the interviewer should
   a. Take note of the interviewee's mannerisms and motions. People tell a lot nonverbally. Note the movement of the hands and feet, the shrug of the shoulder, the raising of the eyebrow, or the blinking of the eyes. The practitioner should try to avoid interpreting the meaning of these motions; but by becoming aware of the total person, the practitioner will be better able to tune in on the conversation and at the appropriate time provide feedback on what has been said.
   b. Let the interviewee know by one's action that the interviewer is intent on hearing what is said. It will be clear to the respondent that the interviewer's concentration level is not high when there is fidgeting, wringing of hands, drumming of the table, shuffling of papers, or aimless gazing around the room. The best way to convey attentiveness is to actually listen.
   c. Try not to get ahead of the interviewee. Active listening requires intentionality and an approach to full awareness of the interviewee, his or her words, actions, and feeling tone.
   d. Listen for patterns of conversation and feeling words.
3. People do talk "in circles." It is important to be aware of recurring themes. There may be two or three such concurrent topical areas that the interviewee is struggling to conceptualize and bring to the surface. It is well to be aware that the speaker has a reason for such repetition.
4. Feeling words or "red letter" words literally leap out of a person's conversation, indicating that something of importance is being worked through.

5. Be aware that, as interviewees are talking to you, they also are talking to themselves. Frequently, they are thinking through their problem as they talk, and the very fact that someone is listening provides an incentive for them to hear themselves and to develop awareness and insights.

6. Reflect feelings. The interview is a two-way interaction in which the practitioner contributes intense empathy, attention, and understanding. This means dedication to the notion that it is the needs of the interviewee, not those of the practitioner, that are important to the process. The practitioner's job is to be active in attending and also to give feedback. Appropriate feedback includes the following:

   a. Briefly summarize "circularity" tracks. By summarizing, the interviewer indicates to the interviewee that there was attentiveness to what was said. The summary also serves to refresh the memory of the interviewee.

   b. Capture and rephrase some point that the interviewee has emphasized or has verbalized tentatively. This helps interviewees to face themselves and perhaps to explore with themselves what they may have in mind.

   c. Reflect the feelings that have been highlighted by emotionally laden words.

7. What the action practitioner should try to avoid. There are a number of pitfalls and traps that practitioners encounter because of inattentiveness to their own inner states:

   a. Parroting what the interviewee has said in a word-for-word manner. Frequently the unpracticed will almost mimic what the interviewee has said in the mistaken notion that this is "reflecting" what is being communicated. Learning to reflect feelings is a difficult skill to learn; but the more empathetically one listens, the easier it becomes. The effort should be to rephrase what has been said in order to capture feelings. In the event the practitioner is wrong, the interviewee will let the practitioner know.

   b. Asking questions. Questions posed by interviewers generally tend to fill the needs of interviewers and almost always interfere with what the respondent is trying to say. The exception to this might be the reflective question. If we really wish to hear what the other person is trying to say, the conversation must be approached through the eyes of the interviewee.

   c. Interpreting. Telling the other person what he or she really means may only reflect the interviewer's biases.

   d. Giving advice. Interviewers interject themselves into the conversational pattern by giving advice. In some rare cases the respondent might accept it; but perhaps the best thing about most advice is that it is not taken.

   e. Showing sympathy. Sympathy helps the interviewees rationalize
      their positions. It implies that the practitioner has the status to give
      comfort to an inferior from a superior position. In fact, it will be
      an indication to the interviewee that what is being said is evaluated
      as "good" or "bad." Further, if one is collecting data, the result of
      sympathetic interventions is likely to move things away from the
      total problem universe and to create a focus on a multitude of
      reasons why the situation of the respondent is so unfortunate.
   f. Indicate disapproval.
   g. Belittle, ridicule, or argue. It should go without saying that indi-
      cations of disapproval, belittling, ridiculing, or arguing with the
      interviewee will diminish the level of trust and sometimes create
      a polarized situation between the interviewer and the interviewee.

It is important to reemphasize two of the points raised previously.
First, the type of interviewing training described in this chapter has
evolved over several decades and has been based in large measure on
the concepts provided by Carl R. Rogers in *Client-Centered Therapy*
(1951). In connection with developing and evaluating the training of
interviewers, several hundred recordings have been made and played
back. Charting the interview process in playback sessions has made
it evident that the reaction to an interviewer interjection is in large
measure predictable. Whenever one intrudes into another person's
conversation, only an entry that is reflective in nature avoids a perception of interference.

Most conversations appear to have a circular pattern. In a normal
conversation involving a subordinate and boss or an interviewee and
interviewer, the one being interviewed moves into the subject incrementally. This may involve testing to see how receptive the listener
is. It may also be because the interviewee is simply getting in touch
with himself or herself and mobilizing ideas. It often works out that
the stated problem is not the real one at all.

Every time a problem resurfaces as the conversational spiral pro-
gresses, it seems to take on new dimensions and frequently new depths.
One might speculate that talking to a person who is listening with
empathy makes it possible to explore and think through problems in
a way not otherwise possible. Thought processes are frequently errant
and random, even when a person is intentionally and consciously
addressing a particular issue or feeling. It may be that the randomi-
zation is diminished by having a sympathetic audience. It is clear that

questions interfere with the orderly progression of the conversational spiral, to the extent that in some cases roles are switched, the interviewee becoming the interviewer and the practitioner the interviewee.

TRAINING IN LISTENING

In providing the type of training that focuses on the listening steps described, one should be under no illusion that knowing about listening and being aware of the nature of questions and conversational patterns alone will lead to improved performance. If the trainee lacks the desire or proceeds without having an experiential base, active listening probably will not take place. To provide trainees an opportunity to acquire facility and experience in listening, participation in a listening laboratory is encouraged. Approaches taken in the laboratory vary, but presented next is one pattern that appears to be fairly successful.

PRACTICING LISTENING

To establish a foundation for skill development, the laboratory starts with concept building through the use of reading materials, demonstrations, queries, and responses and, if appropriate, lecturettes. The training class is then divided into subgroups of three (when the mathematics of the situation permit; if not, subgroups of two or four may be used). Each triad is given an audiocassette recorder and asked to assume three roles: the interviewee, the interviewer, and the observer. The skill-building interviews are as reality-based as possible. If the precise nature of the action research is known, the actual patterned interview will be used, with the interviewee answering as himself or herself and not in terms of a role-playing situation. Keeping in mind the guidelines on interviewing, the interviewer will attempt to put into practice the concepts the group has been learning.

The observer is asked to sit behind the respondent in full view of the interviewer. It is the observer's job to note the degree to which the interviewer is conducting the interview within the general concepts set forth. The observer also notes deviations from the process and raises his or her hands, waving them back and forth, to call the interviewer's attention to the deviation. The interviewee does not see the signal.

The initial practice interviews are approximately 5 minutes. Each member of the triad will take all three roles, with each person having an opportunity to be interviewee, interviewer, and observer. Triads then replay their tapes, listening to themselves, with staff members sitting in on request.

On completion of the replay, another practice session is developed. This time trainees are asked to practice nondirective training skills. Interviews this time are longer, 15 minutes, and are recorded as before. In addition to playback within the triad, it sometimes helps to take an interview or two and analyze it for the entire group. This analysis helps the trainees discern what to listen for as they play back and analyze their own interviews. The exercise demonstrates quite dramatically the predictability of the consequences of intervention.

Field Training

When trainees have listened to the tapes of their second practice sessions, their next experience is in the field. This third experience is only possible when the general nature of the action research is known. Trainees, who are also the incipient client practitioners, go into the organization or communities to be researched. Each one interviews a person on location. This time the trainees go out in pairs. In this situation, one person does the interviewing, the other observes and records the data. When such interviews are concluded, team members share with each other the observations they have made.

At the end of the first field practice, the training group shares experiences and decides on the interview approach they will employ in a small pilot program. At this point, the interview methodology should still be regarded as tentative and subject to revision.

Another training group practice interview session, participated in after the first field experience, generally shows that most participants have developed a heightened level of skill and that observers have a growing ability to be effective in the helping role. At this point, the preresearch training is generally concluded, although retraining is done at appropriate times during the action research process.

Additional Skills

In a motivation study undertaken by the National Training and Development Service for State and Local Governments, the interview training was conducted simultaneously with training in observation, use of unobtrusive measures, journal keeping, and data analysis. The process of learning to hear others is not perfected in one training program, in one action training and research effort, or perhaps even in a lifetime. Those who have been interested in trying to develop consulting and managerial skills that enable us to hear others realize how uncommonly difficult the process is. But the difficulties of hearing others may not be as troublesome as learning to hear ourselves. In any case, hearing oneself is an important skill for the practitioner.

LEVELING: THE ART OF HEARING ONE'S SELF

The degree to which one can be accepting of others has a demonstrable effect on hearing a person with empathetic ears. It requires a lot of work before a person can be nonevaluative in response to others. Also, one may have a very difficult time in accepting the self. Erich Fromm suggested that it is highly desirable for a person to love the self; and, in order to love others, this self-love must prevail (Fromm, 1947).

Developing the ability to love and accept self does not mean creating a conscience that is "good" through pleasing external and internalized authority or bad or "guilty" when it does not. If one is unable to live without the love and approval of authority (or society), one may be conditioned to continually seek means of avoiding rejection.

Fromm believed that the *humanistic conscience* is the expression of human self-interest and integrity, whereas the *authoritarian conscience* is a manifestation of obedience, self-sacrifice, duty, and social adjustment. The goal of the humanistic conscience is productive living. A person is crippled when he or she becomes the tool of others. One has to learn how to listen to, and understand, one's humanistic conscience in order to secure its development and strengthening. The job of listening to the humanistic conscience, then, becomes one of getting in touch with one's self in ways that lead to future enhancement, rather than to self-punishment or feelings of guilt because of one's imperfection. In this mode a person would say, "I am imperfect. This I can accept. I neither castigate myself for my imperfections nor am I joyful. Recognizing who I am and where I am permits me to deal more realistically with the world."

The payoff that comes from being able to hear one's humanistic conscience is revealed in the improved quality of communication with others.

OWNING ONE'S FEELINGS

There is very little likelihood that, with the best of efforts, people can do more than progress toward developing interpersonal communications that are free from manipulation, blame, and guilt. In speaking of his concept of congruence, Carl R. Rogers said, "I regret it when I suppress my feelings too long and they burst forth in ways that are distorted or attacking or hurtful" (Gardner, 1980, p. 502). In a way the process relates to saying what one feels and is able to do by manifestly owning one's feelings.

To hear one's self, then, it is important to be aware of, and to give expression to, one's feelings. In expressing feelings, there seems to be some benefit in seeking to identify causes, rather than to deal exclusively with symptoms. Some illustrations will show that the normal behavior is to conduct one's inner conversations around means at the expense of ends, and of limiting the degree of awareness to stimuli, rather than to psychological responses.

One can imagine a 50-year-old man walking down a street on a wintry day through a neighborhood made clean and white by new-fallen snow. Suddenly, and unexpectedly, he is hit with a snowball. In this case, the pink-cheeked boy who threw the snowball is aware that his aim was true and that he achieved a solid hit. Mission accomplished!

It would not be surprising for the man hit with the snowball to respond with retributive action and counter-aggressive behavior. In the moments following the snowballing, the victim might have a vague feeling of being embarrassed at his spattered condition or being aware that he hurts and feels angry; but it is likely that the anger he articulates is not communicated in terms of embarrassment, hurting, or anger.

More likely it will be communicated in terms of the blame that should be attached to the thrower, the despicable quality of the act, even to the extent of some rather scathing remarks about the thrower's character. All these actions are indicative of symptoms of feeling but in no way permit the attacked person to examine the depths of his feelings. Perhaps he would feel, among other things:

1. Physically injured
2. Not respected
3. Aggrieved
4. Challenged
5. Frightened
6. Hostile and aggressive and desirous of acting out his aggressions

With such information, the victim might understand that there were options available to him. He might then choose to ignore, attempt to escape from, or confront the snowball hurler. Admittedly, the situation is not one that is conducive to authentic communication. One could predict that the snowball hurler will not learn about, nor be interested in, the many feelings held by the attacked person. In turn, the snowballer will also have feelings that under most circumstances would not be revealed to the person attacked. The snowballer might, for example, feel

1. Elated that the aim was good
2. Anxious about a possible confrontation
3. Guilty that someone may have been hurt
4. Hostile because the person hit is evincing aggression

Should the snowballer explore all these feelings, the options of escape or confrontation would likely emerge. There might be defiance or contrition; in fact, there are many possible interpersonal and physical approaches that might be taken. In this scene communication is only partial. The interpersonal transaction is incomplete. There is little chance that either party will see the situation through the other's eyes. Perhaps the responding action is "getting even." Then the victim of the attack will feel better, and perhaps the snowballer will feel worse. If the situation develops as one would normally expect, the aggressor will find some way of blaming the other for his plight. There seems to be no way that a satisfactory human transaction can come out of the situation. It appears to be a completely win–lose situation. It is obviously the kind of circumstance to avoid in as many human transactions as possible.

THE TRAINING PROCESS FOR LEVELING SKILLS

Action research practitioner trainers should not expect too much from their efforts to explain the concept of leveling verbally. However, the learning process is enhanced when trainees develop a cognitive acquaintance with the notion of leveling.

Here are some approaches to training in leveling:

1. Modeling. Insofar as the practitioner is able to practice leveling and listening in transactions with members of the client group, this behavior will serve as a motivation for client learning. One of the ways in which people learn new behaviors is through the process of identification. As clients begin to consider the practitioner important to them, and as they see the behavior as effective and admirable, individuals in the client group will, to a degree, attempt to emulate it.

2. Lecturettes. Some learning may come from lecturettes of no more than 10 to 15 minutes. It is certainly useful for the practitioner to put into words the ideas of leveling; and the speaker may benefit the most from the exercise. The extent of learning by the listeners is more problematic. A great deal of interest, and perhaps learning, grows out of the question and response sessions which some lecturettes stimulate.

3. Written materials. Written materials that clients have the opportunity to read serve to delineate the general concept of leveling, making it possible to engage in training group conversations with a fair understanding of the concept.

4. Skill practice. One way to approach "leveling" training is through role playing. Recording, particularly via videotape, assists a great deal in the effectiveness of the training by providing immediate and effective feedback. This does not preclude role playing without such equipment.

LEVELING PRACTICE TRAINING

There are three steps to learning how to level with client organization people: (1) role playing, (2) practice leveling, and (3) discussion.

Role Playing

Role playing is the first step taken after trainees have had exposure to the leveling concepts explained in this chapter. The role playing itself should focus on four dimensions:

1. Superficial/manipulative
2. Hostile/aggressive
3. Guilt/self-punishment
4. Journey into self (leveling)

For each of the areas on the continuum, the practitioner–trainer provides a script that has credibility in the organizational setting familiar to the client group. The practitioner describes a cluster of feelings, such as words described in the snowball scene in this chapter. The described feelings were that the person who was attacked by the snowball thrower felt physically injured, not respected, aggrieved, frightened, challenged, hostile and aggressive, and desirous of acting out aggressions.

In a series of four role-playing incidents, participants are asked to use each of the four dimensions in approaching the communication situation. For example, in scene I the role players (person A) are asked to use the superficial, manipulative approach, keeping in mind the private feelings (which are stated in role instructions). The second party (person B) in the role playing is simply asked to play himself or herself and to react naturally to person A. Each of these roles is recorded when possible. When recording equipment is used, the roles are played sequentially before playback. If electronic equipment is not available, it is a good idea to pause and obtain participant and observer feedback on each role as soon as it has been played. The reason for this is that the audio or audiovisual recording will provide a memory and an opportunity for a comparison of the different approaches; without such equipment, it is necessary to tap the memory of participants.

Practicing Leveling

The second step involves practice of the most desirable approach. The practitioner–trainer divides the group in triads so the members can practice the journey into self (leveling) as they talk about real concerns. Topics for discussion might include problems that have risen in connection with the action training and research project or problems that pertain to other work or personal situations. The transaction might last from 5 to 10 minutes; afterward the triad is asked to play back and critique the interaction. The practitioner should be available to assist the various triads.

Discussion

Finally, the practitioner–trainer should use all group meetings on action training and research team interaction as an opportunity to raise and discuss the concept of leveling behavior. This is particularly true for meetings in which process observations are made. There is some experience that indicates that, given the training provided in the first two steps, training in the actual meetings becomes more effective. It is in the final step of training that leveling behavior begins to be incorporated into the group norms.

Listening and leveling are basic skills that are needed in one-to-one communication. They are also central to the process of group interaction. Practitioners and managers acting as change agents also need to develop their group leadership skills.

SUMMARY

Setting the contract is a coming together of the practitioner and the client organization to agree on what the situation appears to be, what the AT&R methodology can do in such situations, and a joint commitment to action research and reeducation to bring about change. Through this coming together the practitioner trains the contact people in the organization the rudiments of the AT&R methodology through interviews, values analysis, and direct discussions about the methodology.

The contract aspect is not intended to be a formal proposal or written document. However, the practitioner must judge that the nature and degree of agreement (psychological contract) in place is sufficient for the parties involved to proceed to the next stage of AT&R.

CHAPTER 6

AT&R STAGE 3: RECONNAISSANCE, EXPLORING THE ISSUES

MENU FOR AT&R STAGE 3: RECONNAISSANCE, EXPLORING THE ISSUES

Action   *Training at the "contract-setting" stage addresses developing knowledge concerning issue areas, as well as increasing the skill and willingness of clients to confront and explore them. Reconnaissance, which is an estimate of the situation, gains credence when based on data relevant to the change project. From these data will emerge an array of perceived opportunities, problems, and possible solutions. Participant researchers are encouraged to enter into reconnaissance activities with an attitude of ignorance concerning substantive issues. The researcher will surely bring his or her own values and perceptions to the task.*

Perceived problems, opportunities, and possible solutions will also have surfaced during the orientation and contract-setting stages. Trainers can help client–researchers to become aware of their values and preconceptions in order to minimize interference with the data collection. It is not

*absolutely necessary that clients participate in the recon-
naissance activity, but it is highly desirable. Clients appear
to receive a fair amount of education by being involved in
the data collection (Gardner, 1974).*

Training   *Team building, group participation, and exploring issues
with brain-storming techniques.*

Research   *An issue is defined as some current or impending change
that we can expect to impinge on our mission. Exploring
issues is a kind of brainstorming. The idea is to examine
what we see as issues without getting too deeply involved
with identifying the problems, opportunities or solutions.
It is opening ourselves to letting new information into our
thinking without prejudging it with our problem-solving
values (that comes in AT&R Stage 4).*

Issue Paper Exercise   *In open session and under general "brainstorming" rules the participants nominate important changes
expected to occur in their organization's environment that
should be included in any intermediate-range (1–5 years)
planning effort. Any nomination of organization problems
or opportunities should be noted separately. This AT&R
stage aims for impending changes in the organization's
situation. The changes can be expected to engender problems and opportunities, but those will be identified in the
next stage.*

*The results are then organized into issue statements that
are then discussed by the group. Suggested issue paper
exploration format is as follows:*

1. *What is the issue (in one sentence)?*
2. *Background circumstances of expected change (in one
   paragraph)?*
3. *Recommendations for researching the impact of the
   change on the organization.*

> 4. *The key issue(s)' priorities for action are ranked and agreed on through consensus.*
>
> 5. *Who are the stakeholders that should be included in this exploration?*

Outcome *Team building, the organization's issue statements.*

EXPLORING THE ISSUES

The situation analysis of the first stage determines the scope of issues that confront the organization and portend a need for the organization to change itself. Issues are the original stuff of strategic decision making (Dutton & Duncan, 1987). Strategic decision making involves how the organization arranges its resources to take best advantage of whatever the future brings. What the future usually brings are emerging changes that threaten to change the organization's status quo. Some of these changes are friendly, some unfriendly, and some inconsequential. In examining the strategic issues listed by the East Coast county's strategic management team we can see that some strategic issues have all three aspects. These aspects present themselves in the form of opportunities, problems, and noise, respectively. For example, the "New computer technology coming out at faster rate" issue causes discomfort to operations people who are completely consumed in running the technology they have. However, the new technology may provide valuable solutions to problems arising in the service delivery to the citizens. Finally, there is so much technological innovation coming out that one organization cannot keep up with it all. Much of it is of no use to them anyway. The function of strategic decision making is to become aware of the impending changes, explore them, and arrange resources accordingly.

Typically, during this reconnaissance stage there arises a discussion of the differences between issues and problems. Understanding this difference marks the strategist. Issues are emerging changes in an organization's situation. These changes may be the source of both problems and opportunities, depending on the organization. Therefore, problems and opportunities are what emerge from issues. Problems seek solutions, whereas issues seek resolution.

What may be a problem for one organization can often be an opportunity for another. For example, in the East Coast county, the major issue was that its information technology was becoming obsolete. Funding and replacing expensive systems presented a host of problems. However, the vendors and big seven consulting firms saw this as an opportunity to sell equipment and services. The county agency managers also saw it as an opportunity to replace ineffective systems with more customer-service-oriented ones. To rephrase this using a meteorological metaphor: Weather is the issue, storms and sunshine are the problems and opportunities. Strategy is focused on the precipitation trends—in other words, greenhouse effect—whereas action tactics focus on storm drains and picnic parks.

EXAMPLE IN PRACTICE:
ISSUE EXPLORATION AT EAST COAST COUNTY

"How can we explore the issues if we don't know where we are going?" the budget director asked. "Shouldn't we set our goals and objectives first?" There was an awkward silence in the strategic management team meeting.

"It's a dilemma," the practitioner offered. "How can we know where there is to go if we don't examine the issues first?"

"But, how do you know which issues are strategic if you haven't set a course?" the general services director chimed in.

"Well, you are right," the practitioner answered. "It's a sort of 'chicken and egg' dilemma. We know there are chickens and we know there are eggs. Some strategic issues can be expected to look quite different, depending on whether we are in the 'chicken' business or the 'egg' business. However, many issues will affect both. Which came first is not an issue to either business. What comes next is!"

"What does come next?" the deputy county executive asked.

"I believe we have already identified most of the strategic issues in our discussions about the model and our values," the practitioner replied. "In exploring issues we need to look at what is not on the model chart and what's between its lines. What's there that we should be taking notice of in our planning? It's a kind of brainstorming process. I'm confident that we could go around the table right now and name most of them in the next 15 minutes."

"You're on," the deputy county executive said. "You write them on the newsprint as they come up."

Before long, the group came up with a list of issues, including

1. Diminishing revenues
2. Increasing citizen dissatisfaction with government
3. Aged information systems on the mainframe computer
4. New computer technology coming out at faster rate
5. Moving to the new government center
6. None of our computer systems can talk to each other

Gardner described the reconnaissance stage as an exploration of the organization's internal and environmental issues in order to identify the problems and opportunities in the next stage. From the exploration of the issues in this stage, opportunities and problems and alternative action options emerge to be identified in the next AT&R identification of opportunities and problems stage. The practitioner encourages the participant–researchers to enter into reconnaissance activities with an attitude of ignorance and wonder concerning the issues being explored (Gardner, 1974).

The practitioner often needs to help the people in the organization to explore issues regarding the forces impinging on the organization's focused and diffused social environment. Problems, opportunities, and various solutions may have already surfaced during the orientation and contract-setting stages. They will surface again during this stage of issue exploration. Practitioners can help client–researchers record them but should view them as tentative preconceptions to be sorted out in the next stage and after the issues have been explored.

AT&R AND STRATEGIC MANAGEMENT

Over the years action research and strategic management decision making have been converging. AT&R is an early example of this evolution. At the State Fund Gardner merged AT&R with the State

Fund's entrepreneurial planning. They formed strategic action groups for organization development, sales and marketing, claims, fiscal, and so on, to develop and support the State Fund's strategy for its entrepreneurial plan. Each strategic action group used AT&R methodology to work in the entire organization in the formulation of the strategy of the State Fund's entrepreneurial plan. A significant change in an organization is usually a matter of strategic decision making.

For example, the orientation and contract-setting stages establish the historical context of strategic management (Nutt & Backoff, 1992). These initial stages research the situation according to coordinates of the organization's social space involved. This gestalt approach helps the client organization frame its place in the foreground and relationship to the background.

The reconnaissance stage moves the research focus beyond the organization's current frame into the organization's *terra incognita* if they are to gain new knowledge, values, and practices. Clearly, if the organization's research remains within the known boundaries, it may discover different arrangements of its current knowledge, but it will simply be rearranging the status quo for itself. The strategic issues are those impending changes in the organization and its environment that pose unknown challenges to the organization. AT&R provides methods for the organization to examine those issues to see if they are going to be foul or fair.

WHY EXPLORE STRATEGIC ISSUES?
HOW DO I KNOW WHAT I DON'T KNOW?

In the case of the Republic of Palau's nation building, this reconnaissance stage culminated in providing the ten national policy issues for the new administration. A myriad of opportunities and problems followed, but the new administration's strategy for nation building flowed out of those national policy issues. This stage is one of the most innovative in Gardner's AT&R method. He joined the three elements of issues, exploration, and strategy. First, this stage precedes the problem identification stage and the goal-setting stage that follow.

Gardner set the exploration of the organization's issues as the key step in strategic decision making.

The most innovative element of this step is the exploration aspect. As a professional trainer, Gardner understood that exploration is the key element of learning. Learning is acquiring something from the learner's realm of the unknown. In the first stages the participants focus on the organization's situation in order to frame the known. One of the values of that frame is that then the participants have a notion of the realm of their unknown. How do I know what I don't know? Exploration of the issues is the path to discovering that realm.

What is exploration? Research has shown that exploration is a third kind of thinking, along with intuitive and rational thinking. Exploration thinking is a process of the brain mapping new experience into the thinking system. Weick and Bougon, in describing this cognitive mapping, point out:

> Maps help people perceive large-scale environments beyond the range of immediate perception . . . they deal with phenomena that cannot be observed but rather must be explored. Thus, maps are intimately tied to action. O'Keefe and Nadel [1987] use an early position paper by Ittelson (1973) to highlight the close ties between action and maps: "Most perception research has been carried out in the context of object perception, rather than environment perception. The distinction between object and environment is crucial, because objects require subjects . . . In contrast, one cannot be a subject of an environment, one can only be a participant. The very distinction between self and non-self breaks down cold. The environment surrounds, enfolds, engulfs, and no thing and no one can be isolated and identified as standing outside of, and apart from it . . . " The fact that they surround means that one cannot observe an environment; rather the organism explores it. (Weick & Bougon, 1986, pp. 104–105)

O'Keefe and Nadel define exploration behavior as "a reaction to new items, new places, or familiar items in new places. . . . Only novel [events] will elicit exploration [behavior]" (O'Keefe & Nadel, 1987, p. 224). Their research indicates that during exploration thinking behavior, the brain shuts down intuitive and rational thinking behaviors while it engages in exploration thinking behavior. Also, rational thinking blocks out exploration thinking as well. It is as though one cannot chew gum and walk at the same time (O'Keefe & Nadel,

1987). The difficulty in engaging in exploration thinking behavior comes in because the past approach to decision making was a cause-and-effect, rational problem-solving one.

It is surprising to note that exploration thinking behavior is not necessarily a learned behavior. It is built into our biological system. We just have to be aware of when we do it so that we do not try to rationalize what we are experiencing while we explore. This is the spirit of Gardner's reconnaissance stage when the participants are exploring the organization's emerging issues. Brainstorming and other open, nonjudgmental methods can be used to explore the issues.

At the East Coast county the strategic management team instituted the "issue paper" to conduct the exploration of issues in the county's agencies. The instruction for exploration of the issues encouraged nonjudgmental, brainstorming activities. The issue paper would be circulated for all the stakeholders on all apparent sides of the issue to respond individually or in groups. The emphasis was on brevity, initial impressions, and candid comments.

The key steps of the strategic management team's issue exploration process developed from Gardner's reconnaissance stage of AT&R are the following:

1. Develop issue papers to initiate (invite or enfranchise) research to explore the issue's nature and boundaries.
2. Form issue exploration groups among the stakeholders to explore, discuss the issue, and develop alternative views.
3. Conduct formal strategic issue research pilot projects when high uncertainty and risk are involved.
4. Report research findings and make recommendations for strategic action.
5. Research, report, and discuss strategic decision-making results.

In the case of information technology development for the East Coast county, an issue is defined as a significant change emerging in the county's organizational situation. Or, more specifically, an issue appears as a change in the county's information technology context from which varieties of problems and opportunities can be anticipated. For example, in 1990 key emerging information technology issues for the county information technology included the following:

What is the impact of more and more powerful computer chips in personal computers? What will the developments in minicomputers mean for us in setting up cooperative computing resources in departments? When can agencies be expected to be able to develop their own systems?

Such emerging information technology issues attract interest by being new, strange, complex, unknown, risky, uncertain, and novel. The emerging information technology issues attract the interest of people who may feel that they could be affected (either positively or negatively) by the problems and opportunities expected to arise out of the issue. In this manner, the issue is an attractor around which the interested parties self-organize into a community of interest known as *stakeholders* (Mitroff, 1983). For example, the appearance of personal computers was an "attractor" and the cause of various concerns in the county administration. They were seen by the county's information technology department as a bother and threat. The agencies saw them as an opportunity to be more responsive to the demands that citizens were making on them for service. The budget director saw them as a growing demand for revenue. The personnel director wondered how the County would train employees in using them, and so on.

Usually, encountering something new causes us to cease our behavior of the moment to fix our attention on the source of the novelty. Then, if the unusual situation does not seem to pose an immediate threat to us, we begin to investigate it objectively, as something new. That is, we examine it with a sense of curiosity, openness, and wonder. Also, there is a temporary suspension of judgment while we take in the new experience. Our typical actions are also suspended and redirected toward investigating the nature of the novelty. In this exploration behavior we are allowing new information into the knowledge base of our view of the world. Exploration behavior is a form of learning; it is changing or enlarging our world view—in other words, growing (O'Keefe & Nadel, 1987). Exploration behavior, of course, is much more active in children because they have so much to learn. The whole world is new to them. For adults, exploration behavior is something we often forget to do; we already know so much.

Therefore, issue exploration is a process that uses emerging issues to foster exploration behavior in strategic decision makers before strategic decision makers begin to identify and analyze the attendant problems and opportunities involved. Issue exploration becomes a process of reacting to emerging issues by exploring them openly in order to learn about them before the ensuing problems and opportunities are identified, classified, analyzed, and solved, sometimes in error. Issue exploration is learning of the context of the issue before we categorize its problems and opportunities.

Using this approach, anyone in the county wishing to propose a management initiative for information technology could create a one- or two-page issue paper. The issue paper would describe the strategic issue without pointing at specific problems or opportunities that have to be dealt with. That would be the function of the issue exploration effort itself. Also, the paper would include some notion of who the key stakeholders involved in the issue are, in order to include them in the issue exploration effort. The issue paper would also contain recommendations on how the issue exploration ought to proceed, any budgetary considerations that might be involved in conducting the issue exploration, what expectation the issue exploration might have on the strategic objectives, and some indication of the anticipated time frame involved.

The strategic management team would review and discuss the issue paper. It also would decide whether it should be pursued. Issue exploration was used to help assure the county strategic decision makers that they were deciding on the strategic problems and opportunities, namely those that can be expected to impinge significantly on the county's ability to achieve its strategic objectives. The issue exploration process was designed to provide a means for the strategic decision makers to acquire the new knowledge they need to separate strategic problems and opportunities from the nonstrategic ones. The issue exploration process allows people from diverse areas of the county to make sure their views, information, and professional insights are included in the strategic decision-making process.

Implementation of this new issue exploration process was direct. After the presentation in the strategic management steering committee, the deputy county executive for management and budget simply announced, "That's it, then. From now on we'll make it policy that all management initiatives brought before this committee will be in the form of issue exploration papers before anything else can be done on them. And I'd like to see that the results of these issue exploration efforts we have approved are properly evaluated as well. We need to interject some 'Baconian' research methods in this process."

INITIAL ISSUES EXPLORED:
FROM THE JOURNALS OF NEELY GARDNER

Early in January, Gardner had his first meeting with the six division chiefs who made up the State Fund's executive committee. One of the stated concerns that surfaced had to do with the program promoting safety in the workplaces of policyholders. The State Fund was moving from a technical, enforcing type of safety program to one of customer education.

Gardner observed,

> The change had never been enthusiastically received by safety people. However, they did not seem to be particularly effective in assisting the people working in the other State Fund functions: sales and claims. I agreed to help them explore the role of safety. I would meet with people all over the organization to get their views on the 'Safety' issue, with an aim to providing data for policy formulation.

After a couple of weeks Gardner returned and presented his findings to the division chiefs. The findings indicated clear differences in philosophy about the role of safety. It was also obvious that many people in the field felt that the safety activity was a second-class activity. Persons working in the safety function were taking little pride in their work, feeling that what they did was downgraded and not appreciated by their fellow workers.

As the chiefs discussed the possible issuance of a new safety policy, they had to confront the fact that the "generalist" program in the compensation insurance representative classifications had eroded the level of expertise in a number of State Fund functions, such as sales, claims adjusting, safety, and underwriting. It was perhaps more readily seen in safety, but it was also true in rehabilitation and in sales.

Another issue they confronted was deciding on what the State Fund philosophy should be in regard to decentralization. The meeting ended in an indecisive way, with Gardner being assigned to keep collecting information. At this point, he pressed them:

> I declared I would only continue to collect data if they would agree to act on the data once it was collected. They agreed with some hesitation. Our contract was consummated, but it was clear that some of the Division Chiefs were mentally writing into the 'contract' some psychological, if unspoken, fine print.

As the division chiefs and Gardner shared the discomfort of this rather painful meeting, Gardner noted, "I had a great deal to do before deciding if our psychological contract was truly in effect. It was time to make an estimate of the situation in terms of issues confronting the State Fund." He asked them each to take a few moments and write down responses to any or all of the following three questions, which would be shared later:

- What is going well with the organization that should not be changed?
- What are the issues that should be examined?
- If you could change the organization with "a stroke of the pen," what would you do?

Some examples of the managers' issues to explore are listed.

1. One question that must be addressed is how to exercise control functions of the manager and still proceed with decentralization and the dispersal of claims activities.
2. There has simply got to be a better way to process claims. It is archaic and wasteful of greatly needed resources.
3. Our organization is weakened because it is noncompetitive. Its image is not sufficiently strong, and it is identified as the enemy by those who are in revolt against compensation insurance.
4. Home office staff should support rather than control. Further, there are too many levels of management. The operations division is too large. I would have liked to see a complete dispersal of all functions, including underwriting.
5. Why not consider contract insurance for the retrospective rate, or scale dividends to give better rewards?
6. Why not conduct marketing campaigns and even go so far as to have representatives in Eastern United States?

7. We must develop a better definition of an industrial accident, because the whole picture of compensation is influenced by "rulings" and by the unrest on the part of both the employer and employee.

8. The inability to retain the better salesmen is perhaps the major problem since the State Fund does not begin to pay salesmen what is needed to retain the best.

Exploring these issues became the basis of the State Fund's strategy for organizational change. Exploring strategic issues accomplishes a variety of things. First, it becomes a forum for a group to formulate agreement on what the issues are without getting into the divisive dialogue about problems and who is responsible for causing them and whose solution should be adopted. Personal agenda can remain "under the table" for the moment. Second, exploration provides the opportunity for the decision-making group to acquire new knowledge about critical areas in which they were currently ignorant. Third, exploring issues enlarges the framework and point of view perspective from which the group will be formulating its organization's strategy for action and strategic change. Together, these elements of issue exploration form the foundation of organization learning.

In addition, the issues themselves lay down the ground rules for hashing out the problems, their solutions, and opportunities that will emerge in the next stage four: identify the problems, opportunities, and action options.

SUMMARY

Reconnaissance as issue exploration is of strategic importance. Errors made at this stage of organizational decision making can have the most serious effects on the organization. Chasing after the wrong issues not only uses up limited strategic resources for change, it also leads the organization down the wrong road. By the same token, selection of the right strategic issues allows the organization to place its strategic resources in a position to take the most advantage of future events. The difficulty in determining the "right" issues from the "wrong" ones comes partly from our inability to predict the future successfully and partly from our use of linear rational thinking processes when exploration thinking processes are in order. During the exploration process the two thinking behaviors are mutually exclusive; we can do one but not both at the same time.

It is the exploration and analysis of the organization's issues that provide the research base for the next stage of problem and opportunity identification. The problem and opportunity identification effort of the next phase often surfaces issues that may have been overlooked during this reconnaissance stage. This is the iterative function of AT&R. In many cases it becomes necessary to revisit this stage after completing the next.

CHAPTER 7

AT&R STAGE 4:
IDENTIFYING PROBLEMS
AND OPPORTUNITIES

MENU FOR AT&R STAGE 4: IDENTIFYING PROBLEMS AND OPPORTUNITIES

Action   *Considerable time elapses before identifying problems and opportunities. The first three steps have addressed climate setting, developing understanding of the process, and reconnaissance. In this model the effort is to develop a "feel for the field." So the data collected in the reconnaissance stage are classified and tested for (1) agreement and (2) degree of importance. If the problem identification is occurring in a group that "owns" the information, the task is to develop agreement, if not a consensus (Gardner, 1974).*

Training   *Problem identification and problem solving methods.*

Research   *Cards (3 × 5) are distributed to each participant. A single problem or opportunity is written on each card, and participants are given 15 minutes to work on the exercise. Each participant indicates the importance of the problem or opportunity and which issue is the key source of that problem or opportunity.*

The participants then place the cards under a sign indicating the appropriate key issue. They inspect and evaluate the cards placed by others, rearranging them as appropriate. Open dialogue is encouraged during this last step.

Outcome   *Problems and Opportunities Database cards sorted per key issue.*

SOLVING THE RIGHT PROBLEMS

Executives search for the right solutions to the organization's problems, and they are concerned about the decisions they make in this regard. The right problems to solve, from their executive viewpoint, are those problems that are most important to their organization's strategic objectives for developing the business or mission. Solving the wrong problem can have serious consequences at the strategic decision-making level.

Solutions to wrong problems can mean spending millions of dollars to build a computer system that would be obsolete before it is installed, or missing the chance to enter a key niche of the market, or buying hundreds of obsolete personal computers. Such wrong choices not only waste valuable and limited strategic resources for change, but the costs of solving the wrong problem instead of the right problem can mean critical services will be needlessly missing in the community. However, executives do not really get to solve problems—they have managers for that. But the situation is similar for managers; they do not really solve problems—the people that create the products and deliver the service ultimately must do the problem solving. Executives and managers provide the methods, tools, and resources to enable the line workers to do just that.

The purpose of this stage is to have as many of the people as possible who might be involved in dealing with the potential problems and opportunities that emerge from the organization's issues to participate in this stage of problem and opportunity identification.

Clearly, people in the work units and departments will have a different view about the organization's issues, as well as identifying different potential problems and opportunities.[1]

EXAMPLE IN PRACTICE: DESIGNING A PROBLEM–OPPORTUNITY IDENTIFICATION SESSION AT THE STATE FUND

A newly appointed State Fund vice president and an internal practitioner flew down to Los Angeles from San Francisco to meet with Neely Gardner at his apartment overlooking Marina Del Rey. They were planning the next management retreat at which both the executives and the managers would participate. Gardner introduced his graduate assistant who would be helping them with the executive retreat and congratulated the vice president on his recent appointment as an executive, "What have you noted about your new duties?" he asked.

"One of the first frustrations I discovered as an executive is how impotent you are to make change," he answered. "As a manager," he explained, "you have a budget, you have people, you get the resources they need, and you can make things happen. But, as executives, we don't have a budget, we 'OK' them for everybody else. All we can do is approve and advise."

Gardner grinned at the newly appointed vice president. "Good! That might be a fitting subject for us to use as a theme for the management retreat in San Diego," he explained.

"What? How to be important?" the vice president laughed.

"You've described a key transformation situation for change: the relationship between the executive and management in the organization. We could use that change as the focus of the workshops during the retreat in San Diego," Gardner continued. "What's the role of the executive in the strategic planning of issues, and how that gets translated by the district and staff managers who have to solve the problems coming out of those issues."

"You're right there, Neely," the vice president replied. "It seems to me that there is still a lot of mutual mistrust between the managers and the executives," the vice president said. "And I say that, having just gotten rid of my manager's hat. We need something to warm up the group as a whole. Maybe, you could do your wine tasting thing."

"That's a good idea," Gardner said, adding it to the list he was making. "And what do you think about this?" Gardner pointed to the list on a piece of paper. The vice president read it aloud:

1. Wine tasting as team building exercise
2. Executives lead discussion to identify and explore the key issues (reconnaissance stage)
3. Internal practitioner records them on newsprint & on separate cards
4. Problem card routine
5. Dinner
6. Breakout groups around issues–problems
7. . . . .

"Excuse me, but what's the problem card routine?" the internal practitioner asked.

Gardner described an exercise that would come to be known as "Neely's Card Trick."

"What we do is pass out an ample number of cards like this," Gardner responded, "holding up a 3 × 5 card. We make sure there are stacks of cards on every table. Then we ask the participants each to think of all problems and opportunities that they see coming out of the issues they had identified earlier. They should put only one problem or one opportunity on a single card, but they are encouraged to use as many cards as they can think of problems or opportunities. They are told that they have only 15 minutes to accomplish this task. They are also instructed to then rank the card's contents as to its importance to the State Fund as a whole, using a scale of, say, 1 to 5, with 5 being most important."

"I see," the practitioner observed. "You're having them create a kind of database of organization problems?"

"And opportunities," Gardner prompted.

"Yes, opportunities," the practitioner replied.

"While they are having dinner," the graduate student explained to the practitioner, "you and I can sort the cards according to the issues generated by the executives earlier."

"That's the way we did it last time," Gardner said. "But this time I think we can improve on that. If we sort the database, it tends to become 'our' database and therefore 'our' information. The participants then sit back and relate to it only as 'our' instructional material. I was thinking as you described that activity, what if we have them sort out the cards according to the issues?"

"Sure! Then it would be their database," the vice president said. "And we could take it back with us and use it to start our entrepreneurial plan. I like that idea."

"How's this," Gardner said, catching the excitement, "we have them switch roles?"

"How do you mean?" the graduate student asked.

"I mean," Gardner said, "we can have the managers copy the 'issues' from the earlier newsprint onto cards, then tape the issues cards on the wall with enough space between them to tape up problem–opportunity cards later. Then we have the executives take all of the problem–opportunity cards and tape them next to the particular issue that is doing the most to generate the particular problem or opportunity."

"That's kind of like a manual computer, isn't it?" the practitioner observed. "I'd like to suggest that we take a photograph of the wall to preserve the order of the cards when they are finished. And then we let everyone mill around and feel free to move a problem–opportunity card to different issue groups and to put them in a sort of priority order visually regardless of the number put on it by the originator."

"What does that contribute?" the graduate student asked.

"I'm not sure, but it's something you can do with a database in a computer," he replied.

"I think it's a good suggestion," Gardner said. "The advantage is that with everyone milling about, moving cards, you get a real chance of serendipity and innovation in seeing problems in different ways."

"And we can take another photograph to get that snapshot of our combined thinking as well," the vice president observed.

Gardner went back to his original list. "This brings us to the last entry on our menu of activities: the whole group." Gardner pointed to the newsprint list. "Remember, we are now talking about a group composed of 6 executives, some 30 district office managers, and 12 staff department managers."

This use of cards to help large groups generate ideas has been used in many management situations. For example, this method was used in a national conference on the role of total quality management (TQM) methods in the university setting in Morgantown, West Virginia. It involved more than 200 academic and practitioner participants including the chairs of many of the leading business departments in the United States, as well as executives from the Air Force, Xerox, Motorola, and other leaders in TQM. After the key issues were identified by the main group, they were explored by smaller "break-out groups" that reported back to the main group. Then there was a 15-minute problem–opportunity card completion period that produced more than 1000 responses by the participants. After dinner, a group of volunteers met in a room with a large wall to paste up the cards in some order according to the issues explored by the main group. In some instances new issues emerged from the process, and some issues did not generate any cards. One of the participants agreed to stay up all night in order to key the responses into a laptop computer. The results were reported to the main group the next day.

In the TQM in the university conference the participants had to come to some agreement on which issues were the most important to include in their strategic decision making. This appraisal of the issues was now more meaningful because each issue was accompanied by an array of problems and opportunities. These attendant problems and opportunities not only gave the strategic decision makers a more in-depth view of their importance, but also revealed that many issues shared the same problems. This meant several things. First, solving a particular problem or realizing a particular opportunity could affect other issues at the same time. However, this analysis also reduced the strategic propensity of the decision makers to select the "silver bullet" approach of using one decision to solve several problems. Just as often, solving one problem would only make problems in another equally important issue even worse—the balloon-poking effect: "If we push the balloon in here, then it pops out there."

In the TQM university conference the whole group participated in prioritizing the issues through presentations by expert practitioners and a general critique of the conference results report that had been compiled during the previous evening. This dual problems–opportunities identification session can be accomplished in a workshop setting such as the State Fund executive sessions or the TQM in the university conference. It is limited only by the imaginations of the facilitators.

WHAT ARE PROBLEMS?

It is useful to discuss the difference between the words *issue* and *problem*. Issue comes from the French and Latin usage with an intransitive meaning, "to go out [from here], a going, a journey" (Partridge, 1958, p. 315). Its root in the Indo-European is *ei*, to go. Problem has a transitive meaning, "a thing thrown forward." It comes from the Greek meaning, *pro*, forward, *blema*, something thrown. From the Italian *ballo* English gets the word *ballistic* (Partridge, 1958). We can think of problems as things thrown forward from emerging issues. For example, a baseball pitcher throws a perfect strike to a batter who already has two strikes. There are two outs, the batter's team is one run behind, and it is the bottom of the ninth. If the batter does not swing the bat at the ball, he is out and his team loses. If he swings and misses—the same. If he swings and hits the ball out of the park, the batter's team wins. The perfectly thrown ball is the immediate issue. The actions taken determine the problems–opportunities that are thrown forward with that speeding ball. Problems in an organizational context are events or things that impede the organization in its mission. Opportunities are events or things that help the organization in its mission. In any case, both problems and opportunities stem from the issues in the organization's situation. Problems are solved or not solved. Opportunities are realized or lost. But issues are resolved, one way or another.

Therefore, we can see that issues and problems are intricately linked. However, the issue should not be identified as the problem.

Issues do not have solutions—only problems do. The weather can not be a problem. It changes according to its own laws and whims. However, weather certainly generates plenty of problems for us. Ice ages, hurricanes, and unseasonable weather events do not seek solutions in themselves; it is the problems they cause humans that require solutions, such as insurance, building codes, and improved weather forecasts, and galoshes and umbrellas.

Problems for organizations are changes, or impending changes, in the organization's status quo that cause the people in the organization to want to act in some way to influence the change on the organization's and their own behalf. Clearly, more often than not, problems are not recognized until after they manifest themselves as something gone wrong. This is the "ouch!" form of problem sensing. The AT&R method, as we have seen in the previous stages, takes a strategic intelligence-gathering approach by focusing upstream from problems—namely, on the issues that generate them.

Problems have problems. The problems with problems are at least threefold. They are a multitude, interrelated, and limited in how they may be solved. First, everyone, as well as every organization, has more problems than they have resources with which to deal with them. AT&R addresses this with issue exploration analysis. It is a matter of strategy: Issues determine which problems I shall choose to deal with, and where I shall place my limited strategic resources.

Second, problems are often complexly interrelated with other problems, and their solutions often impinge on other issues, causing even more problems. The solution to one problem often causes problems somewhere else down the line to us or other people. For example, the perfect strike thrown by the baseball pitcher was an immediate problem to the batter. If, instead of hitting a home run he hits the ball so that it will land inside the playing field, it becomes an immediate problem for the opposing team's fielders. But it is a problem of different force to the fielding team players depending on where in the field it is hit. If it is a ground ball and is picked up by the infielders, then it becomes a problem of getting it to first base before the batter gets there, and so on. This phenomenon was the focus of Lewin's force field theory. Lewin saw the ongoing situation as a sort of balance of forces impinging on each other to the point that they equalized each other in a sort of homeostasis—that is, the appearance of status quo. Where the reality we perceived seemed stable and calm before the ball was thrown, behind that stability was a myriad of contending forces balancing themselves from moment to moment. Because balance, in effect, is the stability, a seemingly trivial change in one of the many forces—the swing of the bat—effects a significant, and sometimes dramatic, shift in the balance. If the ball is thrown in the first inning, it is one thing. If it is thrown as the last pitch of the World Series, it is quite another.

Lewin tried to build a mathematical model based on this view. If one knew all the forces and the vector of the direction of their thrust, one could calculate what any particular change would cause in the field as a whole. Current work on chaos theory explains why Lewin's mathematical model was never completed. Human systems, like the weather, have too many forces involved to be included in a working model. And, as in chaos theory, which Lewin foresaw, a trivial event now can have unforeseen major effects on the entire force field involved—the proverbial butterfly wing flutter in Peking causing a hailstorm in Lima, Peru, years later. Gardner adapted Lewin's force field analysis into a tool that AT&R uses to help organizations identify at least the salient problems emerging out of the organization's universe of issues. Therefore, force field analysis can be plotted on a continuum with strict linear cause and effect at one extreme to the chaos of variables at the other. On one hand, it can be practiced in a simplified single table of supporting and restraining forces. On the other hand, the forces can be detailed and interlinked into a complex analysis process. Clearly, the decision-making situation will dictate the depth of analysis that is most appropriate.

FROM THE STATE FUND JOURNALS OF NEELY GARDNER: IDENTIFYING PROBLEMS AS TEAM BUILDING

In most of the action research projects that had been conducted to that point, it was apparent that managers in both the State Fund's home office and the district offices had difficulty relating to the executive committee. Frustration increased until the executive committee and managers councils decided to hold a "giant" team building session that would include the executive committee and district and staff program managers.

When a vice president and a member from his Strategic Action Group for Organization Development met with Gardner and his graduate assistant in the day-long planning session in Marina Del Rey, it was decided to use the team-building meeting as a model that would be used later as a design for regular monthly managers council meetings. The theme of the meeting was, "How we think it is. How it should be." If the managers council were to succeed, ways must be found to permit an exchange of views around major issues and problems that confronted the State Fund on an ongoing basis. Also the three groups, the executive committee, the district office managers, and the staff support managers, had a need to meet with their counterparts in the other groups sharing common tasks and having similar problems. For example, team-building planners recognized that some district managers would have problems not shared with other district managers. Many of these particular problems could be resolved only through one-to-one interaction between the district manager and the executive committee members or with people in staff support departments. In addition, how were the employees to participate in this process? Gardner hoped to develop a design that would make it possible to meet a wide variety of individual and group needs for the 50 participating managers and, ultimately, the employees as well.

The process developed for the team-building sessions in San Diego included several action research methods to facilitate a large group in a comprehensive evaluation of the State Fund's current situation as a "changing organization." The staff from the Strategic Action Group for Organization Development also participated as facilitators.

FIRST EVENING

At 5:00 P.M. of the first evening, participants met in the hotel dining room and were seated in six action analysis groups, each with managers from three categories (executive, district, and staff program managers) chosen at random. The session was designed to maximize the exchange between groups.

As a socializing and intercommunication modeling exercise, they were given the task of blind tasting and rating a series of bottles of Cabernet Sauvignon from different wineries. Several wine bottles were placed at each table; the selection was the same for each group. Each bottle was wrapped in a paper bag in order to disguise its vintner, and new names were written on the bag referring to some organizational problem that was, at that time, in the forefront. (For example: "Chateau Loss-Ratio," "Clos de Claims," "Chateau Entrepreneurial Plan").

The action analysis groups' task was for each group to reach a consensus regarding the order of quality of the masked wine bottles. Gardner opened the exercise with a brief lesson on wine tasting, its criteria, and how to judge good wine as a group. All of the groups began the conversation around the common task of coming to an action group consensus about the type and quality of the different wines. Soon the groups became very cohesive, if not coherent, taking considerable pride in their work. We then took a reading on the total rating of the six groups, compared results, and went to dinner.

After dinner, participants entered groups with others in their own work category; these groups were called basic activity groups. Their first task was to identify and explore the issues (reconnaissance stage). Thus, the executive committee met as a group; district managers formed a group; and staff program managers made up another group. Each group was asked to complete the following statements:

1. The State Fund means _____
2. The State Fund could _____
3. The major changes in the State Fund's situation are _____

It was expected that the responses would surface the declared values held by group members.

As the issue responses were recorded on chart paper by the various groups, they were taped around on the walls of the large meeting room. At the end of the evening participants were invited to walk around, examine the responses, and share their views. The responses were consolidated by the whole group into basic issue areas.

SECOND DAY

The next morning the management groups were reconvened to focus on identifying the State Fund's problems and opportunities relative to the issues explored. In this morning session basic activity groups were asked to provide answers to the following questions in regard to the organization's issues:

1. What are the problems and opportunities posed by these issues?
2. What problems and opportunities do you have with the other management groups?
3. What problems and opportunities do we think they have with us?

Groups then categorized problems and opportunities that surfaced. In answer to the last two questions they were asked to decide whether the problems were (1) interpersonal, (2) intragroup, (3) intergroup, or (4) councilwide. In the afternoon every group met with every other group to attempt to make a beginning toward solving problems discussed and listed in morning sessions.

THIRD DAY

Participants started the morning's work in the action analysis groups to review significant issues and identify those problems that were councilwide. These groups then selected a representative to present their views to the total council.

The final portion of the council team-building effort was a planning session to address the question "Where do we go from here?" with the selected representatives of the groups deciding future steps for the council.

OUTCOMES OF THE TEAM BUILDING

The San Diego team-building meeting marked a change in the discussion pattern of the managers council. It moved from talking about "how we should organize" to "what should we be doing in the State

Fund?" At the San Diego meeting the discussion was quite open, and the educational process seemed to provide a new base for future interaction among all the managers. Also, the problem census provided a database for future actions.

Gardner noticed that members now talked to each other in a less vacuous manner and seriously addressed issue papers that were prepared by council members or their staff. These issue papers concerned the types of problems that surfaced in the San Diego meeting.

The last time Gardner was at the State Fund, he talked to all the members of the executive committee. At that time another meeting format had been developed. The staff program managers and district managers (basic activity groups) were going back to meeting together one month and separately the next. Executive committee members were invited to sit in but not participate directly in proceedings. The executive vice president said that a recent district managers' meeting was the best he had yet attended. In general, the managers council seemed to be serving its originally intended purpose of

1. Giving information to, and receiving it from, its members and the executive committee

2. Giving advice on formulation of new studies and programs and reviewing these studies and programs after formulation and before implementation

3. Reporting on, and receiving reports on, "exceptions" in regard to major policy and operating questions

4. Exchanging information among themselves

In looking at all the evidence available, Gardner concluded that the managers council had contributed to a higher level of coordination than was achieved in the hierarchical organization. Although there were still times when counterdependency was quite high, there was growing understanding of organizational and unit goals and an obvious commitment to the achievement of such goals. Although the council managers, the employees' program advisory council, and other employees of the State Fund were quite self-critical, outsiders who have done studies in the State Fund have remarked on the openness of the organization.

SUMMARY

It is clear that in a changing organization, problem identification cannot be a linear, step-by-step process. Problems cannot be identified in isolation from the rest of the organizational matrix and the various dimensions of its work from which it is derived. Lewin's force field analysis was a method to track and relate forces as they opposed each other in the balance of the status quo of work in progress. Just as with the present failure of computers to create artificial intelligence, so too the mathematics of force field analysis was not up to the task of tracking and computing the changes in all the forces at play in even the simplest of human work activities. However, as a "Practical Theorist" (Morrow, 1969), Lewin's force field analysis has become a useful method of evaluating a large number of interrelated problems and tracking their likely effects in the near future. Further, Lewin's reeducation theory provided a practical method for guiding people to change themselves as a changing organization.

Problems often prompt people in organizations to think about changing. When a practitioner gets called in to help, he or she is usually confronted with a problem situation of some sort. AT&R recognizes that problems come out of the issues that the organization is facing. The role of the AT&R methodology is not to provide a method for solving the problems. There are numerous problem-solving instruments already available to any organization. The AT&R practitioner's role is to guide the client organization to analyze its situation and values, identify its issues before formally identifying the problems and opportunities. Certainly, problems will be surfaced during the processes of the first three stages of AT&R. They can be taken note of and brought up as a primer for this fourth stage.

Only by going back through the first three stages can the problems and opportunities be properly identified with the organization's strategic issues. Furthermore, the constellation of strategic issues will most likely prompt the client organization to identify its problems and opportunities more comprehensively. Problem solutions will come in the action phase of AT&R stages.

More important, without research and analysis of the issues, and especially the problems and opportunities that confront the organization, the organization cannot properly visualize in what ways it must change itself. All of the research in the stages up to now provides the basis of agreeing on the aspirations the organization can have for changing itself in the next stage, aspirations.

NOTE

1. The Chinese view problems as being "dangerous opportunities." Therefore, for the sake of analysis, we refer to both as "problems."

CHAPTER 8

AT&R STAGE 5: ASPIRATIONS

MENU FOR AT&R STAGE 5: ASPIRATIONS

Action   As used here, aspiration *refers to the issues that people
           would like to influence as they begin to solve their prob-
           lems and exploit their opportunities. One approach that
           works well is to prioritize the issues now that the problems
           and opportunities are identified. The participants can
           convert the problem–opportunity descriptions into "How
           to" statements. In answering a "How to" question, in the
           next stage participants generally advance a series of action
           options that represent their range of aspiraions.*

           *Often, the AT&R activities of determining the aspirations,
           analyzing the data, and defining the desired strategic ac-
           tion decisions can take place in one workshop or training
           session, although the number of possibilities for inter-
           action are as great as the trainer's ingenuity and include
           focus groups, Internet chat rooms, and other survey feed-
           back methods. These three stages are largely action train-
           ing activities. For example, in one study, the entire staff of
           the city's daytime employees participated in the training
           session. Council members and citizens took part in parallel
           sessions (Gardner, 1974).*

Training   *Goal setting, writing objectives, creating vision scenarios.*

Research   *The participants select each key issue and its attendant problems and opportunities, and prioritize them. As a group they reword the issue's problems and opportunities into "How to" statements.*

For example,

> *Under "issue": the new computer technology is increasing our clients' expectation of our service response.*
>
> *Under "problem": purchasing is rejecting more and more of our purchase orders.*
>
> *Under "How to" statement: How to have the correct vendor information at hand when we are filling out a purchase order.*

As many as possible of the problems and opportunities are converted to "How to" statements and compiled under the appropriate key issues. They are then prioritized and organized into a basic strategy for change.

Outcome   *Strategic decisions, futures scenarios.*

ASPIRING TO BECOME A CHANGING ORGANIZATION

One of the major differences between planning and AT&R is that goal setting comes after issue exploration and problem identification. There is an ongoing discussion about the differences between goals, objectives, missions, and vision statements. All of these concepts involve future changes to be desired and actions to be taken in order to achieve them. Aspiration is a term of inclusiveness that Gardner used to describe the state of changing that the organization needed to become. In Lewin's terms, the organization needed to unfreeze its status quo, and move toward a new level of organization. However, the aspiration is not to "refreeze" again at the new state, but rather, the new state needs to be a more fluid one that does not require the degree of "unfreezing–changing–refreezing" that Lewin's original paradigm for developmental change requires. The organization's aspiration is to be a continually changing, continually developing organization. Gardner's entrepreneurial aspect of a more democratic (read *participative*) organizational environment puts certain market forces into play that requires this more agile posture.

AT&R need not necessarily be used only at organization-wide efforts. It can be used at project level and work-unit-level groups apart from parent organizations. Any work group can aspire to develop into a changing organization on its own, for that matter. The aspiration stage shows how the AT&R cycle can apply to the effort of any work group to develop itself into a changing organization. The cycle is replayed, to some degree, at each stage. This will be especially true in the following stages of the action phase of AT&R. Finally, as the approach is applied to departments and work units within a department, the cycle can begin anew. The problems from the organization level most likely will become issues for departments. And problems identified by departments may very well become issues for the work units within that department.

ENTREPRENEURIAL ASPIRATIONS IN FEDERAL GOVERNMENT

The federal government has begun to experiment with this approach to develop changing organizations. John A. Koskinen, deputy director for management, Office of Management and Budget (OMB), pointed out,

> The answer for federal managers lies in franchising support activities. This growing form of enterprise government enables organizations, both large and small, to "hire" other government organizations with expertise in administrative areas—from procurement to payroll—to perform administrative support work. This approach to administer support enhances effectiveness, economy, and accountability and allows government organizations to benefit from each other's expertise and better focus their energies on accomplishing other organizational missions. (Koskinen, 1996, pp. v–vi)

Even before NPR (National Performance Review), Ted Gaebler and David Osborne made this entrepreneurial approach to delivering government service known to a broad audience. In *Reinventing Government,* Osborne and Gaebler (1992, p. xix) describe several entrepreneurial and marketing methods practiced by state and local governments. Entrepreneurial government has actually been around for decades. Pioneers such as Frank Sherwood and Neely Gardner began their innovations in entrepreneurial government administration in the 1950s (Serlin & Bruce, 1996, p. 31)

Clearly, introducing changing organizations that have Gardner's entrepreneurial approach can be expected to be controversial. In the case of the NPR franchising administrative services among federal agencies, the first large franchise contract, bid in competition with private-sector firms, landed on the front page of the Washington Post with the headlines, "When the Government Hires the Government; FAA Awards Big Systems Contract to USDA, but to Private Contractors, It Doesn't Compute." Where the federal government's 1994 Government Reform Act established six pilot franchise projects, the private sector questioned whether a government data center could be more qualified than a commercial one.

However, the *Post* article acknowledged,

> [Franchising] might not be such a bad thing. "Ultimately, the government is not always going to win and the private sector isn't either," said Michael D. Serlin, a former National Performance Review official who now works as a consultant on federal contraction issues. "If the result is genuine competition, however, it's the taxpayer who's the winner." John A. Koskinen, OMB Deputy Director for Management said, "The point of these operations is to bring down the costs for government. (cited in Chandrasekaran, 1997, pp. 1, 20–21)

EXAMPLE IN PRACTICE: THE NTDS ASPEN SEMINAR

Aspen, Colorado, was the site of the second National Training and Development Seminar (NTDS) for developing changing organizations, where Gardner first trained people in AT&R. The participants lived and had seminar classes in Snowmass. Their "learning client" was the city of Grand Junction, Colorado, whose mayor had been a participant in the first NTDS seminar the year before. The participants commuted from time to time to practice their AT&R methods with their counterparts in Grand Junction's administration and community groups.

On one of the breaks during the presentation of this fifth stage on aspirations, Gardner and one of the participants wandered out on the deck. There was a panorama view of Aspen down below and the snowcapped peaks all around. They discussed this aspiration stage among the granite spires of the great Rocky Mountains.

"I don't know," one of the NTDS seminar participants asked Gardner. "How come the goal setting is here and not at the beginning?"

Gardner looked down the steep valley toward Aspen. He paused to phrase his answer. "It is unusual, I know," he answered. "You have hit upon one of the more unique features, I think, of this AT&R approach. Changing an organization involves not only the success of the organization but the lives and careers of those involved. In the first stages we are doing mostly research as a kind of strategic homework to help us decide what to do. You have all been going to Grand Junction to gather these data from the citizens and government officials there: the issues, problems, opportunities and all."

"Yes, we have plenty of those," the participant replied.

"And I see that you've worked out a nice matrix to relate them to each other. Fine," Gardner continued. "These next two stages are involved in discovering, inventing, and selecting the action options Grand Junction has available to them to make changes they decide are most important for them to make. But they also have to agree on which ones they will actually make . . . that is committing their resources to . . . and who will actually make the changes. These are the crucial stages for action."

"Like project planning?" the participant asked.

"Not really, that comes later," Gardner replied. "Up to now, mostly policy makers and idea people have participated in our data gathering. No, I know a lot of administrative employees and citizens have participated as well, but only some. Therefore, these next two stages are the transition from data gathering and ideas to action steps for change. They are the transition from strategic decision making of goals and objectives to the tactical decision making for action."

"Aspiration means literally 'breathing life' into something. At this stage, it does not refer to the organization's mission or vision. We dealt with that in the first two stages and in developing the enterprise model. We wait until after the issues, problems, and opportunities are brought forward before this stage of developing the goals and objectives of changing the organization, more exactly, developing the organization into an organization that could change itself whenever needed."

"But that's what's got me confused," the participant said. "Usually, we set the goals and objectives, then we identify the problems getting there, select the best alternative, and then get on with the program. Aren't we kind of duplicating our effort?"

"There are two basic purposes behind this order in AT&R. First, only when you learn something of the territory ahead can you properly fix on where you ought to go and how you are going to get there. This is why reconnaissance and exploration are so important in earlier stages of AT&R. Second, mutual goal setting between the executive policy makers and the line-work units informs the transition process of changing from executive strategic decision makers to the people in the organization who will be changing. Similarly, this transition process can equally occur between the work unit management and the people producing the products and delivering the service to the customers or citizens.

"The first purpose means that much of the groundwork of goal setting has already been done in the previous stages identifying and analyzing issues, problems, and opportunities. Aspiration translates them all into action. Now all of the issues and their attendant problems and opportunities must now be used to tease out all of the possible options the organization has for actions to solve the problems and realize the opportunities. Aspiration is the first step in matching resources to actions. It is the first step in commitment to change and the handing over of the resources necessary for the change to those people that will be involved in the change."

"A sort of handing off of the baton, so to speak," the participant replied.

"You can look at it that way, yes," Gardner agreed. "Let's take an example from your organization at the State Fund. When the executives identified the loss of top sales people as a major strategic issue and outlined pay structure in the state's civil service as a major problem, what happened in your strategic action group?"

"We tried to figure out how to change the pay and compensation for sales people," the participant replied.

"We? You mean your strategic action group?"

"No, not the SAG," the participant replied. "We formed a task force of sales people, personnel people and others . . . computer systems folks because we may need them, and some counterparts at the state personnel board."

"And then?"

"Well, the team did a force field analysis that showed that there were lots of supporting forces and several large restraining forces."

"No, I mean," Gardner interjected, "what did you do first. This force field analysis, how did you go about it?"

"Well, you know," the participant replied, "you draw a line for that status quo . . . "

"Yes, the line," Gardner interrupted. "And then?"

"We drew a second line to represent where we wanted the status quo to move to."

"And what did you call that line? What did it represent?" Gardner asked.

"Oh, I see," the participant exclaimed as though a lightbulb just went on in his head. "That was our goal for change we wanted."

"Which was?"

"To have a pay and compensation system that would keep top sales performers from being lured away by our competitors and taking our top policyholders with them."

"Let me fill in the picture," Gardner said. "Earlier, I had gone through the first four AT&R stages with the executives and managers where they explored the original issue. But they were not going to make the actual changes required themselves. Your task forces of the people involved in the change are. That brings up your task force's force field analysis. Your goal line expressed the aspirations stage we have been studying this morning. What happened next?"

"We decided that the 1-year budget cycle was a small but key constraint that kept us from adopting a commission on sales pay system. The problem was that taking a 1-year planning horizon, getting the state personnel board to approve a sales commission system for us always seemed impossible."

"That's interesting," Gardner observed. "And how did that work out?"

"We tried to figure out how we could change the budget planning cycle. It would be at least 2 years for the personnel board to awake from the dead faint for us just asking for a sales commission system. Another problem was that the State Fund executives were very nervous about a sales commission system in the State Fund as well. Two of the executives were actually dead set against the whole idea in the first place. But they would never come out publicly against it because they knew the personnel board would never let it happen. They assumed a benign neglect stance."

"How were you able to deal with those problems?"

"We found out that some of the lower-level state personnel board people were interested in innovative pay and compensation approaches. They had tried one in the transportation department once, but were unable to get it off the ground. We suggested that the State Fund could conduct a sales commission program as an experiment. If it didn't work, they could blame us. We were an enterprise fund not using public tax money so they would be protected on that account. On the other hand, if our experiment did succeed, it could be used as an example, should they want to try it in other state agencies.

"We promised to have a professional pay and compensation firm set up our pilot system. In all, it took us 5 years to build and prove out the system. It succeeded and the rest is history. We now pay out hundreds of thousands of dollars in commissions to sales people and sales managers every year."

"What about your problem with the executives?" Gardner pressed the practitioner.

"The same thing," he answered. "We tried to figure out how to handle that very touchy situation."

"What did you do?"

"We figured that their stance was one of benign neglect. We decided to adopt it as well."

"How so?"

"Because they had approved the task force goal, we decided that our concern about their true motives was our problem. So we didn't try to get them to reassure us, and pressed on. None of them is timid about intervening if they see a need. In the end the whole program would have to be approved by them in a meeting with the state personnel board. They would have plenty of opportunity to decide on the final outcome. This way, they would get to decide on the basis of State Fund experience and not on the prospect of it."

Gardner smiled. "That will be a perfect example for the aspiration stage. May I call on you for it?"

"Sure," the practitioner replied, "if drawing a goal line on a force field chart is all there is to the aspiration stage."

"Do you see that ridge-like mountain across the valley toward Aspen?" Gardner asked, looking out at the mountain range.

"Yes."

"Before you came out on the deck, I was watching it for some time . . . through these field glasses." Gardner explained. "Here, you look."

The participant took the glasses and focused them on the mountain across the deep valley. "Do you see some people there on the crest of that escarpment?"

"Yes," the practitioner replied. "What are they doing?"

"I think they might be a good example for us as well. Let me try it out on you," Gardner observed. "You see, they are going to jump off that mountain."

"Jump off!?"

"They are hang glider enthusiasts. Let's say that they have worked out an agreement to jump off the mountain. The mountain is their current status quo. They have studied the issues, that is, the weather, wind situations, identified the risks, their equipment, all sorts of strategic considerations, however, they have not yet acted. But at the moment they step to that short running path at the edge to jump off, there is a distinct shift. They now focus on goals beyond the mountain top. They now have to set their aspirations for flight and safe landing. They must examine all the problems that weather, air currents, trees, and the rocks below pose for them. For once they take the leap of faith into the sky, everything becomes tactical for them. The 'How to's' must be at the ready as they encounter the dangers and thrills of the flight.

"But ultimately, they must commit their resources to the sky, in this case, themselves, then action begins. Strategy is by the boards and the sky is everything," Gardner concluded.

"That's a pretty complex metaphor," the participant remarked. "It's quite a jump from pay and compensation systems to these human pterodactyls finding their way back to earth through the thrill of hang-glider flight. But I think I get the point about issues and problems first and aspirations next."

"What the aspiration stage method does," Gardner explained, "is to take all the problems and opportunities arrayed in your force field analysis and turn them around to positive statements by asking "How to" questions of each one: The answers are the options you have to choose from for actions to reach your goal of change during the implementation stage. Come, then," Gardner said. "Let's see if we can find some adventurous birds inside that will fly with us."

MOVING FROM STRATEGY TO ACTION

The aspiration stage is the transition from strategy to action. But one must not take a linear view of it. The process is still organic, and that is where the innovation comes in. The people who must be involved in the change certainly have a much different point of view than executives and managers sitting around filling out 3×5 cards. It is the action options that come out of the aspiration stage that can be later organized into a step-by-step plan for change in the project planning and implementation stages.

But at the aspiration stage there are still two tracks the change process can take. If all the action options chosen are clear and understood, then the process can go directly to the project planning and implementation stages 9 and 10. However, if any of the critical action options are based on unverified and critical assumptions, then it is best to experiment to test those action options to see if the original assumptions are justified. That was the tack the State Fund's sales commission task force took. By *critical* it is meant that the organization's success and people's careers are at risk should the assumption prove in error.

The mechanics of the aspiration stage involves a bringing together of the strategic elements of organizational change: issues, problems, and opportunities that had been raised in the previous stages. Those elements represent the "what and why" that the organization change must accomplish. The other side of the aspiration stage addresses the "how, where, and who" of the organization change that will be made.

There does not seem to be any "right" way to make this transition. On the one hand, all methods have sometimes failed in the past. On the other hand, most of them have also sometimes succeeded. Each situation is different. In any case, because of the role issues play in changing organizations, change will come, one way or another. The question becomes, "What role does the organization want to have in making the changes it will undergo in the future?"

There are three forces working against organizations taking a proactive role in changing themselves for the future. First is the press of current business. They are so busy just keeping up with present demands that they do not have ample time or resources to deal with the future. This is often called *crisis management,* and it is a reality most of us experience in our own lives. Also, solutions are much clearer when there is a crisis, because many of the creative options are no longer available.

Second is the seeming futility of such change. "How can you plan for every expediency you may meet in the future? We have long-range plans, but none of them ever work out. Something always comes up. Besides, long-range planning requires predicting the future—a fool's errand, at best."

Third is that most of the people involved have a vested interest in maintaining the status quo for the organization. It is their job to keep things running according to agreed on objectives, goals, and established procedures. We are all too busy just trying to keep the organization running and doing what it has to do to have time to change it.

However, the aspiration stage of AT&R breathes life into the organization change efforts by remaining firmly in the present, the "here and now," as the gestalt approach recommends. In the aspirations stage there is a variation on Peter Drucker's call to consider what decisions we can make today so that we will be in a position to make more valuable decisions tomorrow. The more literal meaning of strategy is, "How should we decide to place our resources in the field today, so that we will have better alternatives to choose from tomorrow?" The aspiration stage focuses on (how) to organize and allocate resources (where) for better decision advantages for action tomorrow (when). The aspirations are a good source of decision making and results in evaluation criteria in the stages that follow.

FROM NEELY GARDNER'S
STATE FUND JOURNALS: ASPIRATIONS

It was apparent that some of the greatest turmoil caused by the reconnaissance results occurred around the organization structure itself. The president of the State Fund had formed three of his managers into a "think-tank" task group in order to explore the organization's structural problems in more depth. Much of the time, in action training and research, one cannot be entirely certain whether the activity is training or research, or both. In order to take the next step, Gardner felt there had to be some concept building. Because the normative reeducative approach to change requires commitment from those involved in the changing, those involved must participate in the change planning, understand the nature of the expected change, and implement the change.

"Even had I desired to steer the State Fund in the direction of a preconceived organizational format," Gardner noted, "I should have been at a loss. There are so many problems with bureaucracy and hierarchy and so few alternative models. My strategy was not to be prescriptive but rather to persuade people to think experimentally, to see if an organic process might evolve that would help develop the State Fund structure in more useful ways. The process involved action training. The change 'agentry' function was to encourage a process by which the principals could learn, develop concepts, and map directions for possible actions.

"When I sat down with the president and the 'think-tank' staff group, I asked them to assume that the entire organizational structure of the State Fund had ceased to exist. Their thinking was to start from a zero-base with an effort being made to avoid preconceptions. With that as a given, the group set about answering the following questions, which were developed from the previous AT&R steps of issue reconnaissance and problem–opportunity identification. Examples include the following

1. What actual work needs to be done to fulfill the State Fund's mission?
2. What type of communication and coordination seem called for?
3. What organization structure and controls are needed?"

Gardner had supplied the group with some written materials prior to the meeting. These included a paper written by Frank Sherwood (1968) on the "market model" and short descriptions of matrix-type structures, as well as organic theories of organizing. By their previous education and training, task group members were generally knowledgeable about concepts of management development.

That day they not only began to "build a new State Fund" but also paused in the process to discuss the organization theory behind the moves being considered. Gardner's role was largely procedural—that is, suggesting the process by which the organizational problems would be addressed. Occasionally, but not often, he would regress to the role of professor as we explored theoretical issues.

"It was a surprising day for me," Gardner noted, "and I think for the others. Once the notion was accepted that we were in fact starting with a *tabula rasa,* the participants were able to consider functions and goals rather than hierarchical structures."

1. *Work to Be Done.* Dealing with the basic functions was fairly easy. As the president and his "think-tank" task force worked at the problem, they quickly agreed that the major functions were selling insurance, paying claims, working to help in the rehabilitation of disability cases, and promoting safety in the workplaces of policyholders. Almost immediately there was agreement that the center for these functions should most logically be carried on in workplaces close to policyholders, namely, decentralized to the district offices.

2. *Structure, Communication, and Coordination.* Assuming that the major functions would be gradually dispersed to the district offices, it followed that there was a need for management to coordinate the work between district offices in terms of uniform rates,

standard underwriting practices, dividing the boundaries so that the districts did not compete with each other, and other similarly obvious problems. How this would be done was a knottier problem. Obviously, in a devolved organizational structure, a great deal of organizational coordination needed to come from employees in the field.

In spite of much folklore around the concept of coordination from the top, the group agreed that the major part of the coordinating job rested with those who actually did the work. This brought about a discussion of the nature of central support required. After great travail, a vice president who was one of the think-tank staff went to the blackboard and put up an organization chart that depicted all of the home office staff departments and their functional units as separate boxes on the chart (see Figure 8.1).

Group members started to protest that he was breaking the "starting from a zero-base" rule, but he asked for patience. He suggested that they had to work the problem through visually. After discussing the contribution of staff department functions to coordination, he erased all of those staff department units that had no coordinating function. Then, seemingly without thinking, he said, "One of the things we need to do is get rid of the boxes."

He removed the borders around each remaining staff department units leaving those lines needed to depict central coordination. "There," he said, "these functions are free floating. They are not organizational units; they are activities." Discussion brought agreement about which were the major coordinating functions.

A recurring theme in the meeting was the belief that it was vital that employees know, understand, and support what the State Fund was attempting to accomplish in the field of compensation insurance and that they be provided with the knowledge and skill required to achieve such ends. This theme helped in examining the concept of coordination and was to be useful in wrestling with concepts of control.

3. *Control.* Most of the early discussion of controls focused on philosophical issues, which grew out of the group's effort to first define what they meant by controls and next to determine which controls were really necessary. Controls, they decided, would be required to keep track of the relationship between promise and performance. They examined the concept of an automatic feedback

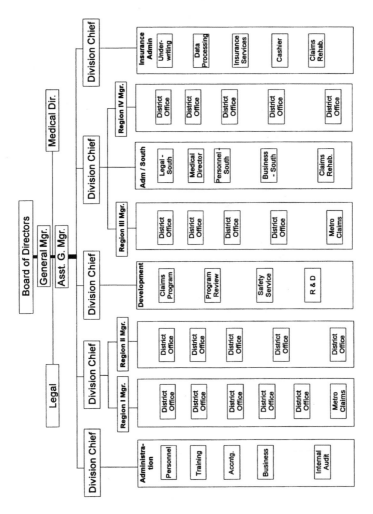

Figure 8.1. Old State Fund Organization Chart

141

management information system that would provide needed performance information to all, but would be nonpunitive. The State Fund had done much work on a computerized system concerned with data on markets, costs, and so forth. But the control mechanism discussed by the group transcended this and explored such areas as employee development, planning, and linking the budget process with the program outcome achievements.

Information, however, is inevitably associated with power. Thus, some way had to be found to avoid hierarchical power problems. Information would need to be divested of authority power connotations. The means of achieving automatic feedback on resources allocated and outcome performance did not emerge from the discussion. It was agreed that the process required a new and creative approach and should be developed as the organization changed.

Measurable objectives became a central theme as the task group looked at program design and resource allocation. Participants went no further than to suggest that the program design function should be collaborative and that resource allocation should be based on negotiation intended to match output with resources. All of the functions required communications, participation, and commitment. At the end of the day it was clear that no grand organizational design had emerged—but there were germs. Gardner had taken extensive notes and so agreed to take the data generated to see if it formed a pattern of some kind. It did, as a "portrait" of a new kind of organization chart emerged during the later analysis.

In the end, the executive retained the control powers of policy making, especially in forming the mission and corporate objectives; allocating resources along program budget lines making long-range plans; and appointing managers. The power devolved to the district managers and staff program managers was to manage the State Fund's business.

SUMMARY

Because aspiration means "to breathe life into," the aspirations need to be articulated in this stage of AT&R for organizations, be they federal government or private sector work units. The aspirations must describe the new status the people in the organization hope to achieve as a changing organization. These aspirations obtain their potential reality and actualization from the research conducted in the first four stages of AT&R. In addition, they will provide the most meaningful guidance for the following action phase stages of AT&R. In the next AT&R stage, action options, the participants will relate the issues, problems, and opportunities to the aspirations in order to generate all of the action options available to them to achieve the new organization to which they aspire. In addition, these aspirations will provide the criteria for measuring the performance of the actions taken.

CHAPTER 9

AT&R STAGE 6:
ACTION OPTIONS

MENU FOR AT&R STAGE 6: ACTION OPTIONS

Action   *Any number of analytical methods might be used to examine high-priority action options (Gardner, 1974).*

Training   *Force field analysis, system and data analysis tools, problem-solving methods.*

Research   *In this approach force field analyses are developed in a workshop setting (see Figure 9.1). The driving forces (vectors) calculated to be supporting receive a plus (+) valence in the force field, and the restraining forces, which inhibit change, receive a minus (−) valence. Some of the vectors may require a greater amount of investigation and study. Certain restraining forces, for example lack of funds, may be so compelling that attaining the action goal might be too difficult or even impossible.*

Outcome   *By the end of the workshop session, participants should be able to determine what significant action options seem attainable, which ones require further exploration, and which ones must be deferred until the critical constraining vector(s) is neutralized.*

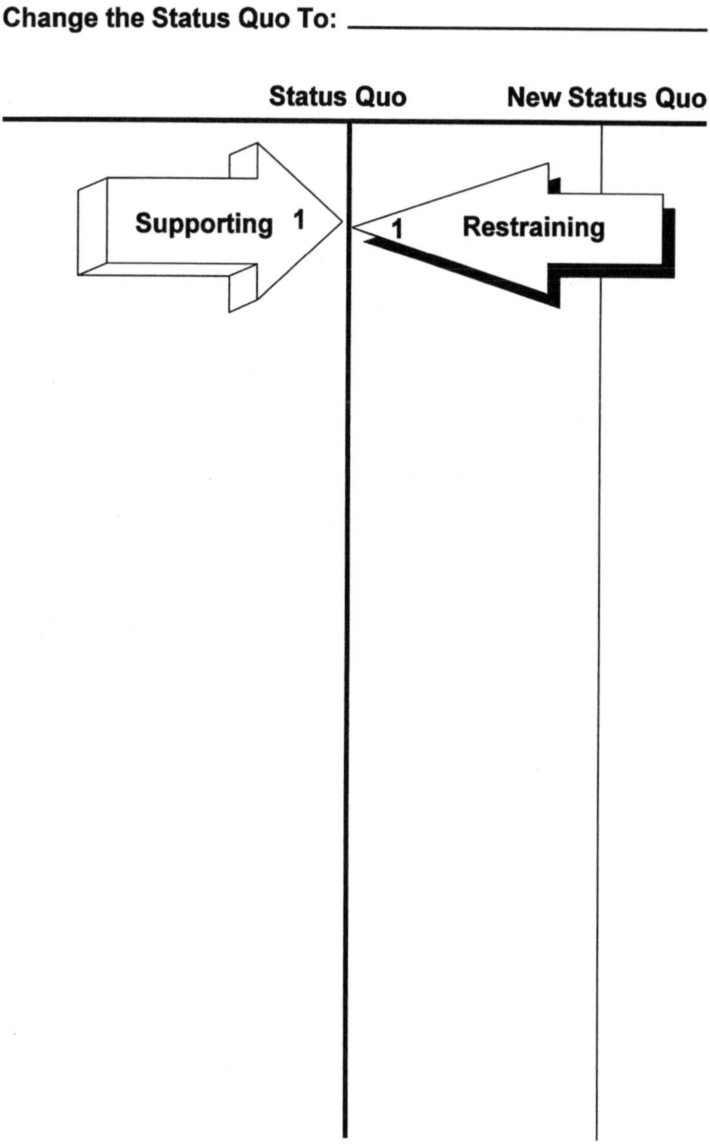

Change the Status Quo To: _____

Figure 9.1. Force Field Analysis

MOVING FROM RESEARCH TOWARD ACTION

Action options is a transition stage from research to action. We have explored the issues, identified the problems and opportunities that emerge from the issues, and set our aspirations on how we want to change our organization. Now, still in the analysis mode, we need to figure out all of the potential actions we can take to change our organization to become more fluid in how it is to engage the issues, solve the problems we select, grasp the opportunities, and become the organization to which we aspire. At the same time, we must become more realistic about how we will allocate our always-limited resources in order to achieve our new organization in a cost-effective way that also takes into account quality of life.

In short, now is the time for problem solving. AT&R can be used with most problem-solving techniques. What it adds are the results of the force field analysis of the issue exploration, problem identification, and aspiration stages already completed. In this problem–opportunity selection process the idea is to evaluate the forces at play to see where the organization's resources can have the most impact in moving the status quo in the direction of achieving the desired organization. These potential influences on any of the forces keeping the status quo are what Gardner called *action options.*

The process involves arraying the problems and opportunities in groups relating to specific issues. Then the participants can develop action options available to the organization to deal with the problems and opportunities for each issue. If there is a large enough group of participants, they can divide up into groups and each group can take a different issue and its attendant problems and opportunities in order to develop the action options. One useful approach is to view problems as restraining forces and opportunities as supporting forces in a force field analysis context. Another approach is to develop a matrix of action options and their relative impact on one or more of the problems and opportunities. The object is to be able to see all the potential action options in relation to all the problems and opportunities. In addition, it is important to be able to view and evaluate these relationships in terms of how they will affect the unfolding issues. Both of these approaches can involve a large number of participants. In developing a process for identifying action options, creativity is important. However, the force field analysis becomes much more complex at this action stage. Working out the relative values and intricate interrelationships requires much more effort and time than in previous stages. Each action option can potentially affect all of the other action options. Seemingly minor action options can have significant effects on major action options that seem to be totally unrelated without thorough analysis.

The action options will generally fall into three main categories. The first category includes actions the organization can control—in other words, the organization can simply decide to do them. The second category includes actions that the organization can possibly influence others to do. The third category involves actions that may or may not occur regardless of any actions the organization can take, but the organization can develop contingency actions to handle those uncontrollable actions should they occur.

The point of developing comprehensive action options is to provide action items to test critical assumptions in the next experimental stage 7, and action steps to take when organizing the program design stage 9. In this way the effort makes the transition from research to action.

EXAMPLE IN PRACTICE:
THE PROBLEM OF SOLVING PROBLEMS

Developing action options recognizes that changing organizations is different from solving problems. An organization is a complex interrelationship among the most complex things on earth: human beings. Therefore, if the organization is to change, then something in and among the people involved must change. Without falling into the relativists' argument that everything is related to everything, when it comes to organizations the solution to any problem must be taken in the context not only of the whole organization but of the people who comprise it. Therefore, before we can consider the AT&R methods for creating and evaluating all the action options available in the organization to deal with all of the problems and opportunities confronting that organization we need to consider the big question: What is *organization?*

During the strategic planning for information technology in the East Coast county the director of information technology presented a solution to the problem of replacing the aging computer systems. After hearing this latest scheme to add more positions and mainframe computers to relieve this situation, the deputy county executive remarked, "Why are we solving this problem again? You managers keep bringing us this problem, we fund solutions for it, and here the same problem comes around again for a new solution? Doesn't anybody ever fix these things? We've replaced the director of the data processing department two times, bought entirely new software for the mainframe, hired expensive consultants, and set up a special strategic planning group in the data processing department. The only result has been that the systems development process finally has ground to a halt."

This is an example of the problem of problems. The solution comes in the actions of the people involved. The deputy county executive's concern was that he was presented the problem, he allocated the resources to solve the problem, and to him that was the end of it. He assumed that he had implemented the solution with his decision, but he could not actually solve it himself. The people doing the work and their managers must actually solve the problems. The executives can only help identify the problems and then get the resources to the people involved with the problem to solve it.

MATCHING PROBLEMS AND SOLUTIONS IN
THE FIRE AND RESCUE INNOVATION PROGRAM

In setting up a program to research and test innovative fire and rescue equipment and methods, the fire chief asked the AT&R practitioner, "How are we to identify the innovative problems we need to solve? If we are going to have a program to test ways to solve fire and rescue problems we need to get some insights about how we are to solve our problems."

"As you know," the practitioner replied, "We researched various problem-solving methods. We were helped by the professors at the university. We found that traditionally there are two general approaches to problem identification: deductive reasoning and inductive reasoning. *Deductive reasoning* seeks to reduce the problem situation to examine its logical component parts for problem identification and diagnosis. *Inductive reasoning* seeks to look at the whole situation to find the principles and axioms that seem to be operating.

"The first approach deconstructs the situation to critique how the component parts relate, how they fit and work together in a linear cause-and-effect process. This approach is the objective, the logical, fact finding approach that searches for a breakdown in the chain of causes and effects. The second approach reads the situation's holistic context in search of new understanding. It is the subjective, creative, graphic, intuitive approach of self-organizing. It is the context interpretation by experts for new understanding."

"So we can use both ways?" the fire chief asked.

"Yes, but despite efforts to combine the rational and the creative approaches there often remains a residual gap between problems and their solutions, causing serious disputes among the people trying to identify and solve the problem. I think that it is this gap that is the cause of a lot of our disagreements in our problem-solving efforts among the firefighters," the practitioner replied. "Perhaps we could do some practical research on that hypothesis."

"A fire and rescue department researching a gap?" the Fire Chief observed in good humor. "That'll look good in the local papers at budget time."

"Actually we're doing some Action Training and Research with a professor from the state university. He is testing a problem-solving computer system that he's developed. Although it may seem absurd to have a gap as a unit of analysis, nevertheless, knowing more about the gap that separates problems from their solutions was useful in expanding our understanding of the nature of problem solving."

"I'm not sure I understand all that in one hearing," the fire chief responded when the practitioner presented the research findings. "But there, enough of theory, just tell me, how do we organize our innovation program to the more practical work of fire fighting?"

"Here's a good example," the practitioner replied. "You know that problem we've been having with the 125-foot aerial ladder trucks and the brick high-rise buildings?"

"You mean when we poke a hole in the side of one of those 'brick ovens' when we're trying to get the rescue people up there as fast as we can?" the fire chief replied. "Now that's a yearly $25,000 problem for us. How do we solve that problem?"

"Well, let's see," the practitioner replied. "It has process dimensions in that the powerful hydraulic telescoping of the latter goes too far and pierces the wall."

"Granted!" the fire chief agreed. "And I can see that the problem has some 'scalar' dimensions in that a small micro-inch change at the operator's control end of that 125-foot ladder causes one of several feet at the other end. That could be merely a training problem."

"That's right," the practitioner agreed. "But we might want to look for solutions in a dimension of a different realm."

"Different realm? What would that be, I wonder?" the fire chief asked.

"It's called *lateral thinking*. Remember that crazy idea that fire truck aerial-ladder operator had about the tennis balls?" the practitioner recalled.

"Yes," the fire chief answered. "I got a lot of grief from my battalion chiefs over that one."

"I think that is because there is a gap in thinking about a tennis court and fire fighting," the practitioner concluded. "And that's why the solution was so hard to see."

"How do you come to that?" the fire chief asked. "What solution?"

"The battalion chiefs could not see how something out of the realm of tennis, a basically horizontal sport, could have anything to do with a fire-fighting problem of a 125-foot aerial ladder poking holes in the vertical brick wall of a building on fire."

"Neither can I," the fire chief confessed.

"By hanging a fluorescent orange tennis ball six inches beyond the end of the ladder, but dangling it below the end where the operator could see the tennis ball touch the bricks, would tell the operator when the 125-foot ladder is exactly six inches away from the burning building. Then, by simply easing off on the control, the ladder would relax the last few inches to rest on the wall without harming it."

"I think we'd better try it out," the chief replied. "A 75-cent tennis ball to save $25,000 worth of damage looks like a good deal. But what about other innovations? Any examples of those in fire fighting? I'm willing to be convinced."

"Sure," the practitioner replied, "But maybe you won't be so happy about this one."

"Why?"

"It involves your favorite Japanese 60-gallons-per-minute fog nozzle project."

"Shoot."

"As you know, it claimed to be able to create water droplets of the .0025 micrometer size."

"That's right," the chief agreed, "And research has proven that that size of water drop was the most efficient size for converting heat into steam . . . a transformation dimension?"

"Yes," the practitioner replied. "But our metered tests in the burn building using a number of different nozzles, including a smooth-bore nozzle at 500 gallons per minute, showed that all of the nozzles had the same effect, they brought the fire under control with the first 10 gallons of water put on it. The fire was so hot that it transformed the first 10 gallons of water droplets to steam, no matter what their size, with equal effectiveness. Efficiency of transformation was not the problem's main feature."

"What was it, then?"

"Scale, I believe," the practitioner replied. "You remember, the original purpose of inventing the efficient 60-gallons-per-minute fog nozzle was for high-rise buildings in which the larger flow nozzles were causing more damage on the floors below with water damage then the fire they were suppressing was. One case was the destruction of millions of dollars of computer equipment on the floor below a small office fire."

The fire chief agreed. "Yes, they flooded millions of dollars worth of computers in a building across the river from us last year with that, but that argues for the 60-gallons-per-minute fog nozzle, doesn't it?"

"Our burn building test also showed that the smooth-bore 500-gallons-per-minute nozzle brought the fire under control with its first 10 gallons because the firefighters always hit the ceiling with the first small bursts of water to break the water stream into droplets. The later, larger water mass that wasn't turned to steam fell on the burning fuel itself, lowering its temperature quickly. In our videos of the test the firefighters with the smooth-bore nozzle were standing up all the time. But when they were using the fog nozzles the firefighters were all belly down on the floor trying to avoid the steam that the fog nozzles had created. Although the small droplets had converted the heat to steam, the original energy was still in the room in the form of steam. One of the complaints the firefighters have about the fog nozzle was all of the 'steam burn' bracelets they showed me. Steam, as you know, is unforgiving to any exposed human skin. The fire's original energy transformed to steam is then transformed to burns on the firefighters."

"Yes, I know. I read their test results and recommendations," the fire chief said. "But I'm interested in why you consider it a matter of scale and not transformation of energy."

"The real problem was not controlling the fire. It was the large amount of water draining down to floors below," the practitioner explained. "Our tests also measured the flow of water over the time of each suppression test. And as we expected, the smooth-bore nozzle poured hundreds of gallons of water on the fire. But we were able to show the firefighters that 95% of the water they put on the fire was done after the fire was under control. If they had simply been more judicious with the water, they would not have had to put any more water on the fire than the 60-gallons-per-minute nozzle. It's just that their adrenaline was up, they saw the fire as the enemy, and gave it all they had at 500 gallons per minute."

"So the solution comes in retraining the firefighters, not changing the nozzles?" the fire chief concluded.

"More than that, I understand," the practitioner continued. "Present practices require that firefighters entering any room of a high-rise that cannot be readily vented must use their fog nozzles first. The training captain is working up new requirements to use smooth-bore nozzles and timing the water release in short bursts in order to keep track of how much water they have used. They will be submitting that recommendation to you next week, I expect."

"Good. No more steam burns," the fire chief concluded. "But tell me, how are you going to work this problem of gaps into our program to research and test innovative fire and rescue equipment and methods?"

"I propose we set up a classic AT&R process," the practitioner replied. "Already, the firefighters want to set up a board of firefighters to review the new ideas we intend to test. We won't have the professor's problem-solving computer system, but the board of firefighters could explore each new idea proposed and identify the problems and opportunities involved."

"How will they do that?" the fire chief asked.

"There's a stage in the process that comes after we explore the proposed nature of the new equipment or method they want to test in which the members of the review board would brainstorm all the problems and opportunities they can think of in regard to the issue at hand, in this case the new equipment. I can then see what the problem situation is and then design the research test and everything. I'll design the whole process and write it up as a proposal for you so you can see how it will all work."

"Fine," the fire chief agreed, "Have it on my desk next Thursday."

FROM THE STATE FUND JOURNALS OF NEELY GARDNER: FORCE FIELD ANALYSIS AND ACTION OPTIONS

Although any number of analytical methods might be used to examine high-priority action options, there is much to be said for the Lewin-inspired force field analysis. Typically, force field analysis is developed in a workshop setting. Members of subgroups list the driving forces (vectors) calculated to be supporting, which receive a plus (+) valence in the force field, and the restraining forces, which inhibit change, receive a minus (–) valence. A few of the vectors may require a greater amount of investigation and study. A restraining force, such as lack of funds, may be so compelling that attaining the action option might be extremely difficult or even impossible.

In participant-oriented action training and research, a practitioner provides the client organization with sufficient process in the previous stages to help define the issues, problems, opportunities, and goals to be addressed in the change.

With the various participant survey tools used in these stages, the organization is given so much data that it can be handled only over a period of time. In short, there is generally an overload of information. From an action standpoint, it is important to work on those issues, problems, opportunities, and change goals regarded by the constituent group as most important and pressing. The participant survey tools help by arraying the issues, problems, opportunities, and goals in terms of perceived importance. The force field method is a means of carrying the process of analysis further. Force field analysis was proposed by Kurt Lewin as a method for analyzing the change process in a social system and determining courses of action. It is valuable for the following reasons. First, it makes readily clear what the forces acting on the desired organizational change and their relative strengths are. Second, it helps participants to see where problems exist and how solutions should be designed. Third, it provides an opportunity to widen participation in the action training and research process (Nichols, 1989).

TRAINING IN FORCE FIELD ANALYSIS

The first step is to train the client researchers to train others in force field analysis. Each client researcher can then train and work with a group of organizational citizens who have been formed into action groups. Members of the action groups should

1. Be willing to work on the project
2. Have the substantive knowledge required to assist in solving the problem
3. Be persons who will be affected by, or involved in, implementing any changes undertaken as a result of the analyses
4. Be held accountable as individuals and as a group for the successful completion of the analysis
5. Be aware that they are preparing an action document that is intended as a blueprint for change
6. Be aware that they will be asked to participate in the changing processes suggested by the action document that they prepare

ACTION STATEMENTS

If the action team is working from the priority list of issues, problems, opportunities, or change goals provided by the participant survey efforts of the previous stages, the team will be given, or choose, one of the items to analyze. In the spirit of the iterative aspect of AT&R, force field analysis can be used as an analysis tool in the earlier stages. For example, it can be used to examine the various issues at the strategic level of planning changing organizations. It can be used at the problem–opportunity identification stage to analyze these items. Equally, it can be a useful tool to analyze the change goals that are considered in the aspiration stage of AT&R. In this action options stage of AT&R the force field analysis tool is applied to the important issues, problems, opportunities, and change goals to develop specific action options and tactical plans of action.

If there are ten action teams, each might address one of the top ten priority items. The next step is to restate each of the questionnaire items into action statements, which should be framed largely in terms of results to be achieved.

To give the statement an action orientation, it is helpful to adopt a "how to change" frame of reference. For example, the statement in the participant survey at the State Fund read, "Convert the accounting systems to reflect program transactions rather than the transactions of the functional organization." In rewriting this statement to give it an action orientation, the item might read, "How to convert the accounting system to a program, rather than an organizational unit, base." Such a statement calls for action.

Although there are other analysis approaches, using force field analysis as a means of writing action options has the virtue of being easily accomplished in a sensible way in a group setting. So phrased, the statement is also likely to facilitate the development of a force field analysis.

RESTRAINING AND SUPPORTING FORCES

The action team next develops a list of all restraining and supporting forces to be considered in achieving the action. As the list grows, it is evident that some of the supporting or restraining forces themselves become rather sizable projects. They also need to be separated and given a more detailed force field analysis. The forces can be weighted with number weights or descriptive ones such as *light, medium,* and *heavy* to indicate relative powers of the forces in maintaining the status quo. The illustrative force field analysis that follows (see Figure 9.2) has been greatly simplified to suggest the basic approach.

Change the Status Quo To: <u>Support Program Management</u>

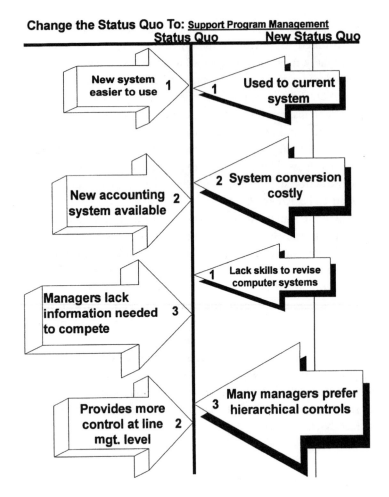

Figure 9.2. Force Field Analysis for Accounting

ACTION OPTIONS

The next step is to develop a list of action options to reinforce supporting forces and to remove the constraints. Action options should be specific to each supporting and restraining force. By mapping the force fields relative to the change in the status quo desired, it is clear that the field is not a win–lose battlefield. There is no need to annihilate the restraining forces in order for the supporting forces to win. The object is to take a strategic view about how the balance of forces can be interdicted in a way to tip the balance to move toward the desired change goal and reestablish the status quo. Each of the forces can be evaluated along the lines of the degree of action options of influence that the planning group's organization has. In general, there are three categories of action options. As noted earlier, there are those forces that are within the span of control of the organization. For these, direct action options can be made. There are those forces that the organization does not control but has significant access to influence. In this case, tactical action options of coordination and cooperation are made. Then there are those forces on which the organization has neither control not influence of access. In the latter case, contingency plans of action options can be developed to minimize the danger and maximize the opportunities that could result in unexpected changes in these forces.

Clearly, leverage is the strategy in force field analysis. What are the best combinations of action options to increase the supporting forces and to reduce or neutralize the restraining forces available to us requiring the least amount of our resources? In some cases, the analysis indicates that the balance of forces in the status quo is already shifting in the direction of our selected change goals and no additional resources are required to achieve the change goal. The situation is going our way anyway.

Another reason for this strategy of leverage is a basic rule of force fields. If you add a force on one side, in order to upset the homeostasis of the status quo an opposing force will emerge on the other side to counterbalance the new force. It does not make any difference whether the new force is added on the supporting or restraining side. However, there is a brief time lapse before the new force emerges, letting the status quo move. Lewin expressed this process for changing organizations as *unfreeze–change–refreeze*. The idea is to stir up the forces to tip the balance in different places along the force field lines and let the status quo move toward the desired goal for changing the organization. Then when the goal for the changed status quo is reached, revise the action option influences and let the status quo not necessarily refreeze but establish itself at a more fluid level. This way, the organization's motor for change will not require such a traumatic unfreezing to resume the change process.

As the force field analysis is completed, it becomes an action document. This, then, is the moment of truth for the decision-making participants:

1. Are they willing to make the changes suggested by the survey responses?
2. If willing, are they capable of removing constraints and reinforcing supporting forces identified in the force field analysis?
3. Does the organization have the resources to make the changes suggested?
4. What is a reasonable time frame in which to make any contemplated changes?
5. How will all those affected by the proposed changes be given a part in the implementation of change?
6. How and to whom will the results of the action training and research and the consequent implementation be communicated?
7. What training will be needed to help involved employees cope with change?

INVOLVEMENT OF DECISION MAKERS

It is important that the practitioner and members of the research team keep in touch with the primary decision makers as the process develops. Brager and Holloway claimed that there are two primary decision makers in an organization: (1) critical actors–organizational members who have the power to adopt or reject the desired change, and (2) facilitating actors—members whose approval, disapproval, or neutrality has a decisive impact on critical actors (Brager & Holloway, 1992). Decision makers need to understand the nature and scope of the survey findings and the obligation for action the findings place on them. If they become nervous at the action stage and are unwilling to take steps indicated as desirable by the research findings, the organization is probably worse off than it was prior to the intervention. After going to the expense and effort of collecting data and after obtaining the commitment of a significant number of organizational members to pursue a change action, a management that runs for cover does itself a great disservice.

It is for this reason that the "psychological contract" negotiated very early between the practitioner and the organization clearly becomes a commitment to act in good faith on the findings of the research and the force field analysis, always considering the organization's capacity to do so. This commitment is more likely to be honored when top management is vitally involved at every step of the action training and research effort.

On completion of the force field analyses and accompanying action options, and given an enthusiastic and adept organizational leadership, bolstered with skill and knowledgeable and ethical behavior by the practitioner, the change process is ready for implementation. By providing an analytical and realistic force field panorama, it is possible to determine whether the action options drawn from the questionnaire items are manageable project items or whether lesser action must occur first.

In the case of the accounting system, with a restraining force stated as, "The organization has no knowledge of what a program-oriented system should encompass," a prior step would be the development of a program-oriented system in the organization. This could turn out to be the major action, or it might be one of several important actions.

Those using the force field analysis approach might well consider the following:

1. Changes made under the force field analysis should be tested experimentally before wide adoption.
2. All changes should be considered temporary changes.
3. All systems should be considered temporary systems.
4. Insofar as possible, all systems should be responsive rather than controlling.
5. Every project or system should have a recycling schedule—a time when it is to be evaluated, examined in relation to its force field, and either abandoned or modified to meet new conditions.
6. It is usually strategically useful to start dealing with major restraining forces first.

Although the force field analysis described previously is related to the participant survey, it does not require such a narrow antecedent action. Force field analyses may be developed at any time to deal with a suspected problem. The process definitely is helpful in moving toward action.

By the end of the workshop session, participants should be able to determine what significant action options are attainable, which ones require further exploration, and which ones must be deferred until the critical restraining vector(s) is neutralized. For example, the issue areas explored in the reconnaissance stage could be graphed in a force-field framework as shown in Figure 9.3.

PORTRAIT OF THE NEW STATE FUND

The State Fund president came to Los Angeles to talk to Gardner. This was to become a pattern over the next few years. The visit served as a counseling opportunity for the president. He spent 1 to 2 hours on each visit to explore his problems, his feelings, his frustrations, and his plans.

At this meeting, after he had talked through his agenda, Gardner unrolled a piece of chart paper and taped it to the wall to show the new pattern that had emerged from the group analysis (Figure 9.4).

"What is that?" the president asked.

"It's a picture or portrait of the State Fund that your think-tank team worked out in our meeting the other day," Gardner replied

"I've never seen anything like that, before," the president said.

"Neither have I," Gardner replied, "but I'll try to explain. There are the basic functions of sales, claims, underwriting, and rehabilitation and the leadership to carry them devolved to each 'field' location. In this picture we are showing the field locations as being the present district offices. In a major way the district offices are the State Fund. In the task group thinking, most of the other activities of the organization are designed for the sole purpose of supporting the field office functions. These functions might be performed in a variety of modes and even in different ones in each location. Reflecting the thoughts of the study group, I thought it might be useful to portray the local unit nonhierarchically. There are a lot of practical reasons why this

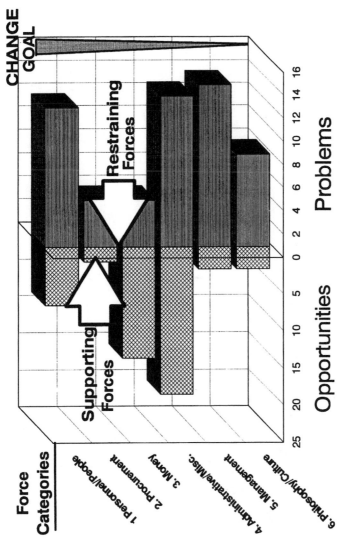

Figure 9.3. Force Field Analysis of Issue Exploration Areas

161

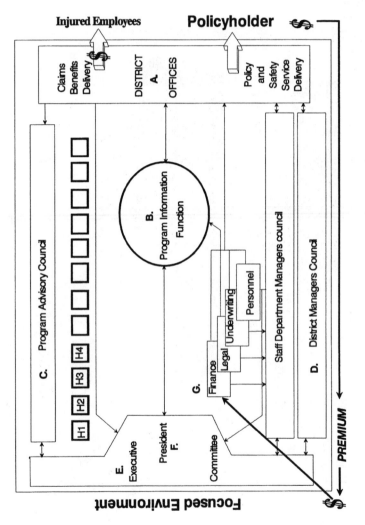

Figure 9.4. Portrait of the Devolved State Fund

may not be possible, but our group was not bound by practicality. Here is one way the cluster of local functions might be shown."

INFORMATION FUNCTIONS

"Your people talked in very vague terms about automated computer feedback that I would agree seems to fit with the Sherwood process described in the market model. This is an information system that feeds back events that reflect the accomplishments of the actors relative to the resources they used. Under an effective information system, the sales function in each district office should be able to tell how it is doing in relation to its expectations. An automatic feedback system should give the same information to the central organization. This information should be neither laudatory nor demeaning. In other words, it should provide neutral data. Regarding people assigned to the information functions, it will be necessary to avoid role demands that encourage them to move into a power and influence position. If we look at item B on the 'portrait,' it represents the information function."

COMMUNICATION

Communication is important to all activities. Some means needed to be found for employees and managers to communicate with the core coordinating group and with each other. Based on these two concerns there are two activities represented by 'councils.' These were not organizations per se, but collectives of persons from the various functions. Each functional office would supply two people to an employee council (item C in Figure 9.4). To reflect what the study group seemed to be saying, Gardner labeled it the program advisory council.

"We did not talk about how the council members should be selected," Gardner explained. "The 'think-tank' study team did suggest that this group should make input to the corporate or coordinating body on proposed new programs and comment on progress in continuing activities. In addition, the program advisory council members should communicate items and events of importance to the corporate body (perhaps represented by the president) and receive information on home office activities to carry back to fellow employees. As I understand what the 'think-tank' study group had in mind, they felt that it was too unwieldy to have the program advisory council be involved in the decision process at this stage of the transformation.

"District managers, as key actors in a devolved organization, will also need to communicate regularly with each other and with the home offices. This can be accomplished through regular monthly meetings (see item D in Figure 9.4). With district offices destined to become the focal point of most State Fund activity, it seems obvious that some mechanism is required to help them share ideas and to contribute their effort to the mutual endeavor. So a district manager's council might be constituted to aid coordination and to influence corporate decisions."

COORDINATION

Coordination of State Fund functions, as far as the corporate entity is concerned, will be through the president and executive committee. You will have the assignment of providing general leadership and vision in the areas of coordination (of insurance communications, information, and all other functions); representation to outside persons and organizations; resource allocation; and policy functions. Figure 9.4 shows the president as item F.

"Here I'm throwing in a concept of my own," Gardner admitted, "which I think you should deal with. You, as president, are generally responsible for the operation of the State Fund. You can operate in the Theory Y mode, delegate widely, encourage a participative approach, but in the end your legitimacy is derived from the will of the citizens of the State of California as expressed in the laws governing State Fund operations and the policies of your board of directors. You have the right to delegate; you have the authority to withdraw the delegation. This need not change your management style. But it should be recognized, and I think it is, that you possess line authority over the operations of the State Fund. Using organization chart language, your relationship to all State Fund activities always follows a solid rather than a broken line."

POLICY MAKING

Gardner was unclear about the policy-making process at the State Fund, but the study group had talked about the executive committee as the molders of internal policy and the board of directors as the body responsible for overall policies affecting the general public. "This is an area that needs exploration," Gardner suggested. "In any case, I have designated the policy function as Item E" (Figure 9.4).

ADJUDICATION

Gardner felt that the adjudicative task could be assumed by the policy committee, although this has dangers. It is difficult to divorce anyone in the organization having policy or program responsibilities from a position of bias. This one needed to be thought through.

STAFF SUPPORT SERVICES

The two other areas shown on the chart indicate specialized staff and support services. The study group did not talk about support services such as accounting, medical, automatic data processing, and legal. They are shown as item G.

"Staff Coordinative services," Gardner continued, "those that were liberated from the boxes to wander weightlessly through State Fund space—can, I believe, be described as project activities. My bias is that these should very much resemble R&D activities that endure for a fixed time then are dissolved, with incumbents being reassigned when the specific task is completed. These functions are shown on the chart as H-1, H-2, H-3, H-4, etc."

The president had listened to Gardner's long explanation with alternate periods of wrinkled brow and infectious smiles. He asked for the newsprint "portrait," folded it, and placed it in a briefcase, and said "These concepts were exciting and pretty frightening." The president left Gardner, promising to think about it and to do some further exploration with the division chiefs and others. Gardner had some concerns too. He felt that he had taken liberties with the task group data, making interpretations he was not sure that he had a right to make. For instance, he had eagerly accepted the ideas of free-floating R&D groups but had added his own bias that these should be self-extirpating. "What if I exerted undue influence and this influence was bad?" In his view, it is the client's role to take charge; the practitioner merely assists in the exploration. In spite of his long experience in large agencies, he did not feel very certain about how humans should organize to achieve a common purpose. On the other hand, he was confident that he knew a great deal about how not to organize.

One of Gardner's confessed biases is that organizations should strive to be tentative and experimental. This concern prompted Gardner to telephone the president the next day. The president agreed thoroughly that any more measures taken to readjust the organization should be in terms of testing concepts rather than rushing ahead with a grand reorganization. "In the first place it would be very difficult to move the entire organization precipitously," the president explained. "Second, and very important, the new concepts might not work."

From that time forward, the idea of engaging in such an experiment began to grow. As the president and his task force members examined the data, the notion developed that perhaps suggested readjustments could be tested in an experimental district office. The office would be a devolved unit, having all of the authority and responsibility of the president for district office activities. Insofar as the president was free, the experimental district office would be free.

It was thought that the delegation should take place after the experimental district office had developed a program statement that would set forth clearly defined, expected results. Such a program might do several things. It might provide a check on the degree of delegation that actually existed in the State Fund. Next it would demonstrate the degree to which support groups, including staff groups and the managers constituting the organizational hierarchy, contribute to the accomplishment of the district office output. Finally, it might test the desirability of articulating objectives at the district level in terms that later could be used for management reporting and for self-measurement.

SUMMARY

Action options completes the transition from research to action. They can be developed in any of the stages, but the important aspect of

AT&R is providing a separate stage where all of the analysis of the research phase of the AT&R cycle is gathered together for all of the participants in the change effort to evaluate and to develop a comprehensive set of action options relative to the gathered facts and shared values. What fell short in this regard was the absence of meaningful participation by people in the work units. However, this would be remedied by designating a pilot office to test the assumptions.

Just as in selecting the issues to be addressed, the problems and opportunities to be identified, and the aspirations for change to be voiced, selecting the action options to be considered has a constricting effect on what action will follow. It is best to keep the scope of the action options considered as wide as common sense will allow. Although selecting an action option does not yet mean a commitment of resources, not selecting an action option does mean that most likely resources will never be committed to that action. That is a decision made in the act of nonelection.

More specifically, aspirations are often built on assumptions about the future—namely how the organization's issues will evolve or be resolved in relation to the organization itself. Assumptions are defined here as professional "best guesses" that may or may not find form in the future. Because these guesses can be expected to involve the viability of the organization, the aspirations and the action options identified to achieve these assumptions need to be tested in some way. Just as interplanetary missions have realistic "sandbox" environments to test the Mars lander and vehicles, the organization can set up pilot experiments, simulations, and other experiments that can test, to some degree, the action options that are key to their aspirations. These key action options become the object of the next stage of AT&R: stage 7, experimentation.

CHAPTER 10

AT&R STAGE 7: EXPERIMENTATION

MENU FOR AT&R STAGE 7: EXPERIMENTATION

Action *When clients agree to undertake a change, they are predict-*
ing success. Even though the change action is based on
carefully developed data, the experimentation stage is a
logical safeguard in a process in which all the action is
considered conditional and subject to testing. Changes
initiated as action options are undertaken either on a
limited trial basis, perhaps in the entire organization, for
a finite time in smaller segments of the community or
jurisdiction. This trial period or limited implementation is
intended to give the client an opportunity to assess the
desirability of change and to correct unforeseen problems
before the change is fully operative. Tentative time-limited
experiments may also give participants a chance to deal
with any unexpected consequences of the change action.

Clients who have conceptualized the action training and
research project are also involved in the implementation
and evaluation of the change action. They have partici-
pated in opportunity and problem delineation, data col-
lection, assessment of aspiration levels, force field analysis,

and determination of the change action to be undertaken. Through these activities they have had an opportunity to understand and to invest themselves in the program. They are in a position to evaluate how the change action is working for them (Gardner, 1974).

Training   *Research design, participative team building, group work dynamics, systems, and work flow analysis.*

Research   *Determine which assumptions about the issue, problem, or opportunity are most critical to people and to the success of the changes envisioned. Devise a prototype of the proposed change that can test these assumptions before the change is implemented. This prototype should not be a simulation of the change but an actual implementation of the critical parts of the change in a "sheltered workshop" or "pilot" by participants who are willing to support the experiment.*

Outcome   *Evaluation of working prototype testing the key elements of the intended changes.*

WHY EXPERIMENT?

There are several reasons to include experimentation in AT&R. First, action research itself is a form of basic scientific investigation in the work processes of people. Its purpose, in Lewin's concepts of reeducation, is to gain new knowledge about how people work together, acquire new valences and values for interpreting our world, and innovative ways to perform our work together. Second, the security of the people involved is a reason to experiment. Their work is an important aspect of their lives; it determines, in part, who they are. It is the means of how they meet their own hierarchy of needs for themselves, for their families, and for their communities, as well as for their organization. Therefore, new work practices, tools, and methods need to be tried out in protected research conditions in order to determine the impact they may have for good or ill. Third, experimentation is needed to verify our assumptions leading to our selection of organizational changes. Much of the strategic decision making is based on certain key assumptions that are not proven. Because we can never acquire complete information about the decision situation, we have to select a change that satisfies. There is much we cannot know until we have actually tried out the change selected. For example, our decisions may include many considered speculations about the future. They also may include work methods, tools, and ideas untried by the organization. Often, new work methods, systems, and tools are promoted by vendors or talk-show experts who talk about how their products or services can improve organizations. However, these innovations are not suitable for every organization. Nor do they perform exactly as the vendors have promoted them.

Therefore, the experiment stage of AT&R seeks to identify these questionable areas and examine them. Action research provides a useful method to test new ideas, methods, and tools. The AT&R method includes the caveat that new ideas and work practices should not be tested only by the organization's research and development units, but that the people involved in the change must also be included among the researchers.

Clearly, all three reasons for experimentation—basic knowledge, security for people, and proof of assumptions—will apply to most AT&R tests; usually one of the reasons will stand out among the others. Therefore, the several examples given will be grouped accordingly.

BASIC RESEARCH

AT&R itself is basically a research method structure. As such, it is able to contribute to the discovery of new knowledge about itself. Experiments should be set up as formal test programs with measurable and specific objectives, test steps, and evaluation methods spelled out for the results. Many of the experimental projects it initiates result in new methods and insights about changing organizations. For example, research into the problem–solution gap for the fire and rescue department resulted in insights about searching for solutions by analyzing the realm, scalar, and process gaps involved in the problem's situation. Research into exploration thinking at the East Coast county's strategic decision-making process verified the importance of exploring issues before problems were identified as is done in the AT&R method. Each of these research efforts constituted a feedback value to improving the AT&R method itself.

EXAMPLE IN PRACTICE:
OVERCOMING RESISTANCE TO CHANGE

Another research effort that added to the AT&R method was initiated at the State Fund to investigate the necessity to include line employees in the changing of their work processes. It is one thing for line employees to see that a change is valuable as part of AT&R methods, but another to get them involved in a meaningful and nonthreatening way. Many times when line employees are included they seemed resistant to participate, at least at first.

The use of the enterprise model as a means to help a group be more open to change in the early stages of AT&R was the result of research done by the State Fund in 1980. They conducted a research project to gain insights on the dynamics of why the AT&R intervention itself engenders resistance to change. Or in Lewinian terms, why does adding a new force seem to engender a counterforce to maintain the status quo? In this case, the State Fund was introducing computer terminals into a particular work unit in each of the State Fund's 32 district offices.

Their idea was that inserting a computer terminal into the work unit would be similar to the initial intervention of a change agent. The working hypothesis was that role confusion was a major element for resistance to change. We all take on job positions and learn them well enough to feel confident in our performance. However, over time, the job duties and functions drift. Things change, organization and client needs change, procedures evolve over time, and so forth. If someone were to come up to us and demand to know precisely what our job is, we might feel a little uncertain. It is not that we are necessarily doing a bad job; it is just that we have not updated ourselves to just what it is as of today.

AT&R methodology would indicate that role clarification before the entry of change should lower this cause of resistance to change.

The State Fund was set up to be an excellent test for this hypothesis. They were on the verge of replacing a Rolodex card-type information lookup system with a computer terminal. This system consisted of a series of large metal tubs holding thousands of 5 × 8 policyholder information cards. The amount of information would vary by the size of the district office's territory. The unit consisted of 2 to 3 people, again depending on the size of the district office. In this regard, the State Fund had three general groups of district offices: Urban, Rural, and Valley Coop–Corporate Farm areas. Within these three areas were several district offices. Target and control district offices were selected in each area for the research. The research was quite simple. In the target districts a change agent would go into the work unit and have the members explain how their work process functioned. The change agent would then feed back to them his understanding of the work process as the members of the unit had explained it to him. When the work unit was satisfied that the change agent understood their work process, the interview was ended. Then they would receive the same training program on the use of the computer terminal in their work process as the control district offices. In the control district offices the work unit got only the training program.

The assumption was that the new computer terminal would greatly improve the quality of the work units' service—no misfiled cards, and so on—and be a less onerous task. As a result of this assumption, we believed that in time all of the work units would recognize this and use the systems equally. However, those members who had role clarification would more readily adopt the computer terminal as a new tool than would those who did not experience role clarification.

In addition, the AT&R research methodology included a computer program that tracked the use of the terminals on a daily basis. The results were dramatic. Figure 10.1 shows the comparison of computer terminal usage from the day of installation, tracking the target and control district offices in each of the three area groups. Clearly, the target district offices adopted the computer terminals earlier and more often than the control offices.

As a piece of research, this is very interesting. In an era of personal computers on our desks that are more powerful than the computer room full of mainframe computer equipment used in that research, what does it mean? Our concern was the orientation stage of AT&R

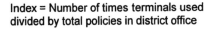

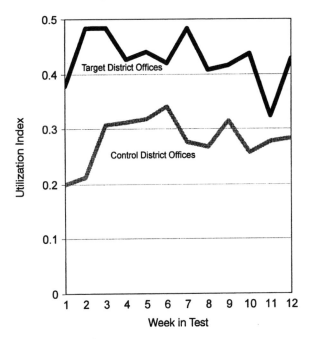

Figure 10.1. Work Analysis to Overcome Resistance to New
Technology—State Fund

and initial entry of the change agent. How could we translate this
research back into our methodology?

What they came up with is the enterprise modeling exercise described in the contract stage two. This exercise is an example of that
computer work-unit role clarification interview "writ big." The
change agent meets with the executive group, the management
group, or work unit, depending on the unit of research of the AT&R
project. This group then describes what goes on in the unit of research
to the extent that it can be drawn up on one page as a flow model of
their enterprise.

For example, the enterprise model (see Figure 5.1, depicted in
AT&R stage 2 contract setting) was developed by the county executive
and its strategic management team. The added value of the enterprise

modeling exercise is that it identifies the key stockholders involved. This can be an important element of the next phases.

The important aspect of institution building–unbuilding is the experimental district office described below in Gardner's journals at the State Fund. Eventually, all of the district offices became entrepreneurial service delivery centers. The staff departments at the home office functioned as service support centers whose clients were the district offices. Under the previous hierarchical organization, the staff department managers viewed their client as being the State Fund executives. Now the managers' programs had to show how well they were supporting the district offices to meet their respective objectives and results. In the managers' council meetings this reality was discussed with an eye to continuing improvements. As the needs of the district offices changed, the support services were transformed as well. The managers characterized this flexibility as "Organization charts written in disappearing ink." And, "Our organization chart should have a note on it like an airline schedule: 'Subject to change without notice'" (Gardner, 1969, p. 12).

A salient example of this flexible organization was the wide use of what are now called *parallel organizations* (Moore, 1989). These groups included ad hoc task forces, formal strategic action groups, and a temporary management analysis group of specialists in work restructuring, systems development, organization development, and service product development. Although the common management view at the State Fund had focused on coordination from the top, the move toward an outcome-oriented service posture prompted increased recognition by the executive committee that the major part of the coordinating job rested with those who did the work.

Instead of organizing a specific department or project team, an action research network was created, linking together the key people who would be affected or otherwise interested. The action research network was embedded not only in the organization but in its environment of significant others outside the State Fund—in other words, the customers, the market, and the community.

The action research network became a temporary, free-floating entity in the organization. It was an organizational scaffolding across the organization that provided the people involved in changing some part of the work process access to the resources they needed and to

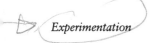

all of the parts of the organization that had to be involved in the change. Instead of using the cocoon approach of taking people away from their regular jobs to form a separate project team, Lewin's action research approach was used. The focus was on the action research network and the reeducation of the work organization itself. While involved in networked action, members continued in their regular job assignments. Such participation in the action group was seen as part of one's regular duties.

The action research network became a quasi or virtual organization without becoming an actual task force or project team per se. The objective of the network, as a virtual organization, was to pursue the intent of the organization's strategic plans and policies. The approach emphasized autonomy in the collaborative process, rather than the behavior norms of a formal project team. It allowed any member of the organization to participate in the work process change but from the point of view of his or her own work milieu. The ticket required to buy into the change effort was simply status as a stakeholder with a special expertise, knowledge, or skill; or a stakeholder who was a user of the work process that was to be changed; or a stakeholder who would be significantly impacted by the change.

When the designated change effort was completed, the scaffolding was not really removed. Rather, in the course of the organizational change, the action research network was woven into the fabric of the organization. It remained as part of the new work process and could be recalled as part of newly learned experiences, without the aid of the action research network developer. In short, not only was the work process changed; the organization had learned and grown as well.

The State Fund's strategic action groups conducted planning within the frame of the action research network. Each group had a coordinator and a starter action research network of key State Fund vice presidents and managers involved in that particular strategic interest area. This was part of the president's and Gardner's notion of sensing one's environment. The following excerpt from the State Fund's monthly newsletter describes the roles of these networked parallel organizations in 1973:

> During the past few years at the Fund there's been a proliferation of work groups known as action forces, task forces, project study teams, etc. They

come. They go. New ones surface. Old ones disappear. What are these action forces? Why do we have them? Who's on them and what are they supposed to do? Who selects membership and how does one go about being appointed to an action force? [Anyone who has] the desire and capability to contribute something to the organization, tell your district or department manager. He or she has an important role to play in the decision and would be your best resource to be named to a planning action force. (Bruce, 1994, pp. 133–134)

The organization development strategic action group was the main vehicle for implementing most of the organizational change activities. The genesis of this action research network was based in several areas of concern. First, although the stated objectives of a formal project might be met in the best cost–benefit manner, it produced a suboptimizing result in which opportunities were lost to the organization as a whole, largely because of the project team's championship of its own specific project objectives. A team's suggested improvement in the work process also affected the way in which the organization did its business. Sometimes, the overall impact of a team's innovation at an organization-wide level had such negative results that they far overshadowed the intrinsic value of the specific work system improvement itself. Without a wide network of communication, the team was not likely to be aware of the larger system costs.

For example, in the 1970s the computer department was documenting the difficult and lengthy development of a statewide distributed data-processing system. Twenty years ago distributed, cooperative data processing was somewhat before its time. More recently, it has become the catchword of modern public organizations. Yet a distributed data-processing system was an important requirement for the development of Gardner's concept of system providing an information feedback service to autonomous work units in the district offices.

Meanwhile, an action research network of mostly district office clerical staff was experimenting with a system that linked the district offices' minicomputers to the home office mainframe. The action research required setting up a working prototype of the distributed data processing network. They used old computer terminals and leased telephone lines. When the statewide computer network was tested and successful, the statewide system was de facto installed because of the action research at the district level. As Gardner had envisioned, another of the free-floating action research activities then disappeared into the fabric of the organization.

Another reason for the use of action research networks was to implement Gardner's concept of communication and consent of the governed in each change effort. In a major organization-wide work system change, so many people are involved that it is never feasible to have everyone on the team. Only a small minority of all the people affected by the work changes can be members of the project team in any meaningful fashion. However, with the informal structure of the action research network, people can come in and out of the process as is appropriate for their needs and the change situation in general.

Still another concern was the tendency for the group dynamics and norms of team building to override the participants' own work-unit culture. Teams take on a life of their own. The participants, in order to be accepted as loyal task force team members, are often faced with disadvantageous work system tradeoffs for their work units. These tradeoffs are unduly influenced by the participants' involvement in a team power dynamic and the inherent need to belong as a team member.

Finally, there was the strong tendency for task force teams to develop sole ownership of a new work system, often to the point of alienating the very work units required to use the new system when it was installed statewide. When the team was dismissed at the completion of the project, the danger was that the ownership and the responsibility for the new work process would dissolve along with the project team. Action training and research relies on the broad scope that the action research network creates to minimize phantom group norms. In addition, the action research network provides connections that are embedded in the organization and furnish ongoing support for change. The new knowledge translated into organizational learning for the State Fund.

One unresolved problem for the Fund in its use of action research networks stemmed from a reverse communication feedback gap. The network teams tended to take on a life of their own. Because they were operating close to the service delivery reality, they were effective in making changes quickly. However, management, especially the executive committee, often found they were uninformed about changes that often had corporate policy consequences. In the case of the data communication network team, the good side was that the whole system was prototyped by work units within existing resources. With success at this level, the statewide data communications system was implemented in the successful outcome.

However, there was a great wailing and gnashing of teeth on the part of the data processing program manager who felt himself outside the decision-making loop. The people who needed the information conceived it as an action research project. The manager's discomfort shows that the State Fund organization had not fully assimilated the concept of self-managed teams nor built an organizational structure that provided sufficient feedback to the manager. A subsequent investigation initiated by the manager and performed by the internal audit department could not identify how this major undertaking was implemented without budgeted resources and outside the structured systems development decision making process.

TESTING ASSUMPTIONS AND SECURITY EXAMPLES

The security reason for experimentation has many examples. The East Coast county's fire and rescue department provides the most obvious and dramatic one. The work that firefighters do is dangerous. Where most people are taught to flee fires in buildings, fire-fighters undergo rigorous training to go 180 degrees in the other direction: They must attack the fire in order to suppress it. Therefore, the fire-fighting organization is understandably a very conservative one, especially when it comes to new ideas. All new ideas can pose a serious degree of risk not only for them but for the people and property they are trained to protect and rescue from danger.

The fog nozzle project to suppress high-rise building fires and the tennis ball to protect buildings from damage from aerial ladders are examples of the need to experiment first before new equipment or methods are introduced into real-life emergency situations. A fire-fighter must have absolute confidence in the methods and equipment when entering burning buildings. Exhaustive testing of methods and equipment is part of everyday life in the fire station.

One interesting research project included the Jaws of Life. This is a hydraulic tool used, in most cases, to rescue people trapped in vehicle wrecks on the highway. It is a powerful tool that cuts open the steel top of a car like a giant can opener. However, it has two problems. First, it is so heavy and large that it takes two firefighters to operate it. This is a disadvantage when trying to wedge into the crinkled side of a burning RV. Second, it uses a very toxic hydraulic fluid that can leak onto the firefighters and victims.

A new tool was being developed that was lighter, smaller, required only one person to operate, and used a nontoxic hydraulic fluid. It was also claimed to be stronger than the ones currently used by the fire and rescue department.

During the first phase of the testing program the lieutenant from the apparatus section had his doubts. "It doesn't track for me," he said. "You read these claims in the *Fire Chief* magazine all the time."

"That's what this testing is all about, isn't it?" a firefighter from the special rescue squad replied.

"How do you want us to test that?"

"We can have a 'Jaws-off,'" the firefighter suggested.

"A 'Jaws-off'?"

"Sure," the firefighter replied. "We can get one of those wrecked cars at the training academy that we use to train recruits on the use of the Jaws of Life tool. We'll come out there with our current tool. We can get the other Jaws guy to bring his new tool to let us try it out. Then we start making equal cuts in the car. We can time them and see who's best. If it works like they say it does, then we'll take both of them on our squad unit on real incident calls. We'll find out just how good it is that way."

On the day of the Jaws-off, the vendor of the new tool arrived early to get ready. The firefighters, garbed in their dull yellow turnout gear, gathered on both sides of the car. On one side two firefighters operated the current tool. On the other side one firefighter was getting instructions on how to use the new tool. Then the test began. The current tool team cut open their side of the roof. The new tool countered with an equally swift cut. The car now looked like a recently opened tomato can. Then each tool took a turn in cutting off the steering wheel column. This was always a difficult cut because of the strength of the column and the difficulty in getting to it. Next they pried the doors off, the current tool on the right side and the new tool on the left. Finally, the current tool went after the post separating the front and back doors. It made a deep crimp in the metal post, but was unable to complete the cut. The new tool came over and made a quick and clean cut just below the crimp made by the first tool. The firefighters then made a second cut above the crimp to produced a graphic Jaws-off trophy to take back to the innovation committee and senior staff.

FROM THE STATE FUND JOURNALS OF NEELY GARDNER: EXPERIMENTATION

Our major experiment at the State Fund was the pilot district office that would try managing the devolved powers of the district office as a kind of mini-State Fund. "When I returned to Los Angeles, I contacted Larry Kirkhart, with whom I had previously talked about the possibility of a research project based on the action training and research approach. Larry and I spent several sessions with Frank Sherwood, a colleague on the University of Southern California faculty, in developing some ideas for the research. Frank Sherwood had been interested in the State Fund from two standpoints: (1) an interest in developing new patterns of organization and (2) as a field to support research of doctoral students."

At the outset Gardner and Kirkhart were interested in three major questions to research. The first was the change in organizational structure and what it might do in terms of mitigating employee alienation. The second was whether a restructuring of the organization would in any way increase or decrease the economic productivity of the unit. The third was a look at the changes that would take place in the Fund's relationship with its external environment. (For a detailed report on this research see Kirkhart, 1972.)

To help orient Larry to some of the State Fund problems and to acquaint him with the State Fund operations, Gardner introduced him to one of the district managers in the Los Angeles area. Gardner felt that the district manager had expressed himself more forcibly in terms of the possible devolution than any of the district managers.

Together Kirkhart and the district manager developed a research design that called for (1) an experimental office, (2) an office Kirkhart called an "aware" office because it would be aware that it was a control office, and (3) an office called the "unaware" or "blind" office because no one in the office would be aware that the comparison was being made. The design was intended to avoid the "Hawthorne" effect.[1]

In keeping with the agreement that Gardner had made with the executive committee, he suggested to the pilot district manager that he develop a program statement. The first "contract" proposal from the pilot district manager resulted from a series of meetings that the manager held with his employees. The document primarily presented a list of problems that employees wanted to have corrected as they moved toward local autonomy. They gave little thought to communicating to State Fund management what the office would contribute in terms of operational production.

The list is interesting in light of Maslow's (1996) concept that one of the indicators of organizational growth is the magnitude of the problems that concern employees. At the beginning of this experiment, employees were thinking about "mini" problems.[2]

Second, they identified things that the pilot district office employees felt the president should do. They fell into these areas:

1. Providing new and better cars to replace the kind the employees are now driving, add air conditioning and radios.
2. Providing expense accounts that at least enable us to come up to the general State regulations. This would mean lunch allowances when ten miles from the office.
3. Enabling the district office to make its own purchases without going through business services.
4. Prepare policies on all applications submitted by the district office without questioning anything other than technicalities or oversights that prevent them from writing a contract.

It is clear from the tenor of this first document that there was a lot of hostility in the pilot district office, both against the home office and, very covertly, against the pilot district office manager himself. Kirkhart also attended the meeting. In his view the pilot district office manager's resistance was showing. The pilot district office employees were asked to present their ideas not in terms of a program to be undertaken but as complaints they might have about their work.

At this point there was no understanding among the parties of what each would do and what each would get. Gardner told Kirkhart that he did not think the document developed at the meeting met the requirements of the delegation contract. Kirkhart conveyed Gardner's concern to the pilot district manager, who then asked a subgroup in his office to refine the statement. The subgroup still did not come up with a contract but continued with a bill of particulars or complaints. Finally, the district manager himself rewrote the contract and apparently achieved agreement from his committee to present it to the home office.

In July, Gardner, Kirkhart, and the pilot district manager went to what was hoped would be the final negotiation with the executive committee. The pilot district manager had given a copy of his proposal to the president and wished to present it personally to the executive committee. Before the executive committee would talk with him, they wanted to meet with Gardner and Kirkhart to discuss the management and direction of the pilot research project.

"For two hours the district manager sat in the reception room waiting, waiting, waiting." Gardner wrote. "I suspect that the outcome of the negotiations went better because of the fact that the pilot district manager was excluded. Although exclusion is against my principles, the discussion was very tender as far as the outcome of the project was concerned."

The president explained the pilot district office proposal. Kirkhart talked about the research design. Several of the vice presidents, quite uneasy with the idea of the experiment, began to raise questions and to pursue "what if" issues. Each question had the potential for stopping the decision to proceed with the pilot experiment. There were some heated exchanges.

"According to my notes," Gardner wrote, "I indicated that I felt my role at this meeting was to be sure that people faced up to the issues that would be involved in the experiment. I also pointed up areas of conflict between those who were arguing the case and tried to deal with the questions and nonquestions that were being asked by people who were opposed to the proposal. It was obvious that the president very strongly wished to proceed with the project. In my opinion it was his desire that carried the day. Without his strong support the project would not have been accepted. Overtly, there were grounds for saying that a consensus existed. In fact, as later developed, some of the parties were not overjoyed with the decision."

The conclusion reached at this meeting was to launch the experimental devolved pilot office, provided that the district manager developed a program statement acceptable to a special review unit organized by the executive committee. The district manager was called in and told of this decision. After some explanation, he agreed to the proposition. Regarding the action training and research process, it should be no surprise that commitment does not proceed at a steady state. Each action changes the situation and the forces in the field within which it operates. The psychological contract must be evolutionary in nature and subject to renegotiation and modification.

Following the executive committee meeting we moved to another part of the building and met with a group that included those who had been present in the morning and with the managers of the various staff services. The president and Gardner explained the basic parameters of the experiment, and the district manager of the pilot office then described what his experimental office would like to do. Questions were asked and answered. The president urged all personnel to cooperate fully with the district manager of the pilot office and noted that the next few weeks would be critical to the experiment. He wanted the endeavor to be launched as rapidly as possible.

The reaction of the managers present was, to say the least, guarded. Although a few of them seemed enthusiastic, most were noncommittal. This is understandable because the presentation of the district manager of the pilot office involved a statement of dissatisfaction with much of the work being carried on by these very staff support managers. What the district manager was saying, in effect, was that organizational activities were impeding the district's performance. The district manager had rather boldly asserted that, as a result of the experimental program, his district office would improve its performance by an order of magnitude:

1. Write a total of 43% more business during the pilot year than in the previous year.
2. Achieve a 15% net premium gain, using as a base period the calendar year just preceding.

3. Create and maintain a pool of people characterized by a high degree of self-reliance, resilience, independence, empathy, perception free of distortion, and feeling-based interpersonal relationships. All of these attributes are encompassed by the term *self-actualization.*

The afternoon following this session, the district manager and Kirkhart met individually with those staff people with responsibility for research and systems, personnel, finance, underwriting, insurance services, and claims. The agenda for these sessions was to have the department heads spell out the limitations they felt were placed on them by the president. By ascertaining these limits it would be possible to delineate the constraints on the experimental office. Kirkhart reported the following:

> No small part of the interviews was spent exploring the basis for the existing evaluative criteria; when these premises were focused on by [the district manager], the gap between what was actually occurring in the field that could be used as performance standards and what was assumed to be the condition in the field was very apparent and was very great. All of the traditional "hard" criteria employee basis for promotion, rewards, etc., began to crumble and become very soft and ambiguous. So one of the consequences of these interviews, in addition to developing a consciousness on the part of the district manager of the limitations placed on the [president], was to confront these several top staff personnel with the fact that the traditional means of evaluation were far from precise, unambiguous, reliable standards relevant to the District Offices. (Kirkhart, 1969; cited in Gardner, 1980, p. 322)

After negotiation with the special program review committee appointed by the president to oversee the experiment, it was decided that the experimental office would be given a degree of autonomy that was limited only by those that constrained the president himself. The office would be provided with a lump sum budget that could be spent in any legal way consistent with the rules and regulations of the State of California Personnel System and Board of Control rules. Staff services, such as data processing, accounting, personnel, and training would not be imposed on the office but would be available to the South Pasadena office as requested. Most reports normally required of the field offices by the larger organization were to be suspended during the experiment. The district office would keep the field records necessary to meet state bookkeeping. Home office records, regardless of character, were to be made available to the district office if that office so requested.

During the 1-year period the experimental office would be removed from its normal position in the hierarchy and report directly to the president. In return for the autonomy, the district office was to operate under a program agreement that presented the broad goals the district office intended to pursue during the course of the experiment, along with specifically expressed short-term objectives that the organization intended to achieve. The experiment seemed to be ready to get under way, but there was one more delay.

From time to time during the negotiations, the district manager of the pilot office found it necessary to go back to the home office in San Francisco for information and discussion of the availability of services. On one of these occasions, Kirkhart went with him, and both were surprised to find that soon after their arrival they were directed to appear in the executive conference room for a special meeting. Kirkhart noted, "Neither of us knew what the unspecified agenda of the meeting might be, but we speculated that a reaction to the delegation had occurred or that a problem between the district manager and the regional manager had been pushed upward in the organization."

At that time the president was out of town. The vice presidents and the southern regional manager were on hand in the conference room. These men, all of whom had attended the earlier approval meeting, believed that final approval had not yet been given to the program; so they declared that the district manager of the pilot office was misreading his role. The regional manager believed that the district manager did not have the authority to travel to San Francisco without his approval.

When the president returned, he was more amused than hurt by this effort of vice presidents to "retake lost ground." He diplomatically told the district manager of the pilot office that the issue would be closed by giving formal approval to the program statement. This saved face for all involved in the transaction. Thus, the setback was only temporary. The program statement was at last sanctioned by the special program review committee established to oversee the experiment.

The final approval was given formally in a special half-day meeting held in the pilot office. The president went to the pilot district office to participate. During the session, employees of the office asked questions and exchanged ideas with the president, Kirkhart, and the district manager of the pilot office. The events that followed demonstrated the dynamic and changing, rather than simply the changed, nature of organization development efforts.

INITIAL REACTIONS TO THE EXPERIMENT

Reactions to the president's first appearance at the pilot district office 2 months prior to the formal approval meeting had been favorable. The employees were both surprised that the president would appear personally and very pleased with his attention. Even then it was clear to the people in that office that the experimental program was under way.

Nonetheless, the district manager faced problems with his subordinate supervisors similar to the problems the president had faced in negotiating with the vice presidents over the launching of the experimental program. Of the district manager's five chief subordinates, two had been trained by the previous district manager and had never accommodated to the current district manager's flamboyant and existential ways. Kirkhart characterized their view of management as entirely authoritarian. The remaining three supervisors were more sympathetic. The district manager had hoped to obtain full support for the project but, as it turned out, received only tacit approval, continuing skepticism, and even resentment on the part of two disbelieving section heads.

On receiving the formal program approval, the district manager abolished the traditional Wednesday supervisory meeting and substituted a weekly meeting to be attended by the entire staff in its place. The purpose of the meetings was to provide an opportunity for all members of the district office to influence the direction of the work of the office and the thrust of the experiment. It was a completely new experience for the employees. The meetings, which involved more than 30 people, were generally quite chaotic, unfocused, and ineffective. In retrospect, it would have been a very good idea for the district manager and his employees to have been trained in group leadership and participation.

One of the characteristics of the meetings was that every time there seemed to be a consensus developing on a decision, two or three people created a diversion. This tyranny of a minority was precipitated by the two supervisors who were not "with" the experimental program. Their strategy was to time their interventions to raise doubts at the moment when it appeared that others were ready to make a decision. The two dissenters questioned the efficacy of persons other than formal managers making decisions. Clearly the two managers intimidated those employees who reported to them directly.

Although employees in the pilot district office still appeared to be operating at a dependent level, it was obvious that learning was taking place. This learning, however, was gained at the expense of organizational effectiveness.

IMPACT OF CHANGES ON THE RESEARCH STUDIES

The changes described previously had considerable impact on the research that Kirkhart was attempting. Once the formal approval of the experiment was given, Kirkhart was ready to use his comprehensive research instruments. He administered a lengthy questionnaire in six different locations in addition to the pilot district office. During the experimental period, the questionnaire was completed at all seven locations on four different occasions. Virtually all the people in each location filled out the instrument in Kirkhart's presence. At least from a volume standpoint, he did not want for data.

Throughout his research, Kirkhart was faced with unmanageable situations. The problem was great turnover in the district offices. He got a virtually 100% response each time the questionnaire was administered, but only 40% of the employees who responded to the original questionnaire were among those answering in the final administration of the instrument. This was a result of rotation, promotion, and resignations.

SUMMARY

Experimentation is the heart of action research. It is in experimentation that the new knowledge is confirmed. Experimentation reduces the risk of negative consequences to the organization and the people in it. In addition, successful experiments that are properly designed with the organization's situation and aspirations in mind, often become, de facto, implemented change. Experiments can be designed with full scientific rigor, depending on the hypothesis being tested, or they can be casual and include the people who will be involved in the change. In the spirit of Kurt Lewin and action research, the important thing to keep in mind is that it should result in some practical knowledge about how the organization should or should not change itself. The results will be evaluated in stage 8, experiment results analysis.

NOTES

1. In the Mayo–Roethlisberger Research (Roethlisberger & Dickson, 1939), in the Hawthorne Plant of the Western Electric Company, it was determined that units improved their performance simply because they were being scrutinized and not because of the changes in environment or management that were taking place.

2. See Maslow (1996, pp. 45–46); see also Dunn (1991). Dunn also applied this term to second-order problems that are ill-structured because the domain of potentially relevant policy stakeholder, options, impacts, and values is unbounded—that is, unmanageably huge (see Mitroff & Featheringham, 1974).

CHAPTER 11

AT&R STAGE 8:
EXPERIMENT
RESULTS ANALYSIS

MENU FOR AT&R STAGE 8: EXPERIMENT RESULTS ANALYSIS

Action   *At the conclusion of the experiment, this model of AT&R calls for an analysis of the results. For the most part the analysis addresses such questions as:*

1. *Are we doing what we said we would do as well as we said we would do it?*
2. *What new data do we need?*
3. *How do we feel about the change action?*
4. *Shall we go ahead with this change action for the next year(s)?*
5. *What can we do to change the change that will make it even better?*

In general, I like to see the intervenor play a low-key role in the results-analysis period. At this time he or she is most useful in training clients to understand and employ AT&R methods. The relationship should approach independence. The clients should be ready to "go it alone" (Gardner, 1974).

189

Training   *Survey and feedback process, research methodology.*

Research   *Devise a survey and feedback instrument that will document the results of the working prototype or pilot implementation. Where the key assumptions were not supported, the AT&R process must be reiterated in order to revise the proposed changes to reconcile with the experiential facts in the test or pilot organization. Where the results do support the key assumptions, the change can be designed and prepared for institutionalization.*

Outcome   *Modified organization change for program implementation.*

ANALYSIS AS LEARNING

The analysis of the experiment results can tell us what new things we have learned. In designing the experiment, we had an argument in mind. It is hoped that the experiment design had the criteria by which it would be evaluated built in. These criteria would be derived from the many stages that preceded the experimental stage, but most notably from the values of the contract-setting stage and the criteria used in the aspirations stage.

There are two kinds of results to analyze. If the experiment has a rigorous design, then new scientific knowledge can result. If the design is linked to practical applications for work, new methods and organization can result. If the experiments are conducted professionally, even those that disprove the argument have value as new knowledge.

For example, the results in Larry Kirkhart's research with the pilot district office at the State Fund did not support most of his arguments. The devolved office organization did not seem to have much impact on the participants' behavior. However, on the practical side, that fact along with the fact that the district office was able to operate in a normal fashion as a devolved district office did prove that all the central command authority from the home office through the hierarchy of regional managers was not needed (Kirkhart, 1972).

EXAMPLE IN PRACTICE: EAST COAST COUNTY'S MINICOMPUTER PROCUREMENT EXPERIMENT

The participation of the Department of Public Works as a pilot to research the role of the minicomputer for the East Coast county's strategic management team began during a telephone conversation with the assistant director of the Department of Public Works. She wanted to know what the strategic management team was going to do about minicomputers. The practitioner gave her the background on the issue-exploration effort and promised to include her in the creating of the issue paper for minicomputers. She said that the Department of Public Works was interested in participating in that effort:

"You know," she said, "we sent our department systems plan to the information technology department, but they have declined to evaluate it because we have included a minicomputer in it. Imagine! Now, what provision is your strategic management team going to make for minicomputers in the agencies?" she asked.

"The issue-exploration effort indicated we needed a pilot experiment to research the pros and cons of our procurement process for acquiring minicomputers," the practitioner explained. "As you know, the information technology branch chiefs have contributed to the issue paper by expressing serious concerns that their programmers could not support minicomputers in the agencies. Each minicomputer vendor had a different proprietary operating system that would require them to staff systems analysts and programmers for each different kind of minicomputer county agencies might want. Any application development support for each different minicomputer would, therefore, require additional information technology staffing as well."

"We at the Department of Public Works have been using minicomputers for years without their support," she countered. "We are not all that concerned about how the information technology will be

supporting us in the future because they don't at this time. They have
been against minicomputers all along, anyway. We have several minis
in DPW already. They were all acquired over these same objections
by the information technology department then. Big deal! We can
handle minicomputers on our own, all right. That's not our problem.
So what's the issue?"

The issue is the fast change of technology and our ability to keep
up with it. The key issue revolves around the county's lack of an
effective process to properly define an agency's system-function
needs before the computer hardware–software solution is put out to
bid. The county uses a request for proposal (RFP) process to solicit
competitive bidding when acquiring computer systems. Therefore, a
task force was formed to develop and test a prototype computer
hardware procurement process. The task force members, including
the assistant director of DPW, had the expertise to do this technical
analysis and evaluation. They decided that if they documented their
process as a technical advisory group for the pilots they would have
the foundation of a technical advisory process for future information
technology development in the agencies.

THE EXPERIMENT: A MINICOMPUTER PROCUREMENT PROCESS

The group then developed the guidelines for the process of evaluating
agency computer system needs. The representative from the information technology department developed a comprehensive technical
review form and process for a countywide technical review team to
help agencies identify and describe their functional requirements in
a group setting. This technical review form and process reflected all
of the concerns and problems that the stakeholders had raised during
the initial issue-exploration phase. In this way, the technical review
process would guide the group in examining these concerns and problems in the process of actually selecting and acquiring the best information technology solution for the two pilot projects.

The Department of Public Works was selected as the pilot agency
to test the experimental computer hardware acquisition process. Under this new technical review process, the Department of Public

Works representative took over the chairing of that group through the experimental project. The DPW was the agency that was going to be most directly affected by the change. Leading the computer selection process was now its responsibility.

The representatives from the various supporting staff departments took on their new supporting role as a departmental computing evaluation group. In this new configuration, the technical review team used the new technical review form and process to help the Department of Public Works develop its specific system requirements as a request for proposal (RFP) to acquire its minicomputer replacement system. In addition, the use of the new technical review form and process also ensured that the concerns and problems of the whole issue regarding the strategic role of minicomputers would be addressed.

For example, the departmental computing evaluation group was able to agree that the core of the issue regarding minicomputers involved nomenclature. The key stakeholders could not agree on the proper definition of a minicomputer. They also found that they were not alone in this situation. The information technology industry could not seem to agree on the difference between mainframes, minicomputers, and personal computers (PCs) either. The spectacular rise of PC technology had blurred all useful distinctions between these categories.

Rather than try to define what even the trade journals could not, the group decided to base the request for proposal on the specific needs and requirements of the department. The responding vendors could propose a mainframe, a minicomputer, or a microcomputer solution. The departmental computing evaluation group decided that if the proposal selection criteria were actually the needs and specific requirements of the department, the subsequent evaluation of the proposals received from interested vendors would put all the concerns and problems in proper perspective. In addition, the strategic decision-making recommendations to the strategic management steering committee would also be based on the experience of acquiring and using an actual minicomputer in DPW.

To the DPW group, the idea of research analysis in which they would have an equal footing with former adversaries was novel and intriguing. This new prospect triggered the group's sense of exploration and discovery. During the development of the new technical review form and process, the group discovered that they had been able to discuss their concerns openly, with an even exchange to win their point.

As the process continued, each member acted for the most part within the expected behavior of his or her work situation. For example, the members from the Department of Public Works came from a civil engineering environment. They stayed close to their rational problem-solving approach throughout the strategic decision-making process.

The central staff departments' computer operations and system analysts participating in the DPW group tended to display a predominantly rational analytic approach as well. They focused on detailed analysis and setting up strict procedures for the technical review process they were developing. To the degree that they were disgruntled about losing their former exclusive technical review power, they expressed anger, fear, and the desire to restore it.

However, when the Department of Public Works representative found himself the chair of the technical review group, it constituted a new experience for him and for the Department of Public Works. In the past, agencies were not even present during the central staff departments' technical review process. And there was little opportunity for agencies to appeal the central staffs' findings and recommendations. Even when projects were approved in the technical review, it was the central staff departments that presented the agency's request to the executives for budget approval.

However, in their new leadership role of the technical review, the Department of Public Works had to come up with their own functional requirements and ones that the county's staff departments would also sign off on as a request for proposal. This opportunity allowed room for the DPW group to be both creative and realistic, because its own criteria would be the main determining criteria that would decide which vendor proposal would be chosen.

As the user requirements were initiated by the Department of Public Works members and staff, they were reviewed several times by the departmental computing evaluation group. Revisions were suggested, made, and agreed on. The request for proposal (RFP) was then handled by the purchasing department and released for responses from vendors. Purchasing also organized a small RFP selection committee composed of three members selected from the departmental computing evaluation group and two additional members from the Department of Public Works. Again, the DPW representative was the chair. In addition, two DPW employees, who were responsible for operating the department's current minicomputers, were also chosen as members of the RFP selection committee.

ANALYZING THE EXPERIMENT'S RESULTS

When the vendor's proposals and bids were received, the results were startling and unsettling to the group. The Department of Public Works was happy because its favored minicomputer choice met and, in fact, exceeded the RFP functional requirements criteria (see Figure 11.1). The bid also came in slightly less than the amount budgeted for the minicomputer, resulting in some budget savings.[1] It was exactly what DPW wanted. Another minicomputer proposal was favored by the information center representative, partly because it was proposed by the same vendor who had provided the mainframe computer that the information center already had. This second minicomputer would simplify central department support. The proposal was rated by the RFP selection committee as having the highest functionality. However, it also was by far the highest cost, almost double the amount budgeted, creating a significant budget shortfall.

The surprise bid was a super client–server proposal. Most client–servers use a single PC as a central processing unit (CPU) to handle everything. A super client–server uses a very fast CPU for its main processing and several parallel CPUs to handle all of the data flowing in and out of the system.

The super client–server proposal had almost as high functionality rating as the best minicomputer, but it cost nearly one half the budgeted amount, resulting in a significant budget savings. The proposed super client–server provided nearly the highest functionality, at the lowest cost.

The selection of the super client–server as the obvious best proposal did not seem to please any of the key stakeholders. However, the strategic importance of the results was clear. Getting twice the functionality at half the cost was a compelling strategy in favor of the

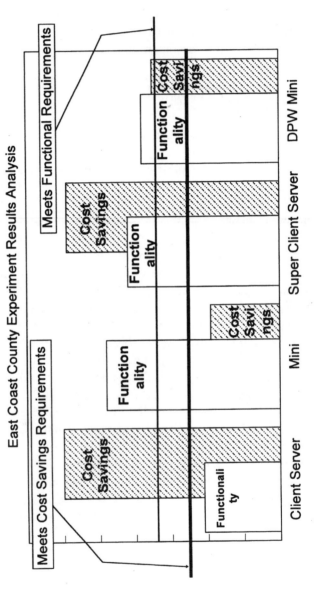

Comparison of Systems Bid - Function & Cost

East Coast County Experiment Results Analysis

Meets Cost Savings Requirements

Meets Functional Requirements

| Client Server | Mini | Super Client Server | DPW Mini |

Figure 11.1 Comparing Bids for Results Analysis

client–server as the county's cooperative computing platform. Therefore, the formal bid evaluation resulted in the RFP selection committee's recommendation for the super client–server and local area network (LAN) solution for the Public Works Department. The departmental computing evaluation group also recommended that the client–server be designated as the cooperative computing platform for the county's goal of creating a cooperative computing environment in the future.

The departmental computing evaluation group's issue-exploration research found that the strategic problems surrounding the acquisition, operation, and maintenance of minicomputers in the county were not going to be of strategic importance. They recommended that minicomputers be considered as a solution to information technology problems on a case by case (tactical) basis, and only then, when the software application was so special and so specific that it would run only on a particular minicomputer—for instance, the minicomputer that runs the DPW's waste-water treatment plant and those used to operate public safety's automated dispatch system.

As in many decision-making situations involving a variety of key stakeholders, not everyone was happy with the result. In this case, it appeared to the client agency, DPW, that the staff departments had once again gotten their way at its expense. The staff departments had been against minicomputers all along, and once again DPW's request for a minicomputer was rejected.

Although any department director would be disappointed to have his or her decision blocked, DPW's reaction was not just sour grapes. The director and his DPW staff had been key stakeholders and most outspoken in their opinions against central staff department interventions that thwarted an agency's better judgement.

The director and his assistant director were both members of the strategic management steering committee. At committee meetings the director was candid about his anti-mainframe and pro-minicomputer sentiments. He constantly used his department as an example of how departments and agencies can run their own minicomputers without central staff department support. Both the director and assistant director had experienced and expert opinions on which solution was best for their department's needs.

THE EXPERIMENT RESULTS ANALYSIS AND THE MANAGEMENT DECISION

The issue-exploration objective of the strategic pilot—to use this real-life deliberation of replacing the two minicomputers in the Department of Public Works as a way to research the strategic problems associated with procuring minicomputers—was put to the supreme test. At the beginning of the issue exploration, all of the key stakeholders thought that the conflict would revolve around which minicomputers would be approved for countywide use, and how to support them; or that maybe only mainframe applications would be allowed. The emergence of the dramatic advantage of the client–server solution was a surprise to all.

Clearly, the strategic decision of adopting the client–server solution toward achieving the county's cooperative computing environment was at odds with the DPW director's decision to acquire a new, but familiar, minicomputer to replace two of his old ones. The director not only had an informed opinion about the choice of replacing the old minicomputer with a bigger model of the same manufacture, he also appeared dead set against acquiring either any other minicomputer or the super client–server solution.

Nevertheless, the departmental computer evaluation group's issue-exploration research had clearly established that minicomputers would not have any strategic role in the county's strategic information technology. They would be acquired only by exception, where the software application was so specialized that it required a specific minicomputer. Therefore, any minicomputer alternative would be a nonstrategic choice.

Further, the group's issue-exploration research revealed that the DPW's particular minicomputer replacement situation was not special in any way that would warrant it as an exception to use minicomputers. Therefore, the RFP selection committee stood by their choice of the super client–server local area network system for DPW. This selection was a strategic decision not only for the Department of Public Works but for the strategic direction of the county's information technology in the future.

The super client–server selection was not unanimous. The members of the director's staff that served on the five-member RFP selection committee were divided on the selection among themselves. Their representative who was chairing the committee strongly opposed the selection. He read aloud to the selection committee several passages from the RFP. These passages had specifically stated in the scope of the contract under the section on special provisions that the purpose of this RFP was to solicit proposals for the hardware, software, and communication needs for a minicomputer, which was to replace two existing minicomputers. The experiment's objectives were to provide a mechanism for the 14 agencies that make up the DPW to attain a centralized automation solution for existing and planned systems, establish a means for centralized processing among the department's agencies, and provide a centralized location for departmental systems.

The committee member from the county's information center countered that the county was considering a strategic move toward a decentralized cooperative computing environment. She pointed out that the super client–server in no way would keep the Department of Public Works from structuring the system into a centralized design. In fact, it would be able to change it to any departmental structure its management wanted. That was one of the main advantages over the minicomputer. She mentioned, knowing the director's distaste for the county's mainframe systems, that if they were so interested in centralizing their operations, they ought to consider using the county's mainframe as a solution as well as minicomputers.

The DPW representative who was responsible for operating one of the department's minicomputers that was not going to be replaced declared himself neutral but agreed that the super client–server was the most forward-thinking solution. The third DPW representative, who was responsible for one of the minicomputers that was going to be replaced, sided firmly with the super client–server selection.

The remaining two members of the committee, the supervisor of the county's information center, and the strategic management team's representative (the first author) supported the selection of the super client–server, as well. This support was based not only on the compelling results of the committee's analysis of the competing bids but the county's policy to have competitive bidding to ensure that the most economical selection would be made.

The supervisor of the information center supported it also because they were staffed and charged with providing central staff department support to personal computers and local area networks but not to minicomputers. A minicomputer selection would require additional staffing of her unit if it was to provide any central staff department support.

The strategic management team representative supported the selection also because it supported the five strategic objectives and goals for a cooperative computing environment the best. The super client–server was a powerful and flexible system that could be shared across the county-wide cooperative computing environment being installed in the new government center by another management initiative. The super client–server represented a strategic opportunity to take a quantum leap into the county's information technology future.

The Department of Public Works was a microcosm of the county. It had 14 semi-autonomous agencies within it. The features of the super client–server fulfilled, in one department, all of the five strategic objectives of the county's strategic plan for information technology development. Here, in the Department of Public Works' pilot project, the county would be able to test all of its critical strategic assumptions about the envisioned cooperative computing environment at no additional cost.

However, the decision to purchase the solution was strictly for the director of DPW to make. In this case, the director and his assistant director were distressed at the committee's recommended selection. The director requested that the RFP selection committee review and reconsider their deliberations in light of the department's stated objectives in the request for proposal. The RFP selection committee's subsequent review merely confirmed that its interpretation of the facts were clear, and the selection remained the same. With the super client–server solution the choice of centralization or decentralization would not be compromised in any way; it would be an option the department management could make (and unmake) at any time in the future.

During the review, the department's committee member in favor of the super client–server selection pointed out that the Department of Public Works needed to recognize that it was merely being confronted by its own data, its own functional requirements, its own criteria, and, ultimately, the reality of its own selection. He explained that to change the outcome to swing in favor of the minicomputer that the director wanted would require a drastic change of its functional requirements.

The RFP selection committee members agreed that a change in the selection would be justified if the Department of Public Works had made a serious error in coming up with its functional requirements in the RFP. They also agreed that another reason for rejecting the super client–server would be if the RFP selection committee had somehow overlooked a deficiency in the super client–server.

On these grounds, the director and the assistant director insisted, through their representative and chair of the RFP selection committee, that the alternatives be reviewed a third time by the RFP selection committee. The Department of Public Works' committee chair pointed out that the super client–server vendor had failed to include certain communication hardware. Although the cost of the hardware in question was less than 1% of the total bid, a third careful review of the request for proposal showed that these items were not in the requirements of the RFP. The vendor did not have to include them. The minicomputer bids did not include them either.

Furthermore, after this third review it was determined that even if the Department of Public Works changed its functional requirements drastically, the results would be the same. There were no realistic changes in the department's requirements that would not result in essentially the same cost and performance spread among the vendors' resubmitted costs and equipment functions. Changing the requirements would be like changing the key of a song. All the notes would move in their exact relationship up or down the scale, and the tune would be the same. The super client–server solution remained as the RFP selection committee's recommendation.

The RFP selection committee submitted its selection of the super client–server to the director and to the departmental computing evaluation group. The director of DPW could decide either to purchase the recommended solution or to discard the request for proposal and start all over with a new one.

The members of the departmental computing evaluation group decided that they were ready to present their strategic recommendations on the minicomputer management initiative. The evaluation group's recommendations included that the county adopt the client–server local area network as the strategic cooperative computing platform of the future. They further recommended that the minicomputer should not be considered a strategic information technology resource. Therefore, the group found that to pursue any of the many problems that had been raised by minicomputers would be committing strategic resources to nonstrategic problems.

However, when the findings were taken to the strategic management steering committee for presentation, the director of the Department of Public Works preempted the group's presenter and said to his peers on the committee,

> I want to preface this presentation with this account. The RFP selection committee has worked hard on this request for proposal and its evaluation. But, I want you to know, I didn't like what they came up with. I sent them back to deliberate again—twice. And twice they came back with the same unacceptable selection. Therefore, I have taken their research to outside experts in the private sector to evaluate their selection. And I want to tell you all here now—that the outside experts looked at the analysis and told me that 'The emperor has no clothes!' They told me that the Department of Public Works was missing a great opportunity if we pass up this super client–server solution. Therefore, I support the selection committee's recommendations, and I am requesting that this committee approve our acquisition of the super client–server solution.

The director of the Office of Management and Budget seconded the PWD director's request and the strategic management steering committee approved the purchase.

FROM THE STATE FUND JOURNALS OF
NEELY GARDNER: EXPERIMENT RESULTS ANALYSIS

Because of the great turnover in the district offices of the State Fund, the initial intention to incorporate a wide and massive database to analyze the experiment was frustrated. In terms of the hypotheses Kirkhart (1972) started out to test, the findings were not conclusive. Yet, from an action training and research perspective, the process itself generated a great amount of change in the organization. The agitation for, and support of, the devolutionary movement was so strong that events in the State Fund had passed the original experiment before it had a chance to run its course. Consequently, much of Kirkhart's research data was transient, reflecting many changes in the procedures, assignments, and organizational structure. Clearly, such changes are discouraging to people conducting traditional social science research but very rewarding from the standpoint of methodology for effecting organizational change.

"As I saw Kirkhart's contribution to the State Fund," Gardner observed, "it was one of providing a great amount of theoretical education for State Fund managers. In order to follow some of his reporting, it was necessary for State Fund managers to 'stretch' themselves intellectually. Kirkhart was well liked and highly respected by State Fund managers. Given their degree of trust for him, he was able to lead them through the dismal swamp of abstract organization theory. This was not an intended consequence of his intervention. As a teacher, he was acting in response to the interest of State Fund managers. In the end, the State Fund adopted the decentralized district office organization. Through the democratic effects of the manager councils and program advisory committee the State Fund proceeded to refine and develop it."

The introduction and initiation of the devolution experiment were characterized by a number of problems related to resistance of change and to dynamic and changing organizational issues and personnel. The top executives, though sometimes skeptical of the change process and its results, were quite supportive of change efforts. Research to test the effects of devolution was initiated, but its consequence was limited by the impact of organizational changes.

SUMMARY

Analysis of test results is where the AT&R research meets the first decision for action. On one hand successful experiments can result in implemented change. On the other hand, the results can often be organizationally divisive. The decision makers' mettle is tested. Once we move from the organizational speculation about what is possible to organizational fact of what we can do, new "political" forces may enter the decision's force field equation. However, if there is sufficient participation by the people who are going to have to implement the change, there is the opportunity for the organization leaders to allow those people to be able to say, "We did it ourselves" (Senge, 1990).

However, the main purpose of the evaluation of test results is to provide guidance and tactical rationale in developing the programs for change in the next AT&R stage 9, program design. These, of course, become the programs for changing the organization that will be implemented and evaluated in the subsequent stages of the action phase of AT&R.

NOTE

1. *Budget savings* is a term that reflects potential public benefit savings through the reduction of costs. Because public organizations cannot refer to profit and loss in any meaningful way, other terms are used for decision-making criteria. See discussion of *benefit savings* for Public Management Information Systems (PMIS) by Bozeman and Straussman (1990, pp. 121–134).

CHAPTER 12

AT&R STAGE 9:
PROGRAM DESIGN

MENU FOR AT&R STAGE 9: PROGRAM DESIGN

Action   *Designing the continuing program for change follows the analysis of the experiment. The major attempt of the intervenor during this program design stage is to keep the notion before the client group that its members are developing a changing program. The design of the program should reflect this changing process.*

Consideration of elements in the force field and collection of new and more sophisticated data are also factors to be incorporated in program design. New investigations may be conducted by task forces or individual experts provided that their data are collected at the request of the client group and that the results are shared with them. In this AT&R model it is expected that the final changing program design will reflect the experience of the experimental program as well as incorporate new dimensions that result from the later and more detailed task group and individual studies (Gardner, 1974).

Training   *Program–project design and management methods.*

Research   *The people involved in the change arrange the action options into a sequence of steps devised to implement the revised working prototype into a permanent change in the organization and its operations. This action plan includes acquiring the resources and training required to make the change a success.*

Outcome   *The program design and its plan of action for implementation and evaluation.*

CHANGE IN REVIEW

The previous AT&R stages can be expected to provide the "stuff" to design, implement, and evaluate the program of changing. In addition, there are many effective methods for designing, implementing, and evaluating programs and projects. Therefore, we will focus on the unique aspects of using AT&R to make the transition. In the end, the people that are tasked to design, implement, operate, and evaluate the program of change will go through a miniversion of the entire AT&R process. However, they will have the benefit of the action research already completed.

For example, the program's outcome goal for changing can be teased out of the research results of the contract setting, aspirations, and analysis of the experiment stages. Some of the people that will now be responsible for the successes of the program, it is hoped, were involved in those stages. In any case, their review can be expected to be more critical from a practical point of view—namely, these are the people who are going to have to do it. Therefore, their views will breathe more reality into the research.

This review process can be expected to rewrite the contract, sharpen the change goals, and add to the action options available to effect the changing agreed on. Clearly, it is a major transition from the various research results and review to the actual design for changing. The first question is a bootstrap issue of designing the best way to organize people to do it. Should a task force be appointed, should it be assigned to a particular department or work unit? Should an outside practitioner–consultant be involved?

There is no prescribable format to answer these questions. Any and all of the alternatives are advisable depending on the situation. For example, when the State Fund designed a program for changing the entire organization from a bureaucratic public agency to an entrepreneurial public enterprise, the program design was complex, involved everyone to some degree, and required a massive reeducation effort to support it. On the other hand, the design for a program to research and test innovative fire and rescue equipment and methods was designed to eliminate itself in a few years. The design was to provide the testing methodology, network with outside research resources, and have the firefighters run the program for themselves. The program design for changing the information technology resource development at the East Coast county relied heavily on using the pilot projects to facilitate the various county agencies' efforts to design, implement, and evaluate specific aspects of the program for changing.

The actual design is an excellent place to begin the coming together of those people who will be involved and have a role in the program's success. Like engineering drawings, designs can be more easily changed than the installed results. The design needs to take into account the elements and decision dimensions of the program. For example, what values must change and how to change them to achieve the selected new outcomes? What new behaviors do we need to acquire and how will we acquire them? What work processes will change and how will we learn to perform them well? Most important, who will have to change in all these considerations? And when? Answering all these questions is the function of the program design.

In addition, once all of these questions are worked out and put in some credible order in the organization involved, a plan of action steps is needed to implement the program and to evaluate it after it is installed and operated for some time. Clearly, these are the most crucial AT&R transition stages. This is where the tire hits the road and where most opponents of the change have staked their hopes that it will all just go away.

ACTION RESEARCH INSTITUTE FOR THE FIRE AND RESCUE DEPARTMENT

The planning and implementation of an ongoing program to research ways for the fire and rescue department to continually change and improve its service involved several tracks for changing. These were process, decision-making, organization, training, and performance tracks.

"I want it to be okay to be innovative around here," the fire chief said. "But I don't want this thing to run wild, either. I want you to include senior staff in the process."

From this design-track point of view, the program first needed a process by which new methods and equipment could be identified, tested, and evaluated by the department in a scientific and safe manner. Second, the program design needed a decision-making structure that would fit with the complex decision-making process of the department from the fire chief's senior staff, through the appropriate assistant chiefs' sections, through the battalion chiefs and fire station captains, and ultimately to the firefighters themselves. Third, the program design needed to fit into the department's organization. It is here that people are assigned to research and test, write budgets, and so on. Fourth, the program design needed to include a training function that would incorporate the research and testing activities and the new methods and the use of new equipment into the rigorous training program for firefighters. Fifth, the program design needed to include a practical way to ensure the professional firefighters' performance of the new methods and equipment that are adopted.

Each of these tracks addresses the organization for changing elements or decision dimensions. The tracks were merely a design convenience, because they are not really separate. For example, the research and testing process resides within the organization. It is decided by many parts of the department and must provide training opportunities for the use of innovations, once funded, added to the organization's procedures for fire fighting in the field.

In this case, the fire and rescue department's program to research and test innovative fire and rescue methods and equipment was designed as an informal consortium or action research institute along the AT&R method model. The consortium was a network of mutual participation entities that included the county's fire and rescue department along with the local universities, government research organizations such as the federal government agencies, the vendors of fire and rescue equipment, as well as other fire and rescue departments. The mutual interest centered around research. The universities that had various fire prevention research projects became interested. Federal agencies had many research projects that required realistic fire situations to test their standards. They also had sophisticated measuring instruments and devices for researching burning materials. The vendors had new fire and rescue equipment they needed to test. Their problem was a lack of professional firefighters to test their innovative equipment in real situations. In many cases, the vendors would invent a new tool or develop new equipment, test it themselves, and then advertise it in professional fire and rescue journals. The fire and rescue departments would then procure examples and test them for themselves. Often, both the firefighters and the vendors would find that many features of the new equipment looked good on paper but in practice had many drawbacks. However, because the equipment was already in production, it was sometimes not feasible to change it. The idea of the consortium was for the firefighters to be able to participate in the testing of new equipment in order to improve the equipment before it was ever put into production.

The county's fire and rescue department was one of the best in the country; the participation of the firefighters in research guaranteed exacting application of tests in real-life situations. Also, the department was awarded houses and buildings destined for demolition for firefighter training purposes. They would set the buildings ablaze to test their fire fighting methods and to train the firefighters in various evolutions of fire fighting under these realistic burn sessions. Participating in the early stages of innovative equipment development was a form of enlightened self-interest. After all, in the end the participants were the primary beneficiaries of improved fire-fighting equipment. By the same token, they were the prime sufferers when they used less safe or less effective equipment. To ensure their participation, the practitioner made it a rule that only uniformed employees could test the new equipment. The practitioner's role was to set up the process, design the tests, and write up the reports from the firefighters' notes, reactions, measured results, and survey feedback forms.

ACTION RESEARCH INSTITUTE APPROACH

By networking between the academics, vendors, and fire departments, an informal action research institute was formed. Within this
consortium alliance, the fire and rescue department set up a version
of the AT&R method as a process to identify, prioritize, test, and
evaluate innovative fire and rescue equipment and methods. This
process was along the following outline:

1. Initial analysis (AT&R stages 1 through 3): The consortium
constantly senses the environment for issues in the fire and rescue
situations. This step involves finding new equipment, describing it,
and identifying what is innovative about it. This step is important
because it provides a stage at which one never has to say "no." All
ideas, no matter how trivial and obscure, have to be accepted and
researched through this first step. The firefighters' innovations committee reviews suggestions for innovations to test from anywhere in
the consortium, which includes the department's firefighters themselves. The purpose of the initial analysis is to determine whether the
innovation had sufficient potential value for the department to spend
any further research and testing resources on it. Their recommendations are then presented to senior staff.

2. Acceptance tests (AT&R stages 4 through 6): This step involves examining the innovative equipment and checking to see if it
is what it says it is. This test includes trying out the various functions,
weighing it, measuring it, and generally examining it. This examination process usually involves the apparatus section of the fire and
rescue department, using typical acceptance testing guidelines. The
results of this examination are written up with recommendations
regarding further testing. The report is evaluated by the innovation
committee. If they recommend continuing, they draw up a plan for
a controlled test. Their recommendations are presented to the senior
staff.

3. Controlled test (AT&R stages 7 through 8): If senior staff
approves, the equipment is then tested in a scientifically controlled
experiment to verify its innovative features and to ensure that the
equipment does not pose a hazard to firefighters. This testing is done

by the training academy using experienced firefighters. During this stage, procedures are developed for use of the equipment in the field. The results of the controlled test are reported with recommendations. The report is evaluated by the innovation committee. Again, if they recommend further research, they draw up a detailed plan for field testing. Their recommendations are presented to senior staff.

4. Field tests (continuation of AT&R stages 7 through 8): Finally, if the senior staff approves, the equipment and procedures are assigned to particular fire stations to test the use of the equipment in actual fire and rescue incidents to see and record how the equipment can improve service delivery. The firefighters report on their findings and evaluations. A final report and recommendations are compiled from all of the testing. The results are evaluated by the innovation committee. If they recommend adopting the innovation, they draw up a detailed implementation plan that includes new and revised procedures for training and use in the field. Their recommendations are presented to the senior staff for approval to implement.

5. Implementation (AT&R stages 9 through 12): If the senior staff approves recommendations to implement the innovation, it is given to the appropriate units for implementation. This would include development of training for the innovative equipment or practice, updating the procedures, periodic reevaluation, and including it in the budget cycle process. Once the program design was approved by the fire chief and his senior staff, implementation of the program was very incremental. For example, the practitioner took the fire chief's pet project, the fog nozzle, through the process. Once the various sections of the department saw how it worked they became very anxious to control their piece of it. The original program design did not include the firefighters' innovation committee. This idea came from the people in the department itself and was included in the program design. This committee included representative firefighters elected from various stations, a training officer from the academy, a fire station captain, and a battalion chief. The practitioner and the deputy fire chief of the section for equipment, training, and communications were ex-officio members of the committee.

Program implementation proceeded as more and more projects for research and testing were considered. For example, the traditional manila ropes were replaced by modern mountain climbing gear for dealing with high-rise buildings. A firefighter expert in mountain climbing put together a training program and tested the use of the gear. His project also included formalizing the procedures in a training program at the academy and was made part of the department's procedures. The protective "turnout gear" that firefighters use was replaced by the new gear incorporating the latest fire protection materials developed by NASA. Personal safety alarms that go off whenever the wearer stops moving were added to lead rescuers to fallen firefighters. The evaluation process was, of course, built into the process at every step. Before long, the idea of innovation was embedded into the department's culture by the firefighters themselves. Innovation became a department norm.

FROM THE STATE FUND JOURNALS
OF NEELY GARDNER: PROGRAM DESIGN

Setting up the program of organization devolution at the State Fund was problematical. The organization was already decentralized into several district offices across the state. The devolution program involved setting up the offices as semi-autonomous organizations that could contract with staff departments for support services.

In the spring of the third year of the pilot experiment, the division chief group, at the president's insistence, reluctantly decided to eliminate the positions of division chief and regional manager and to change the positions of district office and home office manager to program manager. The former division chiefs became vice presidents, to serve on the executive committee, and became responsible for achieving the objectives of the office of the president. This meant that vice presidents would be concerned with policy and major programs with no responsibility for day-to-day operation of any segment of the organization. They would have no line authority whatsoever.

The new executive committee decided to use the concept of the plural executive, whereby responsibility would be shared for overall administrative management. Staff assistants to the executive committee were to be the actuary and assistant vice presidents (previously the regional managers), until such time as the assistant vice presidents could be placed in other positions. The announcement stated that a plural executive sharing responsibility for State Fund management and the accomplishment of the objectives of the office of the president requires an understanding of that office and the roles within it.

The executive committee became the core of the office of president. It was organized to support a participative style of management and use management by objectives, based on the effective use of outcome program budgets. Each vice president was assigned a specific organizational area of management concern. To further clarify the nature of the plural executive, the document went on to state that the executive committee is responsible for the achievement of the objectives of the office of president. No single member of the executive committee was to assume line command over any normal State Fund operation.

PURPOSE OF THE EXECUTIVE COMMITTEE

As members of the executive committee, the powers and responsibilities of the vice presidents included

1. Representing the State Fund in its social environment
2. Conducting the enterprise-wide planning process
3. Setting policy and guidelines
4. Approving and evaluating outcome program plans and budgets presented by district and program managers
5. Appointing, developing, and evaluating managers
6. Setting the dividend (with the board of directors)

To fulfill these responsibilities, the committee was to develop clearly enunciated State Fund plans and objectives supported by written management policy. It would develop an information and review process that measured State Fund performance in relationship to program objectives, resources used, and outcomes achieved in terms of impact on the State Fund's policyholder customers. The executive committee would also provide appropriate corrective action when required. Other functions were to provide responsive State Fund representation in the political arena and to communicate effectively with the board of directors regarding internal and external factors affecting the State Fund plans and operations. Finally, the committee considered it a duty to provide for the fiscal security and stability of State Fund operations and to operate as an effective management group.

PART VERSUS WHOLE THINKING

The vice presidents had talked about directing their major attention to policy and planning matters. However, when the final decision was made to move toward the plural executive format, individuals could not resist a feeling of helplessness in dealing with assigned areas of oversight. These responsibilities were (1) operations (the primary insurance business of the State Fund), (2) organization development, (3) planning, (4) public relations, and (5) fiscal resources.

EXECUTIVE OVERSIGHT IN A DEVOLVED ORGANIZATION

The problem of oversight was to plague the State Fund for the next 3 years. The vice presidents found it very difficult at times not to behave like line managers. People in the district and home office management positions also tended to try to entice vice presidents into line decision making. It is important to understand that these vice presidents had made their way to the top under a very competitive win–lose system and had become vice presidents in part because of their demonstrated abilities to outperform and outmaneuver others. As guardians of a division within the State Fund, vice presidents found it difficult to assume a global view of the organization and fought for what appeared to be best for their own division.

"This point of view was not necessarily evil," Gardner observed, "Nor can it be termed unusual. In my experience, every organization that has created an executive committee composed of line managers and expected them to provide an overview for the organization has had the same results. Executive committee members did decide, with a good deal of persuasion by the president, I suspect, to go ahead with the program on the outcome program budget. In retrospect, I think that tying the budget to the rest of the devolutionary activities was one of the most critical parts of making the experiment successful.

"I am convinced that the only chance of effecting the type of local autonomy the State Fund tried to achieve was to delegate responsibility and authority for resources to the operating manager. The same holds true in the relationship between the line managers and the people who must actually develop and deliver the State Fund's services to its policyholder customers."

COUNCILS AS COORDINATIVE MECHANISMS

With these major changes, it was necessary for the State Fund to devise some coordinating mechanisms to promote the operation of a nonhierarchical, participatory organization. The mechanisms included two councils and an outcome program budgeting process.

With the intervening hierarchy gone, the executive committee believed there would be an obvious need for coordination and communication. Therefore, in conceptualizing its organization, keeping in mind the consent model, the State Fund decided to experiment with two group communication devices, a district managers' council and a program advisory council.

COPING WITH CHANGE

"At this time," Gardner pointed out, "I was meeting with the executive committee as often as my schedule permitted. I did try to assist them in observing their own interaction process. They were not averse to process observation; but, as far as I could tell, they simply nodded their heads and said, 'Yes, as we look at the process, this is what's happening. You are quite right!' However, this acknowledgment did not seem to bring about any correction in the group effectiveness."

It seemed clear to Gardner that the older members of the executive committee were not comfortable in their new roles. The change had divested them of staff who had been available to them when they were division chiefs. There were no stacked in-baskets to give them a sense of security and accomplishment. After all the years of decrying the lack of scanning time and hours to spend on policy formulation, they were faced with unfilled blocks of time. The ambiguity was overwhelming. Restructuring of the hierarchy had its effect on a number of the organizational actors, but the role change of executive committee members appeared to Gardner as the most traumatic.

The committee did undertake one chore that to them was understandable and comforting. This was reviewing program statements prepared in district offices and negotiating with district managers on the distribution of resources in return for the expectation of service rendered. Although the first year program statements were not done very well, the process provided an opportunity for committee members to engage district managers in a meaningful transaction. The contact between committee and district turned out to be valuable to all parties. Still, one of the vice presidents was concerned. He made a visit to Gardner to discuss his fears. If the executive committee could not decide, could not plan, and could not develop policy direction, who could? In his view the organization was soon to be in "big" trouble. The committee was foundering. He thought maybe a team-building session would help. Gardner agreed to join him in exploring the idea with the executive committee.

ACTION TRAINING

The committee agreed to the team-building session, and it was scheduled that spring. A couple of issues were worked quite heavily during this session. One was the issue of decision making.

"My interventions were intended to provide vehicles for the members to address and resolve actual pressing issues that were before the executive group," Gardner explained. "What actually happened was that the group engaged in a great deal of posturing. They were 'walking on and off the stage,' in one concerned vice president's words. I could not see much substance that came from this particular effort. On the other hand, communications improved. There was very frank discussion, and participants made considerable progress toward leveling with each other."

The second major issue involved the functioning of the executive committee itself. The group was able to make a major decision together that was to have considerable consequences. The group decided that on the return home members would devote an increased amount of time to the business of the executive committee and less time to oversight responsibilities. The executive committee decided to meet together each morning at the start of the working day for as long as necessary. They would congregate once more in late afternoon. This was the major accomplishment of the first meeting.

The executive vice president raised another issue at the session. He declared that the State Fund needed to provide a policy framework within which State Fund employees could operate. The executive vice president could not get the rest of the group to understand what was meant by policy, nor could he get the endorsement of anyone to back him up in the direction the State Fund should go. There was some abrasiveness between the executive vice president and the president at this point.

Internal communication of committee members with one another was another problem that emerged. The executive committee was having, and would continue to have, difficulties communicating with home and district offices. How did the plural executive communicate and the rest of the organization's employees communicate to the committee? In point of fact, district managers and others were contacting "their favorite vice president" whenever they had a problem— in other words, they would get in touch with the person to whom they related well, a person they thought would carry their case to the executive committee. A major problem with the executive committee was that it became "faceless" and on some occasions was referred to as the "presidium."

PERSONNEL CHANGES

Over the years, the old division chiefs group, now vice presidents, retired. Program managers from district offices and staff departments were promoted to fill these slots. The president, having seen his changing organization become a reality, waited for the propitious moment to retire. *Propitious,* in this case, meant making sure that the executive vice president, rather than someone outside the State Fund, would succeed him as president.

The State Fund president is, for a public official, very highly paid. He is appointed by a board of directors who are, in turn, appointed by the governor. Tradition has been that the job must be filled on merit, but there is no guarantee that at any time a political appointment will not be made. The president watched his votes on the board of directors with great care and caution. When the votes were assured, he retired and the executive vice president became president.

"Everyone, including me," Gardner confessed, "watched the process of succession with fascination. The new president captivated the managers' council and reassured the program advisory council. He declared his intention to move forward along the changing, participatory organizational path set out by his predecessor."

SUMMARY

The design of the programs for changing the organization focuses the effort for changing on the people who will be most affected by the change. There may be a "grand plan" that coordinates all of the individual programs for change, but it is the people doing the work who will provide the reality check for the individual programs. In this stage the need for communication among all organizational units involved is paramount to a coordinated success. These programs for change need to be closely linked to the organization's budget and management information systems in order to properly support them and to make necessary midcourse corrections during the next AT&R stage 10, implementation.

CHAPTER 13

AT&R STAGE 10:
IMPLEMENTATION

MENU FOR AT&R STAGE 10: IMPLEMENTATION

Action   *There are many ways to introduce and implement a pro-*
          gram. By this stage in the AT&R approach, however, it is
          hoped that those affected know about and have partici-
          pated in the decision to implement the change action. This
          means that the AT&R process has gone beyond the execu-
          tive group or task force and that the participation within
          the organization has been broad. There is considerable
          merit in using the process known as the risk approach in
          disseminating information concerning change actions. In
          this process, the affected persons are brought together and
          invited to contribute (1) critical comments and (2) sugges-
          tions for overcoming problems suggested. It is called a risk
          approach because frequently changes are called for that are
          necessary or expedient and that ask for redesign or even
          abandonment of the proposed program. The risk process
          permits people to deal with their anxieties and to get these
          anxieties out in the open where they can be appropriately
          processed (Maier & Frederick, 1952). It is useful to take

*note in a formal or ministerial way of the adoption of the
program and of the launching of its implementation. If the
process has gone as planned, the change action has considerable chance for success. Unfortunately, there is probably
no way to foresee all of the consequences of implementation (Gardner, 1974).*

Training   *Participative management, work group dynamics, project
management, and research methodology.*

Research   *Implement the action steps of the project plan, constantly
cycling back to previous steps with the new knowledge
learned from the current step. Document the process as
you go along. One major research obligation for AT&R
projects is to add to the body of knowledge about changing
organizations. Each new action step is an opportunity for
new knowledge. The first to benefit from this new knowledge should be the project participants themselves. Therefore, it is paramount to maintain this iterative approach
in each step.*

Outcome   *A change in the organization and its work processes.*

SYSTEMIC IMPLEMENTATION OF CHANGE

Implementing a program for changing organizations is by definition
a systemic program that affects the whole as well as the parts. Organizations are groups of people working together to achieve a common
outcome. Purposefully instigating change in an organization requires
consideration of all of the aspects of work—namely, the people involved, what they can and must do in order to achieve their desired
outcomes. Weber (1946) changed the organization's structure and
decision-making process to focus on the economy of the outcome.
Taylor (1911) and the management scientists changed the work process and decision making of how people are to behave for efficient
work processes. Lewin (1947) and the applied behavioral scientists

changed the way people learned and decided how to perform their work tasks. Clearly, all of these approaches are involved in implementing a program for changing organizations.

Common reasoning would assume that a successful program for changing organizations would feature a harmonious balance among all three approaches. History has shown us that such a harmonious balance is an ideal not often achieved. However, as we saw in the reconnaissance stage of the action training and research method, at the heart of change are issues that generate more conflict than harmony. The magic wand, so called, is to be able to guide the conflict into its most creative mode in win–win outcomes.

Science and our capitalist economy have put us into an ever-increasing pace of change—to the point where change has become the chief engine of our postmodern culture. Our culture has cast us all as change agents. We have to constantly reinvent ourselves, not only at work, but in our multimedia homes as well. In the renaissance age, with the birth of modern science, reinventing one's self was a lifetime project. Now, we have to do it between Super Bowls.

In *The Witch Doctors* (1996), authors Micklethwait and Wooldridge sketch the negative effects of management trying to create changing organizations or using the management flavor of the month method to disguise Weberian methods to inflict draconian change. It is not always a pretty sight. Management gets the idea that it owns the organization and that the employees are merely resources for their command. Members of management often forget that they are organization employees too.

People are not resources but partners in work. Human resources are the skills, knowledge, and abilities of people. Human resources are the resources that individuals bring to the work organization. Employees can work in an organization and still withdraw some or all of their human resources. Consent of the governed in this context means that employees agree to work together for an agreed-on share of the outcome. Change in organizations upsets that agreement and gives cause for employees, whether they are line employees or management employees, to withhold their human resources from the organization until a new agreement is made. This upsetting change may come from outside the organization or it may come, as is the case for changing organizations, from within.

What the action training and research method tries to do is to provide people, no matter where they are in the organization, a guide through the organizational change process. AT&R can be used by individual employees as workers, by management in making changes in the organization to meet new customer or citizen demands, or by professional practitioners who can help others to turn the conflicts emerging from the issues in their environment into creative win–win outcomes.

NATIONAL PERFORMANCE REVIEW: IMPLEMENTING A CHANGE PROGRAM IN GOVERNMENT

The story in the previous AT&R program design stage not only tells about the design of the program to research and test innovative fire equipment and methods, it also tells about how the program was implemented and how it changed the culture of the department to make innovation a more salient feature of the culture. For this stage we will tell a story about implementing another program on a somewhat larger scale—namely, changing the entire executive branch of the U.S. government organization. This program is being implemented by Vice President Al Gore and the National Performance Review. We do not mean to imply in any way that the National Performance Review was an AT&R program. However, an AT&R practitioner was associated in various marginal ways to certain aspects of its inception and implementation along the way. In addition, the story of a project implemented in the National Performance Review, which we will tell, was chaired and staffed with several people familiar with the principles of AT&R, especially the entrepreneurial and outcome resource allocation concepts of Frank Sherwood and Neely Gardner.

There has been plenty of press as well as books and articles written about this large project to reinvent the government. In a sense, the National Performance Review is the implementation of the design for changing the government initiated first during the Economic Summit of the Clinton–Gore Presidential Transition Team, and later spearheaded by Vice President Gore.

It is not within the scope of this book to evaluate the complete National Performance Review program's results in changing the entire executive branch of the U.S. government organization. However, one National Performance Review program for changing government in which an AT&R practitioner was asked to participate was a "Major Recommendation Affecting Governmental Systems: FM06: 'Franchise' Internal Services; The President's Management Council should encourage agencies to purchase common administrative services, such as payroll, computer support, or procurement, competitively from other federal agencies that may be more responsive or offer better prices" (Gore, 1993, pp. 57, 58, 162).

Several of the members of the franchise internal services' planning and work group were familiar with Neely Gardner and Frank Sherwood's entrepreneurial approach to changing organizations. Although the direct influence of these approaches to the reinventing effort may have been marginal, the franchising services program serves as an excellent example of program implementation along the lines of the AT&R method.

Program implementation of such a major change in federal government systems can be expected to include many obstacles to change. For example, implementing franchising internal support services such as personnel, finance, budget, and automated data systems would require an executive order from the president, a change in the law passed by both the House of Representatives and the Senate, approval and support from the Office of Management and Budget, as well as voluntary participation by cabinet-level departments and risk taking on the part of federal agencies to engage in entrepreneurial service delivery efforts that were competitive and whose funding depended solely on the reimbursable funds they earned from other agencies using their services. These are formidable obstacles indeed.

The program implementation can be described in ten basic steps:

1. Conceptualization and reconnaissance of current needs and examples in practice
2. Identification of issues and obstacles

3. OMB, presidential, and congressional approval for pilot agencies for a 5-year experiment
4. Development of prototype with how-to handbook
5. Initial training workshops to organize agencies with potential interest in franchising
6. Revision of budgeting, finance, and personnel (full-time employees) rules for franchises
7. Solicitation, review, selection, and training of pilot agencies
8. First national conference with pilot agencies to assume future leadership role; publication of conference papers for second national conference
9. Second national training conference organized by a user group of agencies interested in franchising internal government services
10. Organization of training–conferences for regional conferences that includes state and local government agencies

It is not difficult to see how the franchise services' implementation program track adhered closely to many of the AT&R stages.

The first step for implementation of this program included refining the concept into a practical design of an entrepreneurial franchising program for federal agencies. At the same time it called for a step-by-step implementation plan for changing government systems that would end up with various federal agencies implementing their own franchising programs.

The NPR's implementation team for the franchising recommendation was established in December of 1992 as the Franchise Services Planning Committee (later the Franchise Working Group). (A more detailed history of this group was included as chapter 2 of Serlin & Bruce, 1996.) The committee was headed by Michael Serlin. Before being assigned to the National Performance Review, Serlin was a founder of the Financial Center for Financial Management in the Treasury Department. Serlin brought together the managers of many of the entrepreneurial organizations already mentioned, along with agency financial officers. The group included members from the Treasury Department, Alcohol, Tobacco, and Firearms, NASA, Public Health Service, Office of Management and Budget, General Services Administration, Cooperative Administrative Support Units, Federal Systems Integration and Management, the Navy, an action training and research practitioner from the American Society for Public Administration's Section for Professional and Organization Development, and the National Performance Review.

This implementation group worked closely with the National Performance Review, Office of Management and Budget, and the Chief Financial Officers (CFO) Council to encourage the growth of the franchising movement across government. They identified the major obstacles to the success of franchises in government. They devised strategies and identified the changes in the law and regulations that would level the playing field to help franchises overcome those obstacles. The franchising planning committee designed a basic model for franchise funds, for setting up individual franchises within such a fund, and for operating under the required changes. They also helped shepherd the franchise provisions of H.R. 3400 and S. 2170 through Congress to become part of Title IV of the Government Management Reform Act of 1993 (Public Law No. 103-356, Sec. 403), enacted October 1994.

Once President Clinton signed the act into law, the committee was renamed the Franchise Working Group and is now called the Committee for Entrepreneurial Government. With Serlin's retirement from Treasury, it became co-chaired by Clyde McShan, assistant CFO of the Department of Commerce, and Charles Self, deputy assistant commissioner for information technology at GSA. The franchise group worked closely with congressional staff, OMB officials, and the Chief Financial Officers Council to set up the process by which the six pilot franchise funds would be selected, monitored, and evaluated during the experimental period.

The main implementation strategy was in conformance with the action training and research method in that it combined issue exploration reconnaissance with problem–opportunity identification analysis. It used training of the potential participating agencies in the franchising organization process, and devolved the power of management of franchises to the participating agencies through setting up independent personnel (full-time employees), budgeting, and accounting processes that guaranteed the franchise the management powers to acquire, allocate, and otherwise make their own decisions. The franchise organization is based on the outcome budgeting approach. The franchises had to get their own clients–customers within the federal government. They had to live by the funds their clients transferred to them. Like the State Fund, if they lose their clients–customers, they disappear. No "sunset clause" is needed. They survive by their performance.

The practitioner arranged to have members of the franchise planning group participate in a Gardner symposium at the American Society for Public Administrators national conference in Kansas City in 1994. They presented a series of papers and discussions that later were published in *Entrepreneurial Management in the Public Sector, Franchising Public Services* (Bruce, 1996).

Joe Coffee, a member from Alcohol, Tobacco, and Firearms, led the organization of the first free workshops to attract and inform potential franchise entrepreneurs in the federal agencies. These workshops were designed to get out the news that the entrepreneurial form of franchising internal government services was going to be a reality soon. The workshops also provided information about franchising, the problems and pitfalls, and brief descriptions on how to set up such franchises. Because the franchising group was made up of people who already were operating as de facto franchises, their teaching and sharing of practical how-to information was on a "user" level.

After high attendance to these free workshops, Coffee led the organization of a national conference, underwritten by the Section on Professional and Organization Development of the American Society for Public Administration. The conference was complete with a handbook to set up a franchise for administrative support services (Halachmi & Nichols, 1996). Afterward, the conference was turned over to the attendees. They organized and presented their own workshops and training conference in 1996. The conference concept and tools were set up by the Office of Personnel Management in separate conferences around the country that included state and local governments as well. The initial implementation strategy was to put the NPR franchise group out of business and let the government agencies become their own franchise groups for changing their organizations.

As the franchise movement grows, the overhead cost of government can shrink as quickly as redundant services are minimized. Remaining support services can be not only more efficient, but, because managers of government programs have a choice, those offering the administrative services will be more responsive in both the timeliness and quality of the administrative support service rendered. Lower overhead and better internal support can translate into better program delivery by federal agencies—win–win government in everyone's book. Franchising is a key component to meeting the public's interest in a government that *works better and costs less.*

FROM THE STATE FUND JOURNALS OF
NEELY GARDNER: PROGRAM IMPLEMENTATION

Stage three, identifying problems and opportunities, describes the design of a team training workshop to identify problems and opportunities. The issue that enacted these problems and opportunities was the actual implementation of the devolutionary organization design for the State Fund's program for a changing organization.

"The last time I was at the State Fund," Gardner stated, "I talked to the new president and all the other members of the executive committee. At that time another meeting format had been developed. The staff program managers and district managers (basic activity groups) were going back to meeting separately on alternate meetings. Executive committee members were invited to sit in but not participate directly in proceedings. The president said that a recent district managers' meeting was the best he had yet attended. In general, the managers' council seemed to be serving its originally intended purpose of

1. Giving information to, and receiving it from, its members and the executive committee
2. Giving advice on formulation of new studies and programs and reviewing these studies and programs after formulation and before implementation
3. Reporting on, and receiving reports on, "exceptions" in regard to major policy and operating questions
4. Exchanging information among themselves

In looking at all the evidence available, it can be concluded that the managers' council had contributed to a higher level of coordination than was achieved in the previous hierarchical organization. Although there were still times when counterdependency was quite high, there was growing understanding of organizational and unit goals and an obvious commitment to the achievement of such goals. Although the council and other employees of the State Fund were self-critical, outsiders who have done studies have remarked on the openness of the State Fund organization.

DISTRICT MANAGERS' COUNCIL

District managers were to meet with the executive committee once a month to exchange information and jointly assess program progress based on a feedback system. Feedback was in the form of management information that recorded the success with which district offices moved toward attaining budgeted objectives and their subsequent impact on the policyholder–customer. As initially conceived, the district managers' council provided an opportunity for the executive committee to receive direct input from the district, to discuss possible policy changes, and to communicate the nature and extent of each new program. It was imagined that management information could be disseminated through the development of an automatic feedback system designed to compare actual performance with expected results contained in the program statements from the various district offices. The president expected that the district managers' council would ensure that the chain of communication between home office and field would be kept open and functioning. Rather than feeling remote from the home office, district managers and other employees in the field would communicate their needs and provide home office management with their thinking and advice.

PROGRAM ADVISORY COUNCIL

It was evident to the executive committee that communicating with district managers who in turn would communicate with their subordinates would fundamentally change the locus of power. The committee wanted to avoid power accumulation through communication. They began to seek means of establishing communication with employees below the district manager level. After serious thought, they decided to experiment with a body called the *program advisory council*.

When initiated, the program advisory council included two elected or appointed representatives from each district office and from each staff support department. The only constraints on eligibility were that the district manager was not eligible and that no person might serve as a district office representative for more than 1 year. Beyond the general purpose of face-to-face communication, the program advisory council was to

1. Advise the president concerning proposed new or developing programs
2. Feed back information on the effectiveness of program execution in the field
3. Receive the president's view of developments in the total organization
4. React to any new program proposals that developed from R&D staff projects

It was made clear that the program advisory council was not to be a decision body. At the same time the president assured the council members that their opinions would have a direct bearing on the decisions made in the State Fund. As might have been anticipated, the district managers' council and program advisory council developed in both predictable and unpredictable ways.

OUTCOME PROGRAM BUDGETING[1]

Once power has been redistributed in an organization to enable the employees to perform their work better, it is necessary to consider the control of the organization's resources. It is possible for the resource distribution system to inhibit initiative and creativity and to stifle individuality. Viewing an organization's business as basically a fiscal system is frequently the source of the inhuman use of human beings. There are undoubtedly economic incentives that encourage willing assistance from employees, but there is also no doubt about the negative power that control of the funds gives to an individual. In other words, refusal of funding support is a powerful weapon. This power was designed to reside in the plural executive function of the executive committee, with its power to approve and fund program outcome budgets presented to it by the program managers.

If any one factor could be considered central to the changes that were taking place in the State Fund, the outcome program budgeting approach has to be considered as one of the more important and crucial factors. Coupled with outcomes program budgeting, there needs to be an effective, comprehensive, automated program information system that tracks the outcome program budgets through the productivity cycle that extends from the budget and expected outcome (with criteria and measures) approved by the executive committee, to resources allocated, to resources used in the work processes, to products and services developed, to delivery to the policyholder–customers and their employees, to the ultimate effect of products and services delivered to customers.

CONTRACTING

In theoretical terms the State Fund's fiscal program was an adaptation of the market model stemming from theoretical work done by Frank P. Sherwood, Robert Dahl, and Charles Lindblom (e.g., Dahl & Lindblom, 1953; Sherwood, 1968). If people are to develop economizing behaviors, they must have something to say about the acquisition and dispersal of resources that they use in their own efforts.

It is significant that the South Pasadena experiment, reported by Kirkhart (1969, 1971, 1972), started with a management by objectives approach. It was during the pilot district office negotiations that the term *contract* began to be used. In brief, what occurs in this form of contracting is that the district office says to the executive committee, "If you will give us so much in resources, we, in turn, will provide you so much in product and improvement in our policyholders workers' compensation experience." There will be differences in perception at this point, both about need and the cost. There may be a haggling over amounts or there may be a negotiation around the social desirability of the particular program proposed. This type of contracting occurred, rather painstakingly, in the Kirkhart experiment as the district manager shaped things to permit him to exercise authority similar to that possessed by the president of the State Fund.

It is interesting that in the State Fund managers and members of the executive committee talked about bargaining and developing a "contract," which was in fact the outcomes program budgeting document. The outcomes program budget is similar to a management by objectives strategy, as the term applies to work unit operation. The work unit develops explicitly stated and measurable expected results to use as a basis for the outcomes program budget. At budget time, these work unit programs are submitted by program managers to the executive committee for its consideration. These documents contain

1. A statement of need, why the program was developed
2. Legal authority for the program
3. How it originated, the situation and alternatives considered
4. Broad objectives, how it will support the State Fund's mission and goals
5. Explicit and tangible program results, program objectives, benefits, and measures
6. A work plan and scheme of how it will be accomplished within the State Fund's organization
7. Program resource requirements and costs, with a benefit–cost analysis that includes alternatives

The statement of need and objectives is not imposed; it is developed out of the requirements perceived by employees and managers at the district level. Participating in setting objectives and developing budget requests has given employees at all levels of the State Fund a feeling of being able to influence their own organizational destinies. Bargaining time is an occasion for intimate interaction between the district or staff program manager and the vice presidents, and it is an educational process for all parties involved. It is interesting, too, that in the case of the State Fund, the negotiation is conducted by parties with direct interests and accountability. Systems analysts or budget functionaries are not relied on for recommendations concerning the budgetary proposals during this negotiation process. Both parties to the negotiation have access to technical expertise; and, if there is a disagreement over expected benefits or costs, third-party intervention is possible. In the end, however, those providing technical assistance have no part in making recommendations concerning action. The transaction is ultimately based on managerial judgment.

The State Fund's move to an outcome program budget was preceded by a thoroughgoing training effort. Despite the training, there were considerable problems. The first year's program statements were put together with great travail, time, and effort. They were not particularly good program statements. It took about 3 years to get the system working smoothly, with yearly improvements in the statements.

NEED FOR COMPATIBLE ACCOUNTING AND
MANAGEMENT INFORMATION SYSTEMS

Budgets can be administered humanistically or otherwise. The outcome program budget was designed to operate within the State Fund and to be handled with a sensitive attendance to human values. Employee participation cannot be reduced to a benefit–cost analysis, and policyholder needs cannot be expressed only as *premium written, claims paid,* and *dividends returned.* Anywhere human beings are involved, there are careers, health, and personal well-being to be considered.

As effectively as outcome program budgeting came to work for the State Fund, it did not work nearly as well as it might. There were some in the executive committee and among the district managers who recognized the importance of relating the accounting system to the budgetary process, but that was not fully accomplished. Part of the difficulty is endemic to the insurance business, which is, at the core, an actuarial spreading of risk among a large number of policyholders over a longer period of time. Therefore, it requires a strict financial and risk analysis acumen in its management and organization. However, it was Gardner's impression that the major organizational barrier to establishing the needed information system for outcome program budgeting was the accounting office itself. Those in the accounting office did not seem to believe that a change in the accounting system was necessary. "You sell insurance, pay claims and dividends, and we just keep track of the numbers."

An information system compatible with the accounting system would constitute a reporting base that would provide automatic feedback to district managers on how their programs are doing. This automatic and timely feedback system would enable managers and work units to take any exploitive or corrective action while the opportunity was still there. It also would indicate to all concerned that the outcome program budget was a major State Fund policy statement designed to influence the day-to-day work program in the district offices and therefore requiring that other State Fund systems be compatible. Sensing these needs, the executive committee initiated the development of a new fiscal information management system that included the outcome program budget.

THE STATE FUND'S CORPORATE PLANNING PROCESS

The planning process that began emerging was compatible with the consent, participation, and outcome program budgeting approaches. There had been a growing conviction on the part of State Fund managers in both district and home offices that there was a need to develop an effective planning process. Planning had occurred in several areas in the State Fund. But it was as late as the fifth study year (1971) when the executive committee decided to attempt the development of an overarching plan that could be used as a dynamic instrument for present and future decision making. As a consequence, the members of the executive committee once again "went to school," attending a seminar on corporate planning conducted especially for the State Fund.

On completing the course, the executive committee began to develop a corporate planning process. This was to provide a framework for decision making. The structure was to be participative in its style and required a pervasive involvement on the part of State Fund managers and supervisors. As it evolved, the State Fund's planning process included five different levels of planning: entrepreneurial planning, strategic planning, practical planning, operating or program planning, and, as an overlay to all the other plans, an organization plan.

Entrepreneurial Planning

For several months the executive committee spent an appreciable block of time each week working on the entrepreneurial plan. In this effort, each vice president developed his own world view in a scenario that was contributed for group consideration. All the scenarios were discussed and a central framework developed. This required the testing of assumptions. In keeping with the philosophy of participation and consent, district and home office managers and the program advisory council were brought in from time to time to make their inputs and to help test the assumptions being made by the vice presidents. As the entrepreneurial plan emerged, one of the biggest efforts was to provide for contingency responses as a means of dealing with changes in a shifting environment. The entrepreneurial plan was designed to provide the foundation for the direction and focus of all other planning in the State Fund.

In the sixth study year (1972), the executive committee and staff presented the entrepreneurial plan to the management council and discussed the implementation of an integrated planning process. It should be noted that this was not an announcement out of the blue to home office and district managers. They had previously been made aware of entrepreneurial planning through individual participation by various district and staff program managers and by regular progress reports. At this meeting the overall planning process was laid out in terms of the five phases mentioned previously: entrepreneurial planning, strategic planning, practical planning, outcome program planning, and the organization plan. A network of assignments was created to establish accountability for the various aspects of the planning effort.

Strategic Planning

The first level beyond the entrepreneurial plan concerned strategy. It involved managers from throughout the organization, depending on their competence, availability, and career development interest. The action areas to be covered by strategic planning were (1) marketing, (2) claims, (3) public relations and influence, (4) organizational development, and (5) innovation research and opportunity development. The strategic plans developed in this phase delineated the specific change elements necessary in each strategic action area required for attaining the entrepreneurial plan.

For example, if the entrepreneurial plan specifies a 22% market penetration overall by the end of the 5-year future period, choices must be made among the various market segments or markets in terms of the composition profile of the penetration. This includes examining the present portfolio. It also means engaging in a thorough examination of industries in terms of growth and stability. Specific targets for penetration would then be set. These would be related to State Fund products and the resources as well as underwriting profitability.

The strategic action area of organization development in the State Fund focused on integrating the vast training and employee development effort that would be required. Also included were provisions for new pay arrangements that would grant commissions to salespeople, career development, a management development and selection process, and the creation of an education center.

Practical Planning

Practical planning for change deals with the way in which strategic plans are to be resourced and implemented. Practical plans provided a set of constraints to guide the districts and departments in the formulation of their operating or program plans. Practical planning groups were made up of representatives of districts and home office departments. When practical plans were approved, district offices and staff departments incorporated them into their outcome program planning. For example, the computer systems development plan affected most district offices and staff departments in one way or another.

Organization Plan

As mentioned, the organization plan is an overlay to other organizational learning. It seeks to make sense of all the planning efforts and to integrate them into the entrepreneurial plan. The organization and its operations will be in constant evolution, but the State Fund's plans must always be translated into actions that it must do today. Plans must be viewed in light of what is occurring in the environment that relates to the State Fund program.

The corporate planning effort went forward successfully. There were some serious delays because of problems in developing the computer systems that were integral to many of the other activities. The planning effort in the State Fund was a major effort to maintain the organization's viability by sensing the environment and using its intelligence system to plan and to recycle its planning in a way that would be felt at the district office level.

The executive committee envisioned two support systems as necessary to activate the planning effort. These were (1) the completion of the automated management information system and (2) training.

State Fund Educational Services

As was suggested in the reconnaissance stage, the training component is extremely critical and should be regarded as an important means of securing change. In order to acquire planning capability, the organization needed a training element. The State Fund educational service center was developed to provide specific training and is worthy of consideration in this context.

The center was an outgrowth of a program to advance safety representatives from *shop safety inspectors* to *safety consultants* who could go into a policyholder's organization and help it improve its safety record (and thus reduce costs, pain, and suffering). The vehicle was to be organization development programs aimed at modifying work behavior. Many of the staff members who developed this program began adapting the approach to other State Fund functions, such as claims adjusting, rehabilitation, and sales.

The center also provided a clerical program that was successful. The organization development strategy of the center was based on the notion that it does not pay just to train supervisors and managers. When they return to their work units, they are still managing the same employees, who have not received the training they need to move into new management methods. The entire culture of the work situation depends on new skills, knowledge, and abilities.

In addition, the future State Fund managers and vice presidents were all line employees at the start. The first president began his career at the State Fund as a clerk in the file room. Investment in young professionals and managers is crucial to the State Fund's future. As we have seen, vice presidents were reluctant to change behavior that had brought them to the career success they enjoyed. Even if they did change, they tended to retire soon after.

The education service center designed and implemented a multi-week professional sequence that brought together the behavioral sciences and managerial technology to prepare State Fund managers as trainers of their staffs. The managers and their employees will all become "trainers of trainers."

However, in some ways Gardner did not agree that this approach was satisfying the State Fund's dream of a center that develops a full and well-rounded insurance person in sales, claims, safety, and underwriting methods, functions, and practices. Many of the vice presidents had this more operational role in mind for a training center.

Another way that the center was helpful in the action training area was to put on a session in which a representative group looked at the work being done by the State Fund R&D project teams. This certainly assisted in furthering the planning effort of the State Fund and brought together managers from the home office and the field in a constructive team effort.

SUMMARY

Program implementation is the key action stage of AT&R. However, organizational change has been occurring all through the previous AT&R stages. In terms of Lewin's reeducation, the gaining of new knowledge and values are key elements of developmental change. Program implementation now engages the third area for change, new physical actions in terms of changing the work processes. This area of change is accomplished in this program implementation stage.

Equally important to new physical experience is the evaluation of it to see if we can accept it as a permanent change. Certain criteria of performance must be identified at the outset and monitored during the implementation in order to make this critical evaluation in the next AT&R stage, program evaluation.

NOTE

1. The term *outcome program budget* is used to avoid confusing it with program planning and budgeting system (PPBS). Although the outcomes budget is programmatic in nature, it differs dramatically from the PPBS model in that it focuses on the impact that the efforts have on the customer's situation. In an insurance industry this can be measured not only by the amount of premium written and sales retention (sales) and the quality of the "business" (underwriting), but by actual experience that the policyholders and their employees have in avoiding accidents (safety) and reducing the severity of those that do happen (claims), how well the injured employees are returned to their normal work status (rehabilitation), and how equitable to the policyholder and their employees this service is rendered (legal). To the degree that the State Fund can attain and balance this insurance service quality better than other insurance carriers, it can return the surplus to the policyholder (dividend) and fulfill its social mission to set the industry standards in all of these workers' compensation insurance functions.

CHAPTER 14

AT&R STAGE 11:
PROGRAM EVALUATION

Action   *Feedback implies some sort of evaluation. Opportunity
         exists to enrich the learning and to increase the effective-
         ness of operations when feedback occurs during and after
         each AT&R stage. In using this AT&R model we suggest
         that a constant and automatic feedback system be used
         (when this can be done) to provide for readjustments as
         the change action operates. But even with an automatic
         feedback system, there probably needs to be an agreed-on
         evaluation date, at which time the change action, to date,
         is seriously and completely reviewed.*

         *There are a number of arguments that favor this iterative
         wrap-up type of action. First, the idea of a changing orga-
         nization suggests that every move is tentative, evolving,
         and sensitive to new inputs and perceptions. Drawing a
         psychological contract to review and renew the program
         at a specific point in time has the possibility, at least, of
         encouraging recycling. Second, an evaluation and review
         that the client–actors have set for a specific time will tend
         to influence timely accomplishment of stated aspirations*

239

*and outcomes expected from the change action. Third is
the argument that in the present environment no one can
be completely certain of the effects of the interaction
between the change undertaken and the field within which
it takes place. Prudence indicates a constant wariness in
this regard. Fourth, a sense of involvement as well as the
degree of learning that occurs among the client–actors is
enhanced by re-involvement in consideration of purpose,
process, and tasks (Gardner, 1974).*

Training   *Program evaluation, constructive critique, documenta-
tion, survey, and feedback.*

Research   *Construct a list of criteria from the previous stages that
best represents the critical factors of the intended change.
Gather key participants together as a group to evaluate the
results per the card exercise instrument. From the results
of this analysis construct a survey–feedback instrument for
the rest of the organization to evaluate. Identify key
success and problem areas. Conduct further AT&R processes to exploit the successes and remedy the problems if
useful.*

Outcome   *Plan for institutionalizing the change, for modifying its
weakness, and for extending its benefits to other aspects
of the organization.*

THE LEARNING ORGANIZATION

In evaluating the programs implemented to develop a changing organization the final organizational learning takes place. This evaluation needs to revisit all of the previous stages in order to define the
criteria of learning. If all of the programs or projects for change were
mere "cherry picking," gathering the "low-hanging fruit" so popular
in most organization change efforts, then little organizational learning will have taken place. These kinds of projects, although they may
have their own intrinsic value, do not add significantly to organizational

learning. In the main, they are trivial, window dressing projects that help to avoid the organizational learning required to establish a changing organization.

It is not uncommon for organizations to take the easy route first, because the members are learning the process. It is only by honest evaluation against all of the criteria developed in the previous stages that the organization can face the daunting task of changing itself into an open, dynamic organization that does not rely on structure to anchor itself to the status quo. At some point the very process of changing needs to become institutionalized, as it were, in the knowledge, values, and practices of the organization. This program evaluation stage provides for that institutionalization to take place.

EXAMPLE IN PRACTICE: THE PROGRAM TO RESEARCH AND TEST INNOVATIVE FIRE AND RESCUE EQUIPMENT

Beginning with value analysis in the early stages and through the evaluation of issues, problems, opportunities, aspiration goals for changing, experiments, and now programs, evaluation is a constant throughout the AT&R method. In a similar fashion, the criteria for evaluating change along the various stages of transition are gleaned from the value analysis, from key descriptors of desired outcomes, and from the principles of AT&R.

It is the evaluation process that prompts people in an organization to keep the organization in an agreeable balance between the elements of the work, as well as maintaining a balance between the decisions regarding desired outcomes, appropriate behavior, and coordinated performance to achieve the agreed-on outcomes. Evaluation is an opportunity to bring the principal stakeholders into a dialog to reconfirm, to adjust, and to redirect the program to be instilled into the fabric of the organization.

For example, at the retirement of the county executive officer, the chair of the board of supervisors asked the fire chief, "Well now, Chief, how's the program for researching fire and rescue equipment and methods going?"

"In the past 3 years," he answered, "we've changed our ropes, our protective gear, our Jaws of Life, automated our dispatch system,

rewritten our procedures for using fog nozzles, and many other innovations. You remember the fire at the concert hall?"

"I remember getting a number of calls from my constituents on
that one, yes," she replied. "You were pretty lucky to find the source
before the whole place burned down."

"We found it because of our thermal camera," the fire chief
explained.

"Thermal camera?" she asked. "What's that like?"

"It makes images from heat instead of light. In a totally dark
smoke-filled room, it can play back TV-like images of people or any
other heat source in the room. We aimed it at the wall in the concert
hall where all the electrical wiring went and were able to trace the
heat to a faulty fuse box. Bingo! We opened the wall and the fire was
suppressed in minutes."

"And how are the firefighters taking all this new stuff?" she asked.
"They're a pretty conservative bunch, I hear."

"Conservative, you bet! So conservative that they have taken over
the program and most of the innovation is coming from them."

"Why is that?"

"The training academy," he answered. "You know how much we
rely on training for every possible eventuality in an emergency. When
we go into an emergency situation, there is no time for wondering
what to do. It all has to have been practiced a thousand times before.
New things have to be worked out in exact procedures and practiced
so everyone knows what's happening. If there's going to be innovation in the fire station, firefighters not only want to learn about the
new methods or equipment, they want to be in on it to make sure
that it is all worked out in training and evolutions before anybody
tries it in a real emergency situation."

"Evolution? What is that, Chief?" she asked.

"I'm sorry," he apologized. "That's just a bit of firefighter jargon.
It refers to the practice of a single firefighter procedure, something
that has to be practiced until it is internalized and becomes automatic.
It is a training exercise module, if you like, that we use to keep ourselves
current with all the procedures we use. It's our guarantee that we will
always be able to perform them when needed in an emergency."

"Looks like we won't be needing a fire chief pretty soon," the
chair observed.

"Sometimes I start to think that myself," the fire chief agreed, "but we on senior staff have a role too. It's one we share with you."

"With the board of supervisors?" she asked.

"Sure," he pressed, "There are so many innovations, problems, and opportunities we could work on. But, as you know, we don't have the resources to chase them all. Someone has to have the big picture view in order to choose which ones to go for. And we have the role to provide what resources the firefighters need to research and take advantage of the innovations we do choose."

"That's a very elegant speech, Chief," she commented.

"And one, I hope," he said, "that you will remember at budget time."

"We'll see, when you present your formal evaluation of the program," she concluded.

FROM THE STATE FUND JOURNALS OF NEELY GARDNER: PROGRAM EVALUATION

The worth of each individual employee was a fundamental principle that the president and Gardner sought to instill in every corner of the new, democratic organization. The participatory management philosophy was expected to appear in the way employees and customers were treated by the State Fund and also in relationships within the organization.

There was a great deal of conflict about this expectation. Gardner pointed out in his journals that some of the greatest turmoil occurred around the organization structure itself. It was here that the paradox of the insistence on the AT&R intervention as a participative undertaking was most evident. Further, the devolution of power to the district offices as autonomous business entities created a great deal of controversy. In such a devolution, or *empowerment,* as it is currently called, there generally has to be a giving over of power to make the act more than a hypocritical gesture. Obviously, those who saw themselves as having to give up power were not always enthralled by such new management practices. Furthermore, there were plenty of employees whose personal values were firmly in support of an authoritarian, hierarchical, central organization. They were equally

committed to their values and to succeeding in their careers at the
State Fund. Therefore, they found themselves having to accept the
new participatory management requirement while hoping that, some
time in the future, things would return to the more comfortable,
authoritarian approach. Such people were often referred to in the
State Fund as Theory X's in Theory Y's clothing (McGregor, 1960).

In point of fact, experience suggests that an organization needs
both values. The new organization provided a structure and the fo-
rums in which participants could thrash out differences and make
their accommodations to X and Y theories, at the same time honoring
a common goal to improve the services of the State Fund. The answer
to the problem was that neither side had to, nor should, win. Ultimate
resolution was not the requirement; exploring the dynamics of the
issue was. The flat organizational structure not only made it possible
for a broader base of participation, but the conflict that occurred
brought greater creativity and collaboration. Gardner's account
shows that settings in which conflict can be allowed to surface, to be
recognized, and to be treated in a problem-solving manner can frequently result in creativity and innovation rather than frustration.
There is a great need for a carefully constructed system of organizational justice in order to keep either extreme from becoming total
master of the organization's values (Gardner, 1980).

In a flat organization everyone must work more closely together
to avoid excessive fragmentation, but when fragmentation does occur, it is easier to see where and why it occurs. Everyone rushes in to
help. When the conflict persisted in the State Fund, the various management and employees' councils and the executive committee functioned as the constructive elements envisioned in Gardner's notion
of organizational conflict and individual justice. However, as we have
seen in Gardner's account, there was not always success in reaching
the desired goals.

The integration of collaboration and competitiveness as organizational values was ever elusive. Both values must thrive in a changing
organization but not at the expense of each other. If one value is
totally dominant, it forms a major barrier to productivity improvement and organization changing. All collaboration without competition leads to a country club culture. All competition without collaboration is anarchy. Both extremes lead to forms of organizational
tyranny. Balancing these modes of organizing has been the concern

of more recent organization change strategies such as total quality management, business process redesign, and reinventing government (Wolf, 1992).

In the ensuing years at the State Fund, the emphasis has moved back and forth between *X* and *Y* values, depending on the State Fund's situation. Typically, hard financial times seem to drive the State Fund managers toward the *X* end of the value spectrum whereas successful market times have moved them toward broad, collaborative *Y* values. Any organization development effort must be able to thrive at both ends. It is one thing to manage change in the organization when top management is of the more open *Y* persuasion, but a different test comes when the more closed *X* value situation is present. The president and Gardner completed the AT&R effort in the early 1970s. Since then, the State Fund has successfully passed through several market recessions and oscillations between *X* and *Y* values. The Fund's emphasis on the worth of the individual has undergone recurrent changes as well.

Many innovative measures in support of the employees' worth occurred in the State Fund's personnel practices. First and foremost was training. Gardner was above all the quintessential trainer (Sherwood, 1990). If one were to characterize the essence of Gardner's approach to changing organizations it is through training and organizational research experiments. Gardner's approach incorporated Kurt Lewin's three assumptions for change through reeducation noted earlier:

> The complexities of re-educative processes arise out of the fact that they must involve correlative changes in the various aspects of the person—[1] their cognitive–perceptual structure, [2] their valuative—moral and volitional—structure, and [3] their motoric patterns for coping with their world(s). (Benne, 1976)

As the organization's work processes change, people are transformed. If there is no organizational program to train the people to think and do differently, only external forces, sometimes undesired, produce change. In a market-driven organization, the environment is often characterized by competition for customers and their changing needs. In a state bureaucracy the environment is further complicated by politics. The elected officials proposing changes this term are often replaced by their opposition the next term. There must be a balance between the organization's investment in resources to change the work processes and an investment in training to prepare the human system for the altered ways of doing things.

In the State Fund of the solidly bureaucratic days, training was seen as a fringe benefit, given to reward loyal performance. But with Gardner, training was viewed as the primary ingredient in creating a changing organization.

In his doctoral dissertation on Neely Gardner, Edward Jasaitis noted, "Gardner's preferred method for budgeting was to attach training funds to various programs. He considered this approach more difficult for obtaining funds but much safer from cutbacks. To him, funds labeled specifically for training were easier to identify, sequester, and cut. The strategy also allowed managers to make trade-offs and provide flexibility in program accomplishment" (Jasaitis, 1992, p. 139). If a line manager and his or her workers are to be held accountable for outcomes specified in plans and budgets, it is unfair, to the point of being sadistic, to withdraw the training resources they require to discharge their new responsibilities.

In the State Fund's new entrepreneurial posture, training was a capital investment needed to achieve excellence and to lower the costs of services delivered. It appeared to be the best strategy to beat the competition. It was important that the State Fund not view employees as its greatest asset but recognize that skills, abilities, and knowledge were owned by its employees. In effect, they are the employee's assets. Within this perspective, job performance was viewed as a collaboration between the employee, the organization, and the customer. Hence, Gardner's concept of participation and consent of the governed was important to the success of the State Fund's new organization. Only by recognizing the worth of the individual employee can the collaboration be freely and fairly channeled toward the organization's mission.

At the State Fund the job was not seen as the sole responsibility of the employee. Job performance was viewed as deriving from several of Lewin's force field vectors of energy and resources. In the past, if the job was not being performed well, the employee was blamed during performance review time. The only change contemplated placed the burden on the employee to modify his or her behavior and to do better. In the new collaborative view Gardner envisioned for the State Fund, success on the job was a result of a context of organization, environment (market–customer), management, work processes, and resources. Improvement in job performance could be realized by changing any one or all of these job performance vectors. The human assets vector was not on the State Fund books of account but rather was controlled by its owners (the employees) in a contract with the organization and theoretically could be withdrawn at any time. Further, an employee did not have to leave his or her job to withhold the human assets so valuable to the State Fund; performing at less than full capacity was always an alternative. Within this philosophical framework it was necessary for the Fund to recognize that the full use of the employee's assets required complete, voluntary collaboration.

CAREER DEVELOPMENT

An innovative employee career planning program was developed to bring all of the job-related force field vectors into focus on performance improvement by helping employees grow in their careers. During the job performance review each employee identified future career goals in the form of specific promotional or lateral job assignments that he or she felt would be best for him or her. By taking a larger look at the employee's personal development, the other job performance vectors could be seen in a more constructive light.

A catalog of all the promotional assignments in the State Fund was developed. It contained positions ranging from lead claims adjuster to president of the Fund. Each post was described in terms of organization needs and resources, as well as Fund management strategies to deal with its changing environment. Included were statements of the duties, experience, and responsibilities required for each job, as well as the special skills, knowledge, and abilities required. In the employee's job performance review, the necessary training and work assignments needed to qualify a person for the next step in the growth process were worked out as well. The employee's career development plan was included in the job performance appraisal for the current position and the appropriate training for the employee included in the program budget. The State Fund was able, therefore, to keep a list of potential candidates for each position, along with those who had qualified on competitive civil service examinations. Thus, at a glance, management could see how deep the bench was for any given position, where to invest in training, and how they could best support the development of careers to match the State Fund's future needs.

Another of many organization development innovations developed to recognize employee worth was the first salary arrangement in California that provided commissions for civil servants. Many of the State Fund's best sales and claims employees would be regularly attracted to the competition by lucrative sales commissions and loss control bonuses. The exiting State Fund employees not only took their human assets with them; their key accounts often went along too. It took 5 years before the Fund was finally able to convince the California state personnel board to allow an action training and research experiment in commissions and bonuses. If it worked, the state personnel board would get the credit, and if it failed, the Fund would accept all the blame. In this case, the action research experiment was successful. The Fund has been paying commissions and bonuses to its employees for many years now.

SUMMARY

Evaluation, evaluation, evaluation. Besides organizational learning, Gardner cited several reasons that feedback in the form of evaluation is important. First, a changing organization is tentative, evolving, and needs to be sensitive to input and perceptions. Evaluation of the change effort programs implemented provide a rich source of pertinent feedback to the people in the organization. Second, scheduling an evaluation and review will tend to motivate timely accomplishment of stated aspirations and outcomes expected from the change actions in each program. Third, no one can be certain of the effects of the interaction between the change programs undertaken and the field within which they take place. Prudence indicates a constant wariness in this regard. Fourth, a sense of involvement that occurs among the participants is enhanced by reinvolvement in consideration of purpose, process, and task. The evaluation sets the stage, as it were, for the final AT&R stage 12, re-cycle.

CHAPTER 15

AT&R STAGE 12: RE-CYCLE

MENU FOR AT&R STAGE 12: RE-CYCLE

Action   *In the Lewin pattern, we begin the AT&R process again. Starting with the orientation stage, the process retraces the AT&R path through the stages of contract, reconnaissance, opportunity and problem identification, aspirations, experimentation, and so forth. At this point the thrust of the project should be quite different from the original project. New action options should develop into innovative and creative change options based on new data evolving from a changed environment.*

The approach detailed by no means exhausts AT&R methods and strategies. As far back as 1948, Chein, Cook, and Harding described four approaches to action research: (1) diagnostic, with diagnosis being done by behavioral science specialists; (2) participant, with the central idea being that the people who are to take the action will be involved in the research; (3) empirical, with observation, recording, and analysis of data; and (4) experimental, with controlled research that contributes more to knowledge than to a dynamic action program (Gardner, 1974).

Training   *Strategic management and planning, program planning and evaluation, human development theory.*

Research   *Apply the AT&R method on the budget and management information system areas of the organization. Integrate these processes into the ongoing managing of the organization's responses to issues that arise in its environment, organization, resources, and operation processes.*

Outcome   *Process to continually develop the changing organization.*

BEGINNING AGAIN ANEW

In the end there is no conclusion. A changing organization is always "under construction." The essence of developing a changing organization is the re-cycle aspect of AT&R. Although Gardner completes his twelve stages with this re-cycle stage, it should be evident that the re-cycle occurs continuously as we pass through the preceding AT&R stages. By now, it is expected that the people in the organization have the skills and experience to change their organization as a matter of routine development rather than a traumatic reinvention project. This feedback–loop effect is also the core of action research. It is the constant going forth into the unknown and relating the new knowledge base to what went before that constitutes the learning organization. And the learning organization is a changing organization.

The following principles, guidelines, and values represent the main thrust of Gardner's AT&R method to help people in the re-cycle stage for their changing organizations:

1. A participative–democratic work organization based on open communication and shared agreement on the work at hand (i.e., consent of the governed; Hamilton, 1775)

2. An outcome-focused service product process that recognizes the citizen or the customer as the ultimate source of the organization's resources as well as the receiver of its service product

3. Institutional flexibility to build and unbuild the work's organization for changing

4. Information systems to provide immediate feedback to people doing their work, whether they are working in the executive suite, the managerial office, or the work unit

5. An organization that recognizes the worth of individuals, their contribution to the organization, and provides organizational justice for them

These principles can work against each other. Such is the dilemma of organization. Situations differ and require a mix particular to each organization in time. However, it seems clear that if any one of them is observed to the continued detriment of another, organization grief may be expected to follow. Re-cycling is aimed at constantly readjusting the focus and reestablishing the balance of these principles. If the people in the organization do not perform this function, then events will, but perhaps in not so desirable a fashion.

FROM THE JOURNALS OF NEELY GARDNER: RE-CYCLING AT THE STATE FUND

The AT&R method is not meant by Gardner as a way of managing the organization. That is another discipline for which many methods abound, each of them appropriate in their special circumstances. AT&R's re-cycle stage is a re-initiation of a guide in applying those management methods in a changing organization. The re-cycle stage seeks, as does the AT&R method in its initial use, to examine and integrate the complex decision-making dimensions of work. The task of this stage in following these principles is to readjust the balance among the peoples' disposition for outcomes, their behavior, and their performance over time.

The list of principles is not exhaustive of the multifaceted unfolding of events, dialogue, and action that governed Gardner's State Fund project. However, it is most representative of the executive risk that the State Fund and its presidents took with Gardner on this organizational odyssey to become a changing organization.

Gardner and the president of the State Fund did not seek simply to change the State Fund's organization but to create a "changing organization" (Sherwood, 1990) that could interact with its environment in an ever-improving process of self-renewal. The major quest was a fundamental shift of values from a 53-year-old, bureaucratic state agency rife with management privilege to a quality participative organization delivering top services to the public. It sought to set the standards of quality for the industry.

Above all, Gardner and the president of the State Fund envisioned an openly participative, democratic organization. "People as a whole are positively charged. If you give them a chance, they are capable of self-management" (Young, 1969, p. 1). At the very outset, the top management at the State Fund was given the charge and permission to reinvent itself in that image. Three layers of hierarchical management were eliminated, bringing work units, line managers, and executives much closer together.

The resulting organization got its leadership from a plural executive committee including the president and vice presidents. The line managers were responsible for delivering worker compensation services to the State Fund's customers and ultimately to the citizens of California. Managers of district offices scattered around the state and the heads of the home office staff departments were the line officials who reported directly to the plural executive. In this structure the claims adjuster, working with injured employees in the district office, was only one level of management away from the executive committee.

The executive committee had no direct, operational management powers, which resided solely with the line managers. It did, however, have five corporate powers: (1) framing corporate policy, (2) entrepreneurial planning, (3) appointment of line managers, (4) approval of program plans–budgets, and (5) declaring the dividend to policyholders each year. To be sure, executive committee advice to managers came under the rubric of "advice one may not safely ignore." Still, there was a real effort to refrain from micromanaging the State Fund. The people in the executive suite knew the operators had to "manage" the day-to-day operations of the State Fund.

WHAT ENDURED IN SUBSEQUENT RE-CYCLE EFFORTS?

Since 1967, the State Fund has grown from a $100 million insurance bureaucracy to one earning more than $1.5 billion as a workers' compensation insurance service organization. It is one of the top insurance organizations in the nation. In 1967 it employed fewer than 1400 people and in 1995 it employed almost 6,000. It has doubled the number of district offices. Three succeeding presidents have presided over the State Fund since the first president retired. How can we assess the influence of the Gardner organization development project on the State Fund today?

The intriguing notion of planned incrementalism based on a consent model may not ensure that the "changing organization" has been achieved, but at least the State Fund has made a conscious effort in such a direction. The consultant, and, it is hoped, other researchers will continue to work with State Fund management as the changing organization of today becomes the "organization of tomorrow," and thence, the "organization of the future" (Gardner, 1969, p. 38).

Clearly, there are too many variables to consider in order to single out the degree to which the Gardner AT&R project accounted for the State Fund's dramatic turnaround and growth of customers and premiums. Perhaps a better way to measure the impact of Gardner's AT&R project is to assess what remains today of the guiding principles introduced into the State Fund more than a quarter of a century ago.

Perhaps the most salient evidence of Gardner's long-range influence is his training-of-trainers approach to AT&R. New State Fund safety representatives are still being trained as safety service consultants. They learn consulting skills, safety methodology, and new technology during a 2-year training program.

In 1990 it was becoming apparent that safety consultants already in the field were missing out on the free exchange of new ideas and methods that occur only during the training period and before they are assigned to district offices around California. An Oakland district office safety service consultant trainee noticed this situation during her own training experience. She circulated an action research survey feedback questionnaire among some 30 senior Safety Service Consultants to document exactly what they felt was needed to keep them up to date. She took the results to the manager of the safety and health services program. Her idea was implemented in a safety and health program that she described at a working conference. It was composed of presentations and discussion groups dealing with issues relevant to State Fund work, such as stress in the work place, computer applications for safety service consultants, underwriting issues that affect safety services, cumulative trauma disorders, and projections of safety services in the 1990s and beyond.

The State Fund's safety and health program manager explained, "Vendors participated in the seminar by exhibiting new products. In addition to the obvious value of this kind of exposure and the formal presentation I am impressed by the exchange of information that happened informally. I am looking forward to future seminars" (State Compensation Insurance Fund, 1990, p. 4).

The Fund's safety and health seminar developed by a consultant trainee is an excellent example of Gardner's vision of the "changing organization." It demonstrates dramatically how skill transfers continued to occur in the generation that followed the work of the first president and Gardner. The seminar is a direct descendant of Gardner's combination of AT&R and training-of-trainers that has been continuing in the State Fund over nearly 30 years. In this instance, the connections are easy to trace back through the safety and health program manager. He was a safety representative participant in the first safety service consultants' training program. In this recent example, a current consultant trainee not only used her training in safety but also her understanding of AT&R. As a result of her efforts, the other senior safety service consultants gained training in new and innovative technologies in their field.

The State Fund has generally retained its flat organization, manager's councils, and executive committee. Each has grown in size as the State Fund has expanded. But an additional level of management structure has been reestablished in the district offices to handle the increasingly complex delivery of policyholder and claims services. Other statewide communication councils were formed by claims adjusters, salespeople, and auditors to share ideas and innovations around the state.

The key idea of the strategic action group for organization development in 1971 was to eliminate the need for internal AT&R specialists by training managers and other employees in the methods, principles, and skills of managing change in large public organizations. These skills, brought into the State Fund by Gardner and his graduate students, were transferred to internal agents. They then trained many other employees through the education services center and through action research network management projects.

In time, in accordance with Gardner's theory, these organizational change units were integrated into the fabric of the organization itself. For example, the training-of-trainers effort now resides in functional groups throughout the State Fund. Unfortunately, the education service center has reverted to a more traditional training support service. The "free-floating" management analysis group of action network developers has been replaced by even more "free-floating" task-force teams networked throughout the State Fund. They have been incorporated into the norms and values of the State Fund's culture.

There has been continued development of information systems for immediate feedback to people doing the work. For example, the statewide distributed data processing system now includes e-mail and word processing functions. Field people are using laptop microcomputers in the field. However, the integrated budget and management information system was never fully realized. This was a result, in part, of the long-term resistance of an accounting–personnel and data processing department nexus that formed against the effort for change. Just as Kurt Lewin's force field theory would suggest, the addition of forces in support of change will trigger new opposing forces. With the emergence of total quality management (TQM) and current information technology tools, the State Fund adopted the PACE program for performance excellence.

A LONG-TERM VALUE CHANGE:
INDIVIDUAL WORTH, "WE DID THIS!"

The effort to create an organization that recognized the "worth" of the individual seemed to have posed the greatest long-term difficulty for the Gardner project. Clearly, the project intruded severely on the personnel department's turf. Although there was considerable creative conflict that emerged, career development approaches have in substantial degree atrophied. Also, some of the innovations the Fund undertook had to be threaded through the policies and practices of the California state personnel board. Fortunately, the board was sympathetic to many of the changes. It ultimately supported the Fund's commission and bonus pay plans, decentralized management, and human resource development functions. In addition, by taking an entrepreneurial approach to affirmative action in the 1960s, women and minority employees have developed as outstanding leaders in professional, management, and executive positions at the Fund.

The employees' program advisory council, which functioned as a vehicle to secure organizational justice for individuals, was abandoned, as was the education center. This, together with the limited adoption of the outcome budget–MIS process, indicates not all of Gardner's ideas for nurturing a democratic workplace took strong root in the State Fund soil. As a result, some of the district offices have grown large and have established their own hierarchical fiefdoms.

However, there is a recognition of employees as critical participants in the changing organization. The most persuasive evidence of the continuing presence of Gardner's original AT&R principles may be found in the thoughts of an executive vice president, enunciated when he announced his plans to retire:

> The Fund's growth does pose a new set of problems. There is a danger we could forget that it's people, not systems that get the job done. If being a manager has taught me anything . . . it's taught me that when there's a problem you don't rush in to blame the people doing the work. It's probably direction or management that's at the core of the problem. Good management and good training: that's what makes us or breaks us. (State Compensation Insurance Fund, 1991, p. 4)

Not everyone has been in agreement about the value of the changes engineered by the first president and Gardner. Gardner was always clear that the State Fund experience was neither his nor the president's work. There has been a large cast of characters who deserve equal credit (and blame), namely the State Fund employees. This view was best articulated by a retired district manager's evaluation:

> Neely made many suggestions on management form and procedures for the good old Fund. We went through a more radical change in the 60s and 70s than any other organization I knew of at that time. We went from a paternalistic management style where all of the communication was upwards to a much more flattened hierarchy where communication was both ways, and more importantly, it was not only possible to communicate, it was expected. In retrospect, it is hard to say just what was because of Neely Gardner and what was because of our own

home-grown people, but I do know that the Fund was a better place to work as we moved on. (Raymond, 1990, p. 2)

It was a unique time and a unique experience. Gardner's enduring, if diffused, impact on the State Fund's culture was forecast in a paper the first president presented in 1969 at the national conference of the American Society for Public Administration in Miami, Florida. He evaluated Gardner's contribution to the State Fund in these terms:

> The Fund, and myself personally, owe a tremendous debt to this man sitting down the table, Neely Gardner. As Training Officer for the State of California, Gardner mounted a training program . . . to bring a large spectrum of training opportunities at a time when this was not the most popular subject to talk about in governmental circles: organization, communication, group dynamics, conference leadership. And all of these connected in a way which encouraged maximum participation.
>
> I was so personally impressed . . . by the value of some of the things I saw and heard, that very soon almost every member of our organization from the front-line supervisor up had been exposed to some area of modern management technique. Without this exposure to some of the wide spectrum of new skills, new training, new concepts, I doubt very much we could possibly have moved in the experiment. (Young, 1969, p. 1)

SUMMARY

The emphasis on the use of the AT&R handbook is primarily on providing nonhypocritical democratic participation on the part of all those people whose work will be involved in the prospective changes. The consultative approaches are taken by management in order to ensure the learning and growth on the part of those involved. Finally, there is an effort to play down the mechanical cause and effect reductionism view of scientific research in favor of the open system or organic approach to researching and experimenting with people's work processes. Together, these three aspects of the AT&R handbook are used as the primary means of developing the organization's internal consensus of what the current social reality of the work situation is and what action options are open to the work group to enhance it.

REFERENCES

Abramson, R. (1978). *An integrated approach to organization development and performance improvement planning: Experiences from America, Asia and Africa.* West Hartford, CT: Kumarian Press.

Abramson, R., & Halset, W. (1979). *Planning for improved enterprise performance: A guide for managers and consultants.* Geneva: International Labor Organization.

Allport, G. W. (1946). Foreword. In G. W. Lewin (Ed.), *Resolving social conflicts: Selected papers on group dynamics by Kurt Lewin.* New York: Harper & Brothers.

Argyris, C., & Schon, D. (1978). *Organizational learning: A theory of action perspective.* Reading, MA: Addison-Wesley.

Baburoglu, O. N. (1992). Normative action research. *Organization Studies, 13*(1), 16–19.

Barnett, Cates Camile (1992). Leadership: Arranging the chairs—reflections on the lessons of Neely Gardner. *Public Administration Quarterly, 16,*(2): 180-188, 1992.

Benne, K. D. (1976). The process of re-education: An assessment of Kurt Lewin's Views. In W. G. Bennis, K. D. Benne, & R. Chin (Eds.), *The planning of change* (3rd ed., pp. 315–331). New York: Holt, Rinehart, & Winston.

Bennett, J. K., & O'Brien, M. J. (1994). The 12 building blocks of the learning organization. *Training, 31,* 41–48.

Bennis, W. G. (1966). *Changing organizations: Essays on the development and evolution of human organization.* New York: McGraw-Hill.

Berger, P. L., & Luckmann, T. (1967). *The social construction of reality: A treatise in the sociology of knowledge.* New York: Anchor Books.

Bergquist, W. (1996). Post-modern thought in a nutshell: Where art and science come together. In J. M. Schaftitz & J. S. Ott (Eds.), *Classics of organization theory* (4th ed., pp. 578–591). Belmont, CA: Wadsworth.

Blake, R. R., & Mouton, J. S. (1969). *Building a dynamic corporation through grid organization development.* Reading, MA: Addison-Wesley.

Blake, R. R., & Mouton, J. S. (1970). *The grid for sales excellence: Benchmarks for effective salesmanship.* New York: McGraw-Hill.

Boss, W. A. (1983). Organization development: A vehicle for improving the quality. In W. B. Eddy (Ed.), *Handbook of organization management* (pp. 253–278). New York: Marcel Dekker.

Bozeman, B., & Straussman, J. D. (1990). *Public management strategies: Guidelines for managerial effectiveness.* San Francisco: Jossey-Bass.

Brager, G., & Holloway, S. (1992). Assessing prospects for organizational change: The uses of force field analysis. *Administration in Social Work, 16,* 3–4.

Bruce, R. R. (1994). Neely Gardner and the state fund experience: 25 years after a large-scale OD intervention. *Public Administration Quarterly, 18*(2), 123–150.

Bruce, R. R. (1996). Introduction: Symposium: Neely Gardner issue: Entrepreneurial management in the public sector: Franchising internal services. *Public Administration Quarterly, 20,* 9–25.

Catlin, T. (1994). *GSA presidential transition on-site support staff planning handbook.* Washington, DC: U.S. General Services Administration.

Chandrasekaran, R. (1997, May 22). Where the government hires government: FAA awards big systems contract to USDA, but to private contractors, it doesn't compute. *Washington Post,* p. 1.

Chein, I., Cook, S. W., & Harding, J. (1948). The field of action research. *The American Psychologist, 3,* 45–48.

Cunningham, B. (1993). *Action research and organization development.* Westport, CT: Praeger.

Dahl, R. A., & Lindblom, C. E. (1953). *Politics, economics, and welfare: Planning and politico-economic systems resolved into basic social processes.* New York: Harper and Row.

Denhardt, R. B. (1993). *Theories of public administration* (2nd ed.). Belmont, CA: Wadsworth.

Dunn, W. N. (1991, December). *Problem-centered inquiry: The principle of bounded ignorance.* Paper presented at a meeting of the Public Policy Symposium Project, Center for Public Administration and Policy, Virginia Polytechnic Institute and State University, Falls Church, Virginia.

Dutton, J., & Duncan, R. B. (1987). The creation of momentum for change through the process of strategic issues diagnosis. *Strategic Management Journal, 8*(4), 297–295.

Eddy, W., & Saunders, R. (1972). Applied behavioral science in urban administrative/political systems. *Public Administration Review,* pp. 56–62.

Fisher, F. (1992). And his memory lingers on. *Public Administration Quarterly, 16*(2), 197–208.

Foss, G. (1987, October). *Decentralization of the personnel function.* A paper delivered at the International Personnel Management Association, San Diego, California.

French, W. L., & Bell, C. (1995). *Organization development: Behavioral science interventions for organization improvement* (5th ed.). Englewood Cliffs, NJ: Prentice Hall.

French, W. L., Bell, C. H., & Zawacki, R. A. (1983). *Organization development: Theory, practice, and research* (2nd ed.). Dallas, TX: Business Publications.

Fromm, E. (1947). *Man for himself: An inquiry into the psychology of ethics.* New York: Holt, Rinehart and Winston.

Gardner, N. (1957). Training as a framework for action. *Public Personnel Review,* pp. 39–44.

Gardner, N. (1969). *Subject to change without notice: Bridging the gap between organization and administrative practice.* A background paper for panel discussion at the American Society for Public Administrators National Conference, Miami, Florida.

Gardner, N. (1970, March). *Guidelines for training senior professional and technical officers.* Paper presented to the U.N. Staff Conference, New York.

Gardner, N. (1974). Action training and research: Something old and something new. *Public Administration Review, 34,* 106–115.

Gardner, N. (1980). *Organization theory and behavior: An approach to managing in a changing environment.* Unpublished manuscript.

Golembrewski, R. T. (1993). *Handbook of organizational consultation.* New York: Marcel Dekker.

Gore, A. (1993). *From red tape to results: Creating a government that works better and costs less.* Washington, DC: U.S. Government Printing Office.

Halachmi, A. (1981). Innovation in the public sector: The case for action research and training. *Management in Government, 12*(4), 303–314.

Halachmi, A., & Nichols, K. L. (Eds.). (1996). *Enterprise government: Franchising and cross-services for administrative support.* Burke, VA: Chatelaine Press.

Hamilton, A. (1775, February 23). The farmer refuted, of a more impartial and comprehensive view of the dispute between Great Britain and the colonies, intended as a further vindication of congress: In answer to a letter from A. W. Farmer, entitled, "A view of the controversy." New York: James Rivington.

Hammer, Michael (1997). *Beyond Reengineering: How the Process Centered Organization Is Changing Our Work and Our Lives.* New York: HarperCollins.

Ittelson, W. H. (1973). Environment perception and contemporary perceptual theory. In W. H. Ittelson (Ed.), *Environment and cognition* (pp. 1–19). New York: Seminar Press.

Jasaitis, E. (1992). *Training and development: The Neely Gardner approach.* Unpublished doctoral dissertation, Florida State University.

Kirkhart, L. (1969, May). *Voyage of change.* Paper presented to the ASPA Conference, Miami, Florida.

Kirkhart, L. (1971). Toward a theory of public administration. In F. Marini (Ed.), *Toward a new public administration: The Minnowbrook perspective* (pp. 127–164). Scranton, PA: Chandler.

Kirkhart, L. (1972). *Organization development in a public agency: The strategy of organization devolution.* Unpublished doctoral dissertation, University of Southern California.

Koskinen, J. (1996). Foreword. In A. Halachmi & K. L. Nichols (Eds.), *Enterprise government: Franchising and cross-servicing for administrative support* (pp. v–vi). Burke, VA: Chatelaine Press.

Lewin, K. (1947). Frontiers in group dynamics. *Human Relations, 1,* 5–41, 143–153.

Lewin, K. (1948). Conduct, knowledge, and acceptance of new values. In G. W. Lewin (Ed.), *Resolving social conflicts: Selected papers on group dynamics.* New York: Harper & Brothers.

Lewin, K. (1951). *Field theory in social sciences: Selected theoretical papers.* New York: Harper.

Lewin, K., Barker, R., & Dembo, T. (1941). *Frustration and regression: An experiment with young children.* Iowa City: University of Iowa Press.

Lindsay, W., & Patrick, J. (1997). *Total quality and organization development.* Delray Beach, FL: St. Lucie Press.

Luke, J. S. (1992). Applied behavioral science in the 1990s: Looking outward more, inward less. *Public Administration Quarterly, 16*(2), 222–234.

Maier, N., & Frederick, R. (1952). *Principles of human relations: Applications to management.* New York: John Wiley.

Marrow, A. J. (1969). *The practical theorist: The life and work of Kurt Lewin.* New York: Basic Books.

Maslow, A. H. (1996). A theory of human motivation. In J. S. Ott (Ed.), *Classic readings in organizational behavior* (2nd ed., pp. 45–56). Belmont, CA: Wadsworth.

Mayo, E. (1945). *The social problems of civilization.* Boston: Harvard University Press.

Mayo, E. (1960). *The human problems of an industrial civilization.* Boston: Harvard University Press.

McGill, M. E. (1974). Evolution of organizing development: 1947–1960. *Public Administration Review, 34,* 58–105.

McGregor, D. (1960). *The human side of enterprise.* New York: McGraw-Hill.

Micklethwait, J., & Wooldridge, A. (1996). *The witch doctors: Making sense of the management gurus.* New York: Times Books, Random House.

Miller, R. (1961). *Cortico-hippocampal interplay and the representation of contexts in the brain.* Heidelberg, Germany: Springer-Verlag.

Mitroff, I. I. (1983). *Stakeholders of the organizational mind.* San Francisco: Jossey-Bass.

Mitroff I. I., & Featheringham, T. R. (1974). On systemic problem solving and the error of the third kind. *Behavioral Science, 19*(6), 378, 392.

Moore, M. L. (1989). Issue analysis, development, and management systems: Parallel participation structures for public-sector OD. *Public Administration Quarterly,* pp. 233–254.

Nichols, J. M. (1989). Successful project management: A force-field analysis. *Journal of Systems Management, 40,* 24–27.

Nutt, P. C., & Backoff, R. W. (1992). *Strategic management of public and third sector organizations: A handbook for leaders.* San Francisco: Jossey-Bass.

O'Keefe, J., & Nadel, L. (1987). *The hippocampus as a cognitive map.* Oxford: Clarendon Press.

Osborne, D., & Gaebler, T. (1992). *Reinventing government: How the entrepreneurial spirit is transforming the public sector.* Reading, MA: Addison-Wesley.

Partridge, E. (1958). *Origins: A short etymological dictionary of modern English.* New York: Macmillan.

Peter, M., & Robertson, V. (1984). The origin and status of action research. *Journal of Applied Behavioral Science, 20*(2), 113–124.

Phillips, B. S. (1966). *Social research: Strategy and tactics.* New York: Macmillan.

Raymond, D. (1990, September). SCIF Retirees' Newsletter. Trinidad, CA: Author.

Remeliik, H. I. (1981). Inauguration speech, January 20, 1980. In *Ministers' portfolios: A guide for nation building in Palau.* Koror, Palau: office of the President, Republic of Palau.

Roberts, P., & Paul, L. G. (1995, November 27). On the line: No matter what you make, the concept of ability is driving your business. *PC Week,* pp. 45–46.

Roethlisberger, F. J., & Dickson, W. (1939). *Management and the worker.* Boston: Harvard University Press.

Rogers, C. R. (1951). *Client-centered therapy: Its current practice, implications, and theory.* Boston: Houghton Mifflin.

Rogers, C. R. (1969). *Freedom to learn: A view of what education might become.* Columbus, OH: C. E. Merrill.

The role of foreign aid in government. (1997). Washington, DC: U.S. Congress, Congressional Budget Office.

Schein, E. (1970). *Organizational psychology.* Englewood Cliffs, NJ: Prentice-Hall.

Schein, E. H. (1988). *Process consultation.* Reading, MA: Addison-Wesley.

Schein, E. H. (1990). Back to the future: Recapturing the O.D. vision. In F. Masserik (Ed.), *Advances in organization development* (pp. 13–26). Norwood, NJ: Ablex.

Senge, P. M. (1990). *The fifth discipline: The art and practice of the learning organization.* New York: Doubleday.

Serlin, M. D., & Bruce, R. R. (1996). Origins of government franchising. In A. Halachmi & K. L. Nichols (Eds.), *Enterprise government: Franchising and cross-servicing for administrative support* (pp. 25–43). Burke, VA: Chatelaine Press.

Sherwood, F. P. (1968). The market and organization theory. *Essays on financial management and behavior.* (Mimeograph). University of Southern California.

Sherwood, F. P. (1990). *The State Compensation Insurance Fund: Neely Gardner's major OD effort.* An unpublished paper presented at the Neely Gardner Memorial Symposium, ASPA, Los Angeles, University of Southern California.

State Compensation Insurance Fund. (1973). Forcing the action. *Insight, San Francisco: State Compensation Insurance Fund, 4,* 6–8.

State Compensation Insurance Fund. (1990). Safety and health development seminar launched. *Insight, San Francisco: State Compensation Insurance Fund, 228,* 3–5.

State Compensation Insurance Fund. (1991). A conversation with exec. VP Lee Grams. *Insight, San Francisco: State Compensation Insurance Fund, 3,* 2–5.

Taylor, F. (1911). *The principles of scientific management.* New York: Harper.

United Nations Development Program. (1995). Building substantive capacity in governance and public sector management. *Management Development in Progress-MDG, 3,* 1–2.

U.S. Congress, Congressional Budget Office. (1997). *The role of foreign aid in government.* Washington, DC: Author.

Walton, R. E. (1969). *Interpersonal peacemaking: Confrontation and third-party consultation.* Reading, MA: Addison-Wesley.

Warren, B. (1966). *Changing organizations: Essays on the development and evolution of human organization.* New York: McGraw-Hill.

Weber, M. (1946). The essentials of bureaucratic organization: An ideal type construction. In H. H. Gerth & C. W. Mills (Trans., Eds.), *Essays in sociology.* New York: Oxford University Press.

Weick, K. E., & Bougon, M. G. (1986). Organizing as cognitive maps. In H. P. Sims, D. A. Gioia, & Associates (Eds.), *The thinking organizational dynamics of organizational social cognition* (pp. 104–105). San Francisco: Jossey-Bass.

Wolf, J. F. (1992). Neely Gardner and Deming's total quality management parallels and connections. *Public Administration Quarterly, 16*(2), 209–221.

Young, R. A. (1969). *The State Fund experience.* Paper presented at the American Society for Public Administration National Conference, Miami, Florida.

INDEX

ABOUT THE AUTHORS

Raymon Bruce works in the Office of Comprehensive Planning in Fairfax County, Virginia. He has worked and consulted in county, state, federal, and international organizations. He was special assistant to the first president of the Republic of Palau, process historian for the Clinton/Gore Presidential Transition Team, and a member of the National Performance Review's Franchise Services Planning and Work Group. He is a presenter in the Enterprise Government Management OPB Seminar Series and has published articles in several journals and books. He earned a BA and MA from the University of Montana, an MS degree in Organization Development from Pepperdine University, and a Ph.D. from Virginia Polytechnic Institute and State University. He has taught at George Mason University and was a Fulbright Senior Scholar, lecturing in Lithuania.

Sherman Wyman has over thirty-five years of experience in urban management, management consulting, academic administration, and graduate-level teaching. He is currently a faculty member and executive director of the Center for Economic Development Research and Service, School of Urban and Public Affairs, The University of Texas at Arlington. Earlier he served as director of the city management graduate program at the University of Kansas and head of the Bureau of Governmental Research at Denver University. He holds a BA from Stanford University, MPA from Syracuse University, and a PhD in Public Administration from the University of Southern California and was a Fulbright Student-Scholar in Norway during 1960-61 and a

Fulbright Senior Faculty Scholar in Poland during the spring of 1997. He has served as Executive Board member of the National Association of Schools and Programs in Public Administration and Affairs, member and officer of five chapters of the American Society for Public Administration, Executive Board member of the Urban Affairs Association, and Executive Board member of the National Association of Manufacturing and Technical Assistance Centers. His consulting assignments in organization development and management training have included local governments and universities throughout the United States, Iran, Malaysia, and Poland; the National League of Cities; International City Management Association, U.S. Departments of Housing and Urban Development, Commerce, and Justice; the Environment Protection Agency; Federal Emergency Management Agency; and the National Traffic Safety Administration.

Frank Sherwood is Professor Emeritus at the School of Public Administration and Policy, Florida State University, where he was the Jerry Collins Eminent Scholar in Public Administration. He is the former director of the School of Public Administration, University of California; former president of the American Society of Public Administration; and Senior Fellow of the National Academy of Public Administration.